Heroes and happy

Manchester University Press

STUDIES IN POPULAR CULTURE

General editor: Professor Jeffrey Richards

Also published in this series

Christmas in nineteenth-century England   Neil Armstrong

Healthy living in the Alps: the origins of winter tourism in Switzerland, 1860–1914
Susan Barton

Working-class organizations and popular tourism, 1840–1970   Susan Barton

Leisure, citizenship and working-class men in Britain, 1850–1945   Brad Beaven

Leisure and cultural conflict in twentieth-century Britain   Brett Brebber (ed.)

**The British Consumer Co-operative Movement and film,
1890s–1960s**   Alan George Burton

British railway enthusiasm   Ian Carter

Railways and culture in Britain   Ian Carter

Time, work and leisure: Life changes in England since 1700   Hugh Cunningham

Darts in England, 1900–39: a social history   Patrick Chaplin

Relocating Britishness   Stephen Caunce, Ewa Mazierska,
Susan Sydney-Smith and John Walton (eds)

Holiday camps in twentieth-century Britain: packaging pleasure
Sandra Trudgen Dawson

History on British television: constructing nation, nationality and collective memory
Robert Dillon

The food companions: cinema and consumption in wartime Britain, 1939–45   Richard Farmer

Songs of protest, songs of love: popular ballads in eighteenth-century Britain   Robin Ganev

Women drinking out in Britain since the early twentieth century   David W. Gutzke

The BBC and national identity in Britain, 1922–53   Thomas Hajkowski

**From silent screen to multi-screen: a history of cinema exhibition in Britain since
1896**   Stuart Hanson

Smoking in British popular culture, 1800–2000   Matthew Hilton

Juke box Britain: Americanization and youth culture, 1945–60   Adrian Horn

**Popular culture in London, c. 1890–1918: the transformation
of entertainment**   Andrew Horrall

Horseracing and the British, 1919–39   Mike Huggins

**Popular culture and working-class taste in Britain, 1930–39:
a round of cheap diversions?**   Robert James

Scotland and the music hall, 1850–1914   Paul Maloney

Amateur film: meaning and practice, 1927–77   Heather Norris Nicholson

Films and British national identity: from Dickens to *Dad's Army*
Jeffrey Richards

Cinema and radio in Britain and America, 1920–1960   Jeffrey Richards

Looking North: Northern England and the national imagination
Dave Russell

The British seaside holiday: holidays and resorts in the twentieth century   John K. Walton

Heroes and happy endings

Class, gender, and nation in popular film
and fiction in interwar Britain

CHRISTINE GRANDY

Manchester University Press

Published by Manchester University Press
www.manchesteruniversitypress.co.uk

British Library Cataloguing-in-Publication Data
A catalogue record for this book is available from the British Library

Library of Congress Cataloging-in-Publication Data applied for

ISBN 978 1 5261 0682 7 *paperback*

First published 2014

The publisher has no responsibility for the persistence or accuracy of URLs for any external or third-party internet websites referred to in this book, and does not guarantee that any content on such websites is, or will remain, accurate or appropriate.

Typeset in Adobe Garamond with Gill Sans display by
Koinonia, Manchester
Printed in Great Britain
by TJ International Ltd, Padstow

STUDIES IN
POPULAR
CULTURE

There has in recent years been an explosion of interest in culture and cultural studies. The impetus has come from two directions and out of two different traditions. On the one hand, cultural history has grown out of social history to become a distinct and identifiable school of historical investigation. On the other hand, cultural studies has grown out of English literature and has concerned itself to a large extent with contemporary issues. Nevertheless, there is a shared project, its aim, to elucidate the meanings and values implicit and explicit in the art, literature, learning, institutions and everyday behaviour within a given society. Both the cultural historian and the cultural studies scholar seek to explore the ways in which a culture is imagined, represented and received, how it interacts with social processes, how it contributes to individual and collective identities and world-views, to stability and change, to social, political and economic activities and programmes. This series aims to provide an arena for the cross-fertilisation of the discipline, so that the work of the cultural historian can take advantage of the most useful and illuminating of the theoretical developments and the cultural studies scholars can extend the purely historical underpinnings of their investigations. The ultimate objective of the series is to provide a range of books which will explain in a readable and accessible way where we are now socially and culturally and how we got to where we are. This should enable people to be better informed, promote an interdisciplinary approach to cultural issues and encourage deeper thought about the issues, attitudes and institutions of popular culture.

Jeffrey Richards

For Ron Grandy and Janet McLaughlin, with love

Contents

List of figures   *page* xi
General editor's introduction   xiii
Acknowledgements   xv

Introduction: the role of popular culture between the wars   1

1 A man imagined: heroes, work, and nation   38

2 The shape of villainy: profiteering and money-men   83

3 That magic moment: the female love-interest and the villainess   133

4 Building character: censorship, the Home Office, and the BBFC   177

   Conclusion: thoughts on heroes, villains, and love-interests
   beyond 1939   215

   Appendix: Censorable items compiled in 1917 from the BBFC's
   Annual Reports of 1913–15   224

   Bibliography   226
   Index   239

List of figures

1.1 *Sorrell and Son* (1927). Stephen Sorrell washing a floor.
United Artists/Kobal Collection   *page* 54
2.1 *Mutiny on the Bounty* (1935). Officers at dinner.
MGM/Kobal Collection   109
3.1 *A Star Is Born* (1937). Esther in a maid's uniform.
United Artists/Photofest, Inc.   151
3.2 *A Star Is Born* (1937). Esther removing Norman's shoes.
United Artists/Photofest, Inc.   154
3.3 *Queen Christina* (1933). Queen Christina in masculine dress
on the throne. MGM/Kobal Collection   160
3.4 *Queen Christina* (1933). Queen Christina in feminine dress
with attendants. MGM/Kobal Collection   161

General editor's introduction

Bestselling books and hit films have much to tell us about the preoccupations, values and preferred role models of society in any given period. In this thoughtful and detailed study, Christine Grandy explores bestselling novels and cinematic hits, both British and American, to assess the extent of their engagement with contemporary concerns about the economy, gender and the nation in inter-war Britain in the aftermath of the traumatic upheaval of World War I.

Rightly rejecting the idea that such popular works are purely escapist, she argues powerfully that the main thrust of the culture was to endorse the worth of a capitalist democratic society with defined traditional heterosexual male and female gender roles. She focuses on the depiction of heroes and heroines (whom she significantly dubs 'the love-interest'), villains and villainesses. In books and films like *Sorrell and Son*, she sees the culture working to re-establish pre-war masculine role models as patriotic soldier, breadwinner and *pater familias*. The male villain is the polar opposite of this value set and among the ranks of inter-war villains in for instance the *Bulldog Drummond* books and films are regularly to be found figures concerned with profit and the undermining of the national economy and social well-being – profiteering businessmen, arms dealers – the so-called 'merchants of death', sinister foreigners (Oriental masterminds, rebel Indian princes, Russian Bolsheviks) and renegade Establishment figures.

For women, who had achieved a degree of emancipation by gaining the vote and experiencing wartime employment and wage-earning, popular culture prescribed a feminine preoccupation with love and finding and serving Mr Right, so films show women giving up their careers for love, as in *A Star Is Born*, and forsaking wealth and power for love, as in *Queen Christina*. Villainesses by contrast seek wealth, status and power at all costs.

Grandy also examines the role of the censors in underpinning the value systems enshrined in popular culture, particularly the Home Office with its bans on novels promoting deviant sexuality and the British Board of Film Censors seeking to eliminate from films anything likely to upset the status quo political, social and moral. Grandy's book, with its focus on the national picture, can usefully be read alongside Robert James's *Popular Culture and Working-Class Taste in Britain, 1930–39* (2010), which establishes a comparative local study of Portsmouth, Derby and South Wales. Together they enrich our understanding of the nature and operation of popular culture in the inter-war period.

Jeffrey Richards

Acknowledgements

This monograph will, at the very least, make it clear that I have read a lot of terrible novels and watched some slightly less terrible movies. A number of unfortunate souls have conspired in my obsession with mass culture and the following is only a small acknowledgement of their support. My supervisor at York University, Stephen Brooke, has mentored me for more years than either of us would likely care to admit and has been a tremendous influence in ways that are difficult to acknowledge. He is an inspiring lecturer, a kind and supportive supervisor and friend, and I hope to gain in my career just a fraction of the good will he fosters among colleagues. Marc Stein substantially improved this project as he pushed me to clarify concepts and claims, all while applying his steely editing eye. Kate McPherson also provided encouragement and coffee at key moments in the completion of this project. Jim Martens from Red Deer College made me think early on about history as something I would actually like to study, while the Ontario Graduate Scholarship made my studies financially feasible. I would also like to thank Jeffrey Richards for his early enthusiasm and Manchester University Press.

I simply would not have finished the dissertation that this book is based on without the deadlines and valuable advice offered by members of the following reading groups: the Southern Ontario Modern British Seminar, the Masculinities Reading Group, York University's Women's History Reading Group, and the British History Writing Group. Mark Abraham, Kristine Alexander, Sarah Glasford, Laura Godsoe, Ian Hesketh, Sean Kheraj, Bethany Lander, Suzanne Carlsen, Monique MacLeod, Ian Mosby, and Laural Raine offered support, advice, beer, and so much more throughout this. Ben Lander read the majority of my chapters and his sense of humour and grounded perspective has been constant in the face of an occasionally irrational person. Michelle Firestone-Cruz, a star in her own field, took an early and active interest in the mystifying vocabulary of graduate work in history and continues to be a pillar of support and the best person to attend an embarrassing Friday matinée with. Brooke Spearn, Scott Dowling, and the girls, consistently provided a refuge that reminded me that story-time is important, but that there is life beyond that. Tannis Gibson attended practically every movie that came through the local theatre of Banff, Alberta when we lived there, an experience that informed this book in oddly persistent ways. My thanks to her and Jason Weidenhammer.

As I began converting the dissertation to a manuscript I benefited from the input of generous colleagues and friends. Catherine Ellis, Stephen Heathorn, Brad Beaven, and Amy Bell offered me valuable advice early on and my wonderful colleagues at Nipissing University, particularly Hilary Earl, guided me through this process and celebrated the book contract, and more, with me. Matt Houlbrook has offered support and advice over the years, and then topped that all by introducing me to my future partner. The final revisions to this book took place in a rather bizarre period between marrying said partner and moving to England. I spent three months living at my dad's place, a feat not to be taken lightly in one's thirties, and revising the manuscript in his shed in the middle of a hot Nova Scotia summer. My partner, Adam Houlbrook, not only toughed out a newly wed existence that was rather outside the norm and dealt with the seemingly interminable amount of paperwork and delays required for our particular form of transatlantic togetherness, but also painstakingly edited the final manuscript. He continues to demonstrate an almost eerie eye for all things John Buchan, but above all, I am truly humbled by his support in so many things, both big and small.

Finally they say that one's doctoral work is really about one's self, a comment perhaps dubious in its claim, but one which has nevertheless remained with me. In my case, this dissertation is indeed about me to some extent, but more accurately it is about and for my parents, Ron Grandy and Janet McLaughlin, who inculcated in me an early love of reading and action films. They are written on every page and their love and support, even when they have not entirely understood what I have been doing for so many years, has been constant. I dedicate this to them in small acknowledgement of all they have contributed to me and therefore to it.

Introduction:
the role of popular culture
between the wars

'Everybody wants to forget it', said Bertram, with a touch of passion in his voice. 'The Profiteers, the Old Men who ordered the massacre, the politicians who spoilt the Peace, the painted flappers. I'm damned if I'm going to let them!'

Philip Gibbs, The Middle of the Road (1923)

Philip Gibbs published *The Middle of the Road*, his bestselling novel about a disillusioned ex-soldier, five years after World War I ended. In those five years, initial celebrations quickly gave way to dismay by soldiers and civilians as they faced the social, economic, and political upheavals unleashed by a relatively new type of twentieth-century warfare. Britain was left to grapple with the loss of over 700,000 men at the fighting front and the return of soldiers traumatised by the mechanised warfare they had just experienced. Disillusionment with the initial ideals of the war and with notions of honour, sacrifice, and national strength was further exacerbated by the failures of a post-war economy that could not easily absorb the four million demobilised men expecting to return to their jobs, some which had been temporarily filled by women. Adding further insult to injury was the prominent post-war role of 'the Profiteers, the Old Men who ordered the massacre, the politicians who spoilt the Peace', who demonstrated that the modern warfare ushered in by World War I could in fact be profitable to some. These developments were accompanied by rapidly rising prices of goods and a general shift in the economy away from traditional forms of manufacturing and towards types of light industry that depended more heavily upon unskilled labour. Britain's victory seemed hollow in such circumstances and 'depression' became a familiar term as unemployment figures reached unprecedented heights in the winter of 1920, when two million men were out of work. After that winter the number of unemployed men rarely fell below one million, and reached a staggering three million men in 1932.[1] Alongside this economic instability was international political uncertainty as the conditions of the Versailles Treaty crumbled, fascism reared its head in Europe, and the prospect of another war to end all wars loomed.

Yet as historian John Stevenson has noted, interwar developments were nothing if not contradictory. Economic stagnation in the old manufacturing areas of the north was matched by economic recovery and growth in the south-east, south-west, Midlands, and London. Those that had work retained far more of their wages to spend on non-staple items. It was at this time of economic uncertainty that a dynamic mass consumer culture emerged. While many suffered economic hardships, others were able to purchase radios, cheap novels, and ready-made clothing, and many, including the unemployed, went to the 'pictures'. Popular culture became a crucial aspect of the rising consumer society. Cinemas were steadily built throughout the 1920s and 1930s and were accompanied by a vibrant trade in film magazines, which advised readers how to dress like their favourite stars and featured photographs to that same effect.[2] Affordable and condensed novels like *The Middle of the Road* (1923), in comparison to the expensive three volumes of the nineteenth century, were produced and sold in numbers that justified the common use of the new term 'bestseller'. Gibbs's novel, for example, appeared in twenty-two editions within two years of its initial printing.[3] Libraries and booksellers set up book-lending systems so that readers could get their hands on the latest and greatest books by their favourite authors. Newspapers also experienced unprecedented sales and marvelled at their popularity, with the accessible paper the *Daily Express* reaching a circulation of two million in the period. Such a brisk trade in a consumer culture that promised constant renewal and offered up images of other and better worlds seemed to fly in the face of the economic, social, and political upheaval in Britain between the wars.

The purpose of this monograph is to examine the immensely popular film and book narratives that developed between the wars and to situate these narratives against the period's simultaneous social, economic, political, and gender crises. I demonstrate that far from being a means of escape from the pressures of the world, the films and novels most popular with British audiences, whether of British or American origins, engaged with concerns about economy, gender, and nation after the war. Contrary to the belief of Gibbs's hero, Bertram, in the epigraph, I contend that the war was not forgotten within the pictures and novels that audiences chose to consume. From overtly topical social issue novels like Philip Gibbs's *Middle of the Road* to the tropical *Mutiny on the*

Bounty (1935 [UK 1936]), which was Britain's second most popular film in 1936, the heroes, villains, and love-interests of these narratives mirrored the contemporary concerns of those turning the page or viewing the screen.[4] Variations of the old men and painted flappers that Gibbs references in his novel, as well as characters like the disillusioned but ultimately heroic ex-soldier, Bertram, can be found in novels such as H. C. McNeile's *Bulldog Drummond* (1920) as well as films like *Grand Hotel* (1932). The novels and films that the British chose to consume featured heroes, villains, and love-interests that not only reflected but moderated post-World War I concerns about class, gender, and nation.

By 'nation', I mean both the realms of citizenship and politics and popular rhetoric about 'Englishness', a concept of national belonging promoted by historians such as Robert Colls and Wendy Webster among others.[5] The interwar period, as Alison Light has argued, was a time when notions of a domestic and inward-looking 'little' England seemed to compete with the unsteady reality of Great Britain. The novels and films I examine here do speak, more often than not, to love of England in particular and were conspicuous in noting English might and English heroics. Yet, that explicit and notable discussion of Englishness was conducted around and regarding institutions foundational to Britain's growth as an empire and state. The British military had a particular role to play in this story, as we shall see. Consequently throughout this I discuss concepts of Englishness within Britain as a nod to the sometimes contradictory, yet ultimately coinciding, uses of these terms. I argue that the film and fiction that British audiences popularised between the wars were preoccupied with a defensive effort to rehabilitate and maintain men as both masculine breadwinners and soldiers for the nation.

This endeavour to buttress the breadwinner and soldier roles through characters like the hero, love-interest, and villain continually endorsed the worth of a capitalist democratic society in the 1920s and 1930s. Many of the features that defined these characters, such as differentiated and unequal gender roles for men and women as well as compulsory heterosexuality, were centred upon the respective position of that character within a capitalist economy. Heroes were distinguished by their fulfilment of the independent male breadwinner role, while the deviancy of the villain's character lay in his inability or unwillingness to work for his wealth. Female love-interests contributed to the modern industrial landscape of these narratives not as workers but as subservient supporters of the male heroes. Villainesses demonstrated the peril of abandoning this supportive role by showing that female wealth and independence posed numerous problems to society and also made one ultimately unlovable. Consequently popular film and fiction became a potent means of conveying the absolute necessity of maintaining a capitalist economy and the breadwinner at its centre, by tying it to the heady and presumably timeless concepts of good, evil, and love. A study of the hero, villain, and love-interest that embodied these concepts will reveal the extent to which popular culture remained in constant dialogue with, and actively reinforced, a capitalist economy in a period when that economic system faced a substantial crisis.

This commitment to the breadwinner and soldiering ideal was not limited to just producers and consumers of mass culture, but was also endorsed by the state. I argue that the British Board of Film Censors (BBFC) and the Home Office encouraged the maintenance and production of this formula through their censorship of the hero, villain, and love-interest characters. By examining the films and novels that were passed by the censors in conjunction with those that were not, I show that the priorities of these censoring bodies were to maintain the role of the heroic soldier and the independent breadwinner. Narratives that produced images of the successful and independent bread-winner or soldier were easily approved by these organisations, while others that troubled this relationship were not. Thus the BBFC and the Home Office granted governmental sanction to what existed on the page and the screen and proved themselves active participants in the production of popular culture in Britain, even prior to the outbreak of World War II in 1939.

What results from my study is a social and cultural history that focuses explicitly on the ideology embodied in the novels and films that British audiences consumed between the wars and situates this ideology within the social, economic, and political climate of the day. The study illuminates the principles and beliefs at work in the popular films and novels that British audiences consumed in the early age of mass consumption. By looking at the ideology produced by popular culture in conjunction with other discourses about work, gender, and nation in Britain, we can see important sites of convergence between them which demonstrates that popular culture, even at its most outlandish and fantastical, was anything but entirely escapist.

The audience and popular culture

The growth of a popular mass culture between the wars was, as Q. D. Leavis pointed out, noticeable, and to some such as her, alarming. Book publishing and film production industries had developed in a remarkably short period of time and were producing goods that were immensely attractive to British audiences. This was truly culture aimed *at* the masses and consumed *by* the masses. Yet this development begs a central question: did popular culture house a coherent and developed ideology between the wars? Further to this, does consuming popular culture necessarily imply an acceptance of the system of beliefs and ideas – the moral framework – that it produces? At the centre of the latter question is a debate about whether the audience is a passive consumer of popular culture or an active agent that exerts a measure of control by either directing popular culture's purpose or resisting its message. Aspects of this debate, about the agency of historical actors, have preoccupied academics for years.[6]

An influential historian of media in the interwar period, D. L. LeMahieu, argues that audiences of a mass common culture moulded a democratic form of media.[7] LeMahieu claims that mass culture granted voices to those who were otherwise marginalised within the press and British society at large, such as the working classes and women. He points to changes in the language of the press: *The Times* began to mimic the more informal language of the *Daily Mail* which in turn emphasised 'human interest' stories that appealed to the working classes, the upper classes, and women. LeMahieu sees in this a cause for celebration, as 'an emerging common culture provided a shared frame of reference among widely divergent groups'.[8] For LeMahieu mass culture was truly democratic in that it encompassed all and was not entirely dictated by film studios and publishing houses. He argues that producers of popular film, fiction, and radio spent far too much time trying to gauge the preferences of the audience to ever have complete control of the product that entered the market.[9] Robert James's recent study *Popular Culture and Working-Class Taste in Britain* takes up LeMahieu's conception of the positive and democratising aspects of mass culture.[10] James argues that the working class consumed largely positive images of themselves and that these images offered them 'comfort', 'reassurance', and 'confidence' in the 1930s. James's work offers an interesting contribution to the field, yet in the process of trying to rescue popular culture from the accusation that it is a 'round of cheap diversions', James also tends to confirm that viewpoint, as he does not problematise the consumption of 'comfort' and 'confidence' by the working classes. Little room is given to the possibility that repeated images of working-class cheerfulness, or indeed middle-class success, may have served other aims – aims that positioned popular culture as an effective means of stabilising a strata of society experiencing high unemployment and exposed to the appeals of socialism, and to an extent fascism.

The work of LeMahieu and James on the democratic vision of popular culture can be most usefully contrasted against the approach of the Frankfurt School, and particularly Adorno's work on the 'culture industry'.[11] In Adorno's seminal essay, penned in 1947, he argued that popular culture allows people to exist as passive consumers and workers within a capitalist economy.[12] Adorno had witnessed the immense power of media to shape and manufacture a people's view of society under the Third Reich. The interwar period had seen the development of a new understanding of the relationship between public opinion, media, and the state, an understanding taken to its most terrible conclusion in the policies enacted in Germany by the Nationalist Socialists.[13] Adorno's cynicism with media was profound and his essay goes beyond the appearance of the customer as 'king' to explore the structure of experience that dictates the fantasies of the masses. He argues that the key to the maintenance of the culture industry is a form of pseudo-individualisation, which, by offering minor variations on the formula, is able to cloak the fundamental sameness of the culture industry's products. Thus the hero is presented, above all, as an individual, even while heroes are disturbingly similar from film to film or novel to novel. The willingness of the masses to subscribe to pseudo-individualisation and the repetitive formula offered by the culture industry, in his theory, reflects the need of the masses to subscribe to a collective aspirational fantasy, which in turn breeds what Michel Foucault would term 'docile bodies'.[14] In this way popular culture is a vital way of maintaining an ideology that supports a capitalist democracy.

My approach to popular culture adheres to Adorno's vision of the culture industry, with some important differences. This study is concerned with the dominant narrative arcs in mass culture and as expressed through key characters. Introductions of characters and the resolutions endorsed by mass culture are consequently given considerable weight here as central conveyers of the ideology of mass culture. Yet this study grounds the production and dissemination of this ideology in a period that faced unemployment, the spectre of communism and fascism, and a capitalist economy under immense strain. This historical grounding illustrates that the production of sameness in the popular culture formula was itself the result of an ongoing conversation as writers and filmmakers in the 1920s and 1930s flirted with socialism and addressed, to varying degrees, the complexities of unemployment and capitalism. The accommodation of the external world to the culture industry was and is, in my opinion, necessary to the ongoing effectiveness of the dominant ideology disseminated by the culture industry. This makes the culture industry less static than Adorno imagined. It produces less of a concrete formula than a constantly changing collection of calculations intent on maintaining the appeal of the hero, villain, and love-interest – characters that I argue encapsulate the formula itself and may provide the most potent testament to its impact. These characters are influenced by the audience who views them and indeed must be influenced by them in order for the culture industry to maintain its potency. This explains changes in attitudes and behaviour in novels and films from the 1920s to the present day, yet still accounts for some remarkable similarities between mainstream films and novels of today and yesteryear.

In focusing on only bestselling novels and hit films, I do imply that audiences possessed some degree of agency when they chose to consume particular films and novels from the selection available to them, although I would emphasise that the agency of audiences in this period was limited by the selections offered to them. The workings of the film and book industry are not examined in detail in my study, yet their roles in putting novels and films on shelves and in theatres is a constant contributing factor to the selection of narratives I examine.[15] However as LeMahieu notes, and as attendance figures provided by Sue Harper attest to, the most heavily financed film could be a flop. Audiences did, to an extent, exercise choice by attending some films more than others and promoting some authors to bestsellers above others. This emphasis does not necessarily trouble Adorno's totalising vision of the culture industry, but rather provides a perspective on the audience's contribution to the formula that appealed to them. It would be folly to presume that audiences did not actively contribute to the maintenance of a discernible formula through their consumption. In an economic climate defined, according to Marx, by great and everlasting uncertainty about work and wages, how could audiences resist something that could embody a step away from that daily grind? It would be difficult to fault audiences for recognising a culture that granted them a measure of pleasure in their daily lives, just as it would be difficult to fault producers for giving the audience what they 'wanted'. Yet the 'wants' that audiences articulated, and producers responded to, I argue, were largely dictated by notions of heroism, villainy, and love firmly anchored within a modern industrial and military oriented economy.

The new wants and desires in the nascent age of mass media were entrenched in widespread concerns in Britain about the shape of the brave new world after World War I. This was truly an age of anxiety when instability reigned in a number of forms, prompting a historiography which speaks of the *Morbid Age* and *Making Peace* along with *The Slump* and a host of other concerns.[16]

Matt Houlbrook has noted how this age of anxiety translated into a persistent preoccupation with the dangers of performance, while Susan Kingsley Kent has emphasised the destabilisation of heterosexual roles in the aftermath of the war.[17] My study further emphasises a concern with unstable identities and performance in the aftermath of World War I. Preoccupations with performance marked out the relatively conservative genre of low and middlebrow film and fiction, spotlighting what heroes could 'know' or not know about those people surrounding them. The ability to locate the 'truths' of the post-war period and see through these performances was central to a remaking of the soldier hero within mass culture.

The mass culture of the 1920s and 1930s, in many ways, worked to develop an epistemology of both love and villainy rooted in these concerns about performance. Queer theory is particularly useful for providing a framework to understand the universal and timeless 'truths' constructed in these narratives and the performances which clouded these truths.[18] Foucault argues that from the nineteenth century onwards modern society has been encouraged to seek universal truths, ultimately located in sexuality and desire. He writes, 'Not only did [nineteenth-century society] speak of sex and compel everyone to do so; it also set out to formulate the uniform truth of sex. As if it suspected sex of harbouring a fundamental secret. As if it needed this production of truth.'[19] The production of this truth in the popular culture of the 1920s and 1930s was embodied by the happy ending and a related dismantling of both male and female performances. Performance is problematic and must be stripped away in the face of a heterosexual 'truth' embodied in the breadwinner hero. Female love-interests give up a performance that privileges wealth and ambition for her 'true love' and the disguise of the villain as a normal or even admirable man falls away to indicate his naked desire for wealth and power. Artificial performance in these interwar works becomes a signifier of potential chaos and is largely rejected within a formula which locates post-World War I stability within the role of the ex-soldier and the breadwinner. Consequently the relationship between truth and love that was produced in these narratives were presented with mass culture as an effective means of governing a population in crisis.[20] This 'truth' becomes a central aspect of the culture industry formula that Adorno argues for and becomes a 'want' of the audience in turn.

The extent to which audiences imbibed or understood mass culture's conception of truth and performance is difficult to assess in any time period. For the 1920s and 1930s, there are few sources beyond the anecdotal that document audience reaction to cinema or novels, though we can gauge popularity through limited figures on books sales and cinema attendance. Any attempt to assess the extent to which audiences adhered to or internalised ideology from popular culture must proceed with the proviso of the complexity of the task.[21] That being said, there are important broad points that need to be made about the composition and beliefs of the audiences of popular culture in the 1920s and 1930s, which help us to understand the possible resonances between audience and ideology in popular culture.

What little we do know of audience response to popular culture between the wars indicates that those who were the main consumers of popular culture tended to imitate those situated above them in class or celebrity status.[22] Audiences paid close attention to what they saw or read and incorporated this knowledge into both their daily lives and their fantasies of their ideal worlds. The sources that historians have located chiefly relate to film-going in the 1930s and indicate that audiences imitated and often internalised the styles, actions, and behaviours that were presented to them. Annette Kuhn's interviews of seventy-eight men and women who were asked about their childhood memories of film-going in the 1930s reveal the relationship that children in the audiences had with those they saw in the pictures. Kuhn identifies 46 per cent of those interviewed as working/middle class, middle class, or upper middle class. The rest are considered working class.[23] She demonstrates that tendencies towards imitation existed among both working- and middle-class audiences. Two subjects, Nancy Carrington (NC) and Nancy Prudhoe (NP), remember their attempts to imitate and dress like the stars:

Int [interviewer]: Did you ever try to look like the film stars?

NP: Y-e-es! (almost cheering)
NC: Copied the styles. Didn't we? I mean there was no makeup. You know, a bit of beetroot, you know. (laughs)
NP: Ye-es.
NC: Beetroot and the blue you'd get out of a (blue-bag?)
NP: Ginger Rogers. I used to try and 'cause you was a dancer and I used to go dancing a lot as you know.
NC: Yeah.
NP: And I used to try to make myself look like Ginger Rogers. Not that I ever looked like her but, you know.
NC: Yeah.
NP: You'd think you were. (whoops with laughter)[24]

Men also imitated the stars they saw on screen, as one elderly man recalls:

> I know my friend used to wear a dark shirt and tie like the gangsters. And when
> he come out of the cinema, he used to strike a match under his fingernail just
> like they did. (laughs) He was holding the door once for somebody and soon as
> they got there, he let it go, you know. The sort of thing a gangster (laughs) would
> do. It impressed him.[25]

This memory not only highlights the role that imitation played in how
audience members related to the screen but, in retrospect, proves the concerns
of morality groups, featured in Chapter 4, who bemoaned the influence of
cinema upon young girls and boys who imitated the gangsters and other
characters they saw.[26] This practice of imitation extended to American films
seen by youngsters as well, as Jimmy Murray remembers:

> You'd be doing a Bing Crosby, holding the pipe, in the corner of the mouth or
> wearing a trilby like Edward G. on the side of the head. Bogart or something.
> Bogart. That's how you *associated* with them. In a way. But in your coat, you
> had your hand in your pocket like. A little (pause: 2 seconds), no way to shoot
> anybody like but still (laughs). You did little things what they, eh, what *they* did.
> [original emphasis][27]

Imitation became a way for audience members to 'associate' with those stars
they saw on the screen. They were able to bring the experience of film-going
into their lives through imitation of the dress and actions of those on the screen.

Memories such as these indicate, to a small extent, that audiences related
to the narratives they consumed. Studies of audience reception in the interwar
period are limited to Kuhn's study and a few others but they do give us some
insight into the ways in which audiences used and responded to popular film
and fiction. Often they declared they were interested in these narratives for
escape, such as the woman responding to the Mass Observation questionnaire
in 1938 who wrote, 'When going to the cinema we go to be entertained and
amused, and I think there is enough crime and tragedy in the world without
seeing it on screen.'[28] Films, and presumably novels, could act as a tonic that
allowed the worker to maintain his everyday life, according to Jim Godbold:

> Especially when you think you lived in a small market town and nothing ever
> happened. And people just went to work and girls went into service. And got
> half a crown a week. Just one half day off and that. You've gotta think in them
> terms, you see. And you would be impressed by eh, going to the cinema and
> seeing how gangsters went about. And Fred Astaire and Ginger Rogers and all
> that. Very impressive and that. It put sorta new heart into you really, you know.[29]

Godbold was able to subscribe to the role of the worker with the new heart
placed in him by the film and fiction industry and its gangsters and dancers.

Yet when one looks further into the responses of audiences one sees that such escapism was not such a simple process, and that audiences, to a certain extent, internalised the messages presented by films. Certainly the account by historian Carolyn Steedman of her mother's life growing up as working class in the 1920s and 1930s indicates that images of escapism and an ideology supporting the male breadwinner powerfully affected the day-to-day life of both mother and daughter.[30] The impact was largely negative as her mother's belief that 'goose-girls may marry kings' led to her own pronounced cynicism and depression as social mobility through marriage failed to materialise in her world. That this bitterness about men, marriage, and wealth was so severe also indicates that she believed that the fantasy and the reality were not so irreconcilable. For her, the fantasies of a better life that story-tales offered were not a type of escapism completely disconnected from the real world; rather these were opportunities to be taken or missed. I would argue that the world of film and fiction had to be recognisable to the audience in order to gain popularity and for this reason could not be a world completely detached from what they knew. As Kuhn's interviewee states, 'All these films were sort of made for you. You know you could see yourself in. Well I did anyways.'[31] In order to see themselves in the narrative, it had to be relevant to their lives. The film or novel may provide an escapist bubble, but that bubble was entirely formed by and surrounded by its historical and social environment and the dominant moral framework of the day. Doreen Lyell recounts the appeal of film-going in the 1930s:

> It was uplifting. And then again it was, em, there was always a moral message. I mean the good people didn't have much but in the end they were always happy and contented. And the bad people seemed to get away with something for a time but in the end, the morals were always there.[32]

The 'good and bad' people in the film both embodied and then instructed audiences about these collective morals. These characters provided an entry into the audience's experience of the fictional narrative. The context could be Shangri-la, America, or the Shanghai express, yet these characters produced a similar moral framework that featured heroes, villains, and love-interests.

J. P. Mayer, a University of London lecturer, undertook his own study of the impact of film on British audiences, leading to the publication of *Sociology of Film: Studies and Documents* in 1945. His study includes the responses, in full, of sixty-eight film-goers to questions posed by Mayer within the pages of *Picture-goer*. Conducted during World War II, his study nevertheless gives us insight into how audiences reacted to interwar films. Ordinary Britons responded in writing to two questions Mayer presented in an advertisement in February of 1945: '1. Have films ever influenced you with regards to personal decisions or behaviour? (Love, divorce, manners, fashion, etc.) Can you give instances? 2. Have films ever appeared in your dreams?.'[33] Respondents were instructed that there was no word limit and that the 'best' answers would receive rewards ranging from five shillings to a guinea. Mayer's film-goers by and large affirmed that films influenced them, while others declared that it had little impact on their decision making. The study's usefulness for this project is highlighted by the respondents' willingness to identify specific films from the interwar period and the influence of characters and narratives on their behaviour and outlook. One woman, identifying herself as a fifty-year-old 'Housewife and Part Time Red Cross Worker', recounts the impact of the 1933 film adaptation of the 1925 bestselling novel *Sorrell and Son* on her:

> The film that made a profound impression on me is not by any means a current one but one nevertheless that has remained in many people's memory like myself. To wit *Sorrell and Son* at the time of seeing this film films which starred 'J.B. Warner' [*sic*]. I was in 'Domestic Trouble' and feeling very morbid and miserable and also extremely sorry for myself, after seeing *Sorrell and Son* I came away from the Cinema with a sense of shame and made up my mind to be more courageous, independent and understanding.[34]

This woman took comfort and inspiration from a film based on a bestselling novel that I examine in detail in subsequent chapters. For her, the heroic figure of ex-soldier Stephen Sorrell became a means of relating to her own 'Domestic Trouble'. Further chapters return to the responses of Mayer's subjects on specific films I address. Their responses grant us some insight in the ways that audiences internalised the ideology of films through popular characters, and also occasionally adapted it. Certainly our fifty-year-old housewife had little trouble applying a masculine ideal to herself as a woman.

Work has been done by scholars of media studies as well as historians on the role that audiences play and have played in resisting or manipulating the narratives of mass media in the vein of our housewife. Janice Radway is chief among those working in this field and the trend that has arisen in recent engagements with popular culture, such as the modification of popular narratives by fans themselves, so-called 'fan fiction', demonstrates the willingness of audiences to shape and respond to mass culture in their own ways.[35] Lawrence Levine has further argued that audiences in the past responded and used popular culture in ways that challenged and sometimes subverted its assumptions; this was undoubtedly the case in many instances. My chapter on portrayals of women's work argues that this work was devalued on the screen, yet women certainly did work, and identified with male protagonists. Popular culture did not prevent, and at times encouraged, this through its very narrative arc. Yet new work is being done in media studies which has moved beyond a celebration of the fan's seeming agency to an understanding of the ways in which fans and fan fiction remains a profoundly conservative genre.[36] Certainly, it is difficult to argue with the powerful place that cinema and the single-volume novel held in the interwar period. This was the heady day of mass culture before the immense cynicism that arose from the post-World War II media landscape, related to the use and abuse of media during the interwar period and the 1920s and 1930s.[37] Post-World War II audiences had a much more nuanced and cynical view of media in part because of greater understandings of the terrible uses of media under the Nationalist Socialists, and in part because of a greater understanding of Britain's own use of propaganda.[38]

As Chapter 4 demonstrates, the British Board of Film Censors and the Home Office made considerable forays into shaping the media in the 1920s and 1930s. It was the relationship between the morals of the characters in films or novels and the morals of the audience that so concerned the BBFC and the Home Office in the interwar period. These agencies, more than anyone, realised the ideological impact of film and fiction upon audiences. The rigorous production and deployment of state-sponsored propaganda in World War II and a rapid shift in the censorship policies of the BBFC to favouring polarised depictions of Germany and Britain indicates the strength of this belief in the ability of film to mould minds.[39] The statement that opens Chapter 4 by the president of the BBFC says as much: 'I cannot believe that any single film can have any lasting effect on the public, but the result of the same themes repeated over and over again might be most undesirable.'[40] Themes that did not promote proper morals could not contribute to the dominant ideology upon which 'Englishness' was based between the wars, an ideology that contributed to a liberal democratic capitalist economy which in turn privileged the role of the male breadwinner and soldier. Thus this ideology, this 'theme' in popular culture, had to be carefully cultivated through censorship.

Who was this audience for these messages? Which class or classes were consuming popular fiction and film in the 1920s and 1930s? The short answer is the working and middle classes. Although both classes experienced considerable shifts in composition and size, the working and middle classes were relatively stable in their consumption of the new media of mass culture. The working classes had dominated early cinema attendance, and were joined by the middle classes as cinema producers and exhibitors actively courted them through lush picture palaces and the development of the feature film, rather than the short film. By the 1930s the middle class had largely been secured as a staple audience for the cinema. The middle classes were particularly important as Britain's economic and political spheres became markedly more middle class in composition and outlook.[41] As Ross McKibbin has argued, the sheer growth in the size of the middle classes and middle-class occupations throughout the interwar period indicated both its surprising flexibility and its primary role in the economy and nation. The conservatives, which dominated between the wars, were generally regarded as the political party of the middle classes, while middle-class jobs continued to proliferate in the form of small businesses and positions within an expanding government bureaucracy at the municipal and national level.[42] By the end of the 1930s the middle class had emerged as a 'technical–scientific–commercial–managerial class'.[43] The expansion of the lower middle classes who worked primarily within the service and white-collar sectors was particularly notable. Members of the lower middle class occupied clerical positions within offices and jobs as shop assistants in department stores, adamantly defining themselves by white-collar rather than blue-collar labour. Miles and Smith note that this class was 'newly dominant' by the 1930s and constituted 40 per cent of all families in England.[44]

Members of the middle class not only increased in the 1920s and 1930s but also, for the most part, flourished. Unemployment did not affect the middle class in the way that it did the working class and the growth of middle-class jobs remained relatively steady throughout the period, with middle-class salaries rising with inflation. This was the general trend after the rocky years from 1920 to 1923 had been weathered. Those years had ushered in what was seen as an economic crisis among the middle class. The economic policy of deflation, as a response to the collapse of the wartime economy, immediately and negatively affected the middle class. Salaries and wages fell faster than prices, and savings were affected. Coupled with this was the spectre of unemployment for the middle class as soldiers from all walks of life, including officers, had difficulty obtaining immediate employment after demobilisation. Yet, greater than the long-term impact of the crisis, which was minimal, was the climate of fear it produced in members of the middle class.[45] Even as that class enjoyed a sustained period of economic and political dominance in Britain, it was haunted by the prospect of economic instability and unemployment. The multiplying gradations that distinguished the upper middle class from the lower middle class and the often considerable differences in income between the two further added to this sense of instability. McKibbin notes that middle-class income was defined as being at minimum £250 per annum but that groups defined themselves as middle class according to their labour and whether it was factory work or not.[46] The middle classes as such encompassed a range of people from clerks and shop girls to those in the professions. This was a group whose aspirational tendencies were built into its very composition and the prospect of slipping from upper middle class to lower middle class seemed tangible to many.[47] Yet the dominant narratives of mass film and fiction emphasised the appeal and security of the middle classes above all else.

The images that both working-class and middle-class audiences consumed in the 1920s and 1930s were primarily those of middle-class success, with working-class characters occupying peripheral roles. This accords with a general sense by historians that, by this period, 'ordinary' Englishness was defined as middle-class Englishness.[48] James Hinton points out that in a Mass Observation survey on class and identity just prior to World War II, the majority of respondents identified themselves as middle class even when they were not.[49] Middle-class domination of the economy and nation was reflected not only in British film and fiction but was further mirrored by the popularity of narratives coming from the United States, which emphasised the middle-class 'everyman' as their centre. The prevalence of the middle classes, from the upper middle-class hero in novels by Philip Gibbs and films such as *Lives of a Bengal Lancer* (1935) to the beat cop detective in Sydney Horler's novels and the middle-class crime dramas of Agatha Christie, indicate that popular culture was a powerful tool for articulating middle-class interests and norms, which in turn were the norms of a capitalist liberal democracy. Popular culture in the form of novels and films offered all ranges of the middle classes the opportunity to read about and gaze upon themselves, and the working classes the potential to look ever upward.

Largely absent from popular film and fiction were representations of the contemporary aristocracy. They rarely appeared, particularly in American films, signalling that the era of aristocratic landlords was not to be idealised in popular culture. When the landed gentry did appear in British products they were treated with a reverence that the nineteenth century did not afford them. With the exception of the womanising and cruel Lord Tybar in A. S. M. Hutchinson's *If Winter Comes* (1921), fictional villains were seldom depicted as upper class. Instead, as Chapter 2 demonstrates, that role increasingly fell to the nouveau riche, who were described in negative terms that drew upon past representations of aristocratic villains. These nouveau riche villains were not adequately working for their wages and often acquired wealth through unsavoury means. They were 'bad apples' who highlighted the goodness of middle-class characters who worked for their wages. The upper class was portrayed with a careful and often doting respect, as though they were rare unicorns out of their time and place. In Michael Arlen's *The Green Hat*, the narrator speaks in hushed terms about the contrast between the aristocratic Iris and the real British politician Horatio Bottomley, a former MP (1906 to 1912, 1918 to 1922) and editor of the weekly magazine *John Bull*, who called for enlistment in the war and then was jailed in 1922 for selling fraudulent war bonds:[50]

> For I was what Gerald [Iris's brother] was not, what she obviously was not. I could somehow 'cope with' my time and generation, while they were of the breed destined to failure. I was of the race that is surviving the England of Horatio Bottomley, the England of lies, vulgarity, and unclean savagery; while they of the imperious nerves had failed, they had died that slow white death which is reserved for privilege in defeat.[51]

In Arlen's novel Iris faces another slow white death as she and her privilege decline throughout the novel. Narratives such as these positioned the aristocracy as unable to endure the post-World War I world. Even the hit film *Cavalcade* (1933) by British playwright Noel Coward, which viewed British history from 1899 to 1933 through the eyes of an upper middle-class husband and wife, situated the aristocracy as a nostalgic throwback to the last century as the husband and wife solemnly watch the parade of Queen Victoria's funeral. The aristocracy became, in these popular novels and films, something to be protected by their hardier middle-class counterparts, who were engaged more actively in the economy and in the struggle with the working classes. It was the middle class and a middle-class economy that would get them all through this crisis.

The working classes were featured in popular film and fiction more so than the aristocracy, yet they were usually relegated to peripheral or marginal roles. British films occasionally elevated a member of the working class to the role of the hero but these were inevitably women. The popular silent *Squibs* films (*Squibs* (1921), *Squibs Wins the Calcutta Sweeps* (1922), *Squibs Honeymoon* (1923)) featured the British Betty Balfour as a working-class heroine, as did the majority of films starring Gracie Fields in the 1930s. The image of an organised working class was tempered by the feminine and often absent-minded young woman at their fore as well as her own dreams of class mobility. More often than not, the working classes provided comic relief and were often prone to sentimentality, such as the gardener in Warwick Deeping's novel, *Sorrell and Son* (1925), who grumbles about guests wrecking his tulips, yet cuts a large bouquet of them when asked to by a pretty girl.[52] In films they occupied the same largely comedic roles. American films, presumably less interested in deploying hierarchies of class, nevertheless also used working-class characters as comedy relief or, in Frank Capra's films, as a benevolent and silent group in need of representation by the protective middle-class hero. This was an idealised vision of class relations in a period initially marked by trade union militancy, and most memorably, the general strike of 1926. This class tension was reflected in the bestselling novels from the 1920s, which habitually avoided even the term 'working class'. In *Bulldog Drummond* by H. C. McNeile, the hero, Drummond, refers to the evil appeal of communism as an effort to 'gull the working-man'.[53] The articulation of a working-class identity, let alone working-class collectivism, had a limited place in this period. This reflected the unease around class that resulted from the economic, social, and political instability throughout the period. In the 1930s widespread depression in Britain and the United States made Capra's compassionate images of silent unemployment more palatable, somewhat in line with images of Jarrow marchers, yet this was still a limited representation. What was clear throughout the 1920s and 1930s was that the images consumed by the working and middle classes were images primarily of the middle class.

The middle classes articulated themselves strongly against the working class through their participation in the expanding white-collar industry and their avoidance of menial factory work in the early twentieth century.[54] Even as the working class emerged from the war with a higher standard of living, high wages, and greater confidence in their importance to the economy, the aftermath of the war saw great changes to this group.[55] This confidence declined with the collapse of 'heavy' industries such as shipbuilding, steel, and coal and the emergence of 'light industries' which relied on assembly line technology and unskilled labour to produce products within the chemical, rubber, and canning industries.[56] The emergence of light industry, although a bright spot of growth between the wars for those women and young male workers employed in it, did not deflect the larger story of male unemployment which defined the working classes during the 1920s and 1930s. Even as the working classes were finally enfranchised in Britain, considerable sections of it were marginalised through sustained bouts of unemployment and a contraction of working-class occupations. Yet for those who did enjoy periods of employment, a wider availability and affordability of things like ready-made clothing and home appliances bridged the gap between the lives of the working and middle classes.[57] It was this range of groups who read the novels discussed here and attended feature-length films. Cinema became a weekly fixture for many working-class and middle-class people. Both classes could afford the novels released in a range of prices at the local bookseller or for lending at the local library.[58] Thus the working and middle classes intersected at the sites of consumption that surrounded film and fiction in the 1920s and 1930s.

Locating popular culture

The sources that are used here are the films and novels that were the most popular with the British public in the 1920s and 1930s. Why, one could ask, is popularity the central organising principle in this study? I argue that there can be no other dominant organising principle when it comes to a marriage of social and cultural history. I am interested in the novels and films that ordinary people paid to see or read, be it in flea-pit cinemas or at lending libraries, and what these narratives communicated to British audiences. I define 'popular' as those works that audiences themselves consumed in the period, rather than works that have survived the test of time and achieved notoriety in whatever form. Large numbers of people attending a film does not necessarily indicate that those viewers unanimously enjoyed it; however, nor can those numbers be ignored. Only 9,711 people saw *All Quiet on the Western Front* (1930) at the Regent Cinema in Portsmouth, in a year when most films could expect to have an average of 12,000 people attend with a 'hit' film bringing in over 20,000 audience members.[59] The amount of people consuming a narrative gives us important information about behaviour and hints at beliefs in the period. Audience members may, after all, profess their dislike of a particularly lowbrow film, yet pay good money to attend it once and even twice. Thus at the heart of this study are the narratives that large amounts of Britons consumed in their valuable spare time. A great number of these novels and films can be cast as the disposable fiction that Richard Hoggart so mourned from his vantage in post-war Britain, yet the very disposability of these works and their inability to survive beyond their time period is what makes these so vital to the cultural historian.[60] These narratives, which in hindsight appear sexist, racist, and elitist and are perhaps rightfully consigned to obscure second-hand shops or film archives, nevertheless tell us much about sex, race, and class in the 1920s and 1930s. For that very reason, the low and middle-brow works of the period that were most popular with British audiences deserve considerable attention from historians.

My focus on the works that ordinary Britons read and watched aims to bring much-needed attention to both the ordinary men and women at the centre of a widening democracy, and to the growth of a truly mass and increasingly Anglo-American culture in the interwar period. It departs from recent accounts of the interwar period which tend to depend upon sources from the upper class and upper middle class.[61] My work sidesteps the intellectuals, the bohemian elites, and sexual radicals in favour of something less refined, and clearly more conservative. Unlike Jonathan Rose's excellent study of responses of the working class to highbrow culture, I am interested in the works that he notes, 'cease to offer much after one has read a few volumes', as evidence of something repetitive but powerful about the period.[62] My study also contributes to existing scholarship on Anglo-American cultural exchange, by including the predominantly British novels and both the American and British films that were popular with British audiences.[63] There is some suggestion in existing information on reading patterns that British novels were bestsellers with both British audiences and American audiences. More importantly, however, the secondary sources on reading in the interwar period that I rely on do little to highlight or even problematise the popularity of American novels with British audiences. American novels simply do not have a huge presence in the sources I examine. The exception would be western novels, and particularly those by Zane Grey, which with their dependence on adamantly American landscapes, if not production, should be treated separately. The history of film-going, in contrast, acknowledges the popularity of a range of American films with British audiences, a topic that is explored later in this introduction. Based upon this disjuncture in studies of film and reading history, I chose to focus only upon the bestselling novels of the period, without searching out the relatively few American novels popular in Britain.

Along with the novels and films themselves, I use popular periodicals such as the *Daily Express*, which was the British newspaper with the highest circulation between the wars with around two million readers.[64] Other less popular newspapers make the occasional appearance. Some contain book or film reviews or articles on the impact of film or fiction. These were discovered in collections of clippings assembled by the Home Office or by examining newspapers published near the publication dates of key novels and films. These papers vary in political orientation from the leftist *New Statesman* to the conservative *The Times*, but the emphasis remains, for the most part, on the *Daily Express*. I also use cinema magazines with high circulations such as *Picturegoer* and *Film Weekly*, which provide the most active discussion of

Britain's popular culture and are particularly fruitful in highlighting some of the tensions, or lack thereof, surrounding American dominance of the film industry. The fourth chapter relies almost entirely on Home Office records on 'obscene literature', as well as the scenario reports and records of the British Board of Film Censors (BBFC). These records involve, in the Home Office's case, collections of press clippings documenting the varying attitudes of the press and the literary elite towards censorship, as well as the actions and responses of the Home Office secretary and his clerks to formal complaints. These files also include internal memoranda between key figures at the Home Office. The BBFC's scenario reports include detailed descriptions of the plots of films that their censors assessed and specific suggestions for censorship of films or scripts, as well as internal discussions of controversial films. They also include reports by the BBFC on the state of cinema and minutes of meetings with private interest groups such as the Birmingham Cinema Enquiry and the London Public Morality Council.

Aside from these sources on censorship, it is the 'bestseller' novel and the 'hit' film which are at the core of this work and identifying the most popular examples is no easy task, in part, because the meteoric development of this media made for confused record-keeping. Historian Billie Melman points out that the term 'bestseller' did not even come into common usage until after World War I.[65] It was only then that the collective impact of changes in papermaking, the printing press, and methods of distribution such as railway and steamer were fully realised by the publishing industry. A book could then be printed at a relatively rapid rate and distributed more widely at a cheaper price. This development was met by a growing reading audience that had steadily developed after the 1870 Education Act made schooling mandatory for children under 13 years of age and which resulted in a literate society at the outset of World War I.[66] A working and expanding middle-class audience could now afford to read the novels that flooded the market at a variety of prices. The mass printing, dissemination, and consumption of novels became such a phenomenon that some warranted the word 'bestseller'. The 'hit' film had a similarly sudden birth. In Britain at the outset of the century, short silent films were usually shown in music halls or churches to a primarily working-class audience, before the first purpose-built cinemas were created in 1907.[67] By 1914, 5,000 cinemas had a weekly audience of 7–8 million. By 1917 attendance had more than doubled, with 20 million people going to the cinema per week and the 90-minute feature film firmly in place.[68] In 1934, 903 million people attended the cinema and by 1940 yearly audiences reached over 1 billion.[69] Middle-class attendance at the cinema contributed to this increase as more and more viewed the feature films in the often-palatial picture palaces that aimed for respectability.

By the 1920s, the existence of the bestseller and the hit film was becoming steadily more secure, even while both were still very modern media. Audiences, reviewers, and producers alike at first marvelled at the popularity of the bestseller and the hit film. Literary critic Q. D. Leavis was fully cognisant of the freshness of the term 'bestseller' for novels when she embarked on a self-described 'anthropological' approach to the appearance of this beast in the middle of the British library in 1932.[70] Her study *Fiction and the Reading Public* mourned the supremacy of the bestseller but was also a testament to its sudden and complete dominance of the bookselling market. Hoping to understand and explain the appeal of the bestseller, she sent a questionnaire out to sixty unnamed authors whom she placed into a variety of categories:

A. 'Highbrow'
B. 'Middlebrow' read as 'literature'
C. 'Middlebrow' not read as 'literature', but not writing for the lowbrow market.
D. Absolute bestsellers.[71]

Earlier in her book she cites authors such as E. M. Forster, D. H. Lawrence, and Virginia Woolf as authors of serious literature, so we can presume they would fall under the highbrow category while categories 'B' and 'C' seem rather similar and consist of the likes of Warwick Deeping and A. S. M. Hutchinson, whose works are examined later. The 'Absolute bestsellers' are those such as *The Sheik* (1919) by E. M. Dell and 'thrillers' by 'Sapper' aka H. C. McNeile, whose popularity among library patrons she likened to a drug habit.[72] Leavis provides valuable figures that indicate the sheer popularity of bestsellers. According to Leavis, those occupying the highbrow category could expect sales of 'a steady three thousand, with greater sales of five, ten, or even fifteen thousand', while absolute bestsellers 'have a buying public of a quarter or half a million, and in some cases of a million'.[73] This was a huge disparity in sales that indicates the extent of the impact of the middle and lowbrow novel upon the reading public and signals the need for historians to concentrate on such a widely consumed medium.

As popular as these novels were and aside from the ambivalent attention paid to them by Leavis, it is difficult to find references to them in the literary press beyond the early 1920s. For instance, the writer 'Affable Hawk' from the political and literary weekly the *New Statesman* wrote of Margaret Kennedy's new bestseller in 1925, 'I have just read *The Constant Nymph* ... Everybody has been reading it, and if I have been asked once I have been asked a hundred times, "What do you think of it?".'[74] Although Hawk granted the novel a favourable review, it did not take long for the highbrow press to distinguish between the bestseller and quality literature. *The Green Hat* (1924) by Michael Arlen was reviewed fairly generously by the *Times Literary Supplement*, which wrote, 'Here, as before, he seems to be at great pains to be vivacious and superficial; yet seriousness will keep breaking in. The result is both irritating and amusing.'[75] The *Times Literary Supplement* was less kind in 1927 when evaluating another brisk seller by Arlen, *Young Men in Love*: 'His lechers are ineffective in what they take to be love because they would be ineffective in anything. There, even more than in his frequent bad taste, his flashy and slovenly style, his assumption of complete knowledge of the world, his melodramatic tricks, is the explanation of his failure.'[76] By the end of the 1920s the *Times Literary Supplement* was able to distinguish between the 'tricks' of bestselling novelists and the quality literature that was being produced. At this point, reviews of the most popular novels of the day were seldom seen in the literary weeklies, with the exception of some middlebrow works by authors such as Philip Gibbs, whose war correspondence was often mentioned by the *Times Literary Supplement* in its reviews of his novels.[77] A study of bestsellers in this period must cope with books that were incredibly popular, yet not reviewed or discussed in the highbrow literary journals that have survived.

Occasionally the lowbrow novel did receive a review in newspapers such as the *Daily Mail*, the paper notoriously labelled by Lord Salisbury as 'a paper written by clerks for clerks'.[78] The *Daily Mail* enthused about the latest Bulldog Drummond book by H. C. McNeile aka 'Sapper' under the headline 'Thrilling new "Sapper" Story. Bull-dog Drummond Sequel'. The article served as advertisement for the book rather than a critical review, and included an excerpt of the story. The article introduced it as follows: 'Bull-dog Drummond is one of the popular heroes of modern fiction, and in this breathless story, with its murders, its plots, and its poison that kills as it touches, he is at his best in daring, in resource, and in grim resolution.'[79] This approach to reporting on the phenomenon of the bestseller mimicked what was happening in film magazines. Magazines like *Picturegoer* and *Film Weekly*, although they reviewed films, tended to provide a platform for their promotion by featuring flattering articles on upcoming films as well as film stars. These fan magazines were supported by others aimed at cinema exhibitors such as *Bioscope* and the *Film*

Spectator, which advised cinema managers on how to best 'sell' their pictures to audiences. Exhibitor catalogues that were sent to cinema managers also attempted to illustrate the incredible popularity of particular films and the novels on which the films were sometimes based. However, sources such as these provide more insight into the effectiveness of the publisher or producer in securing advertisements than they do into the popularity and reception of the novels and films themselves. In sources aimed at the cinema manager every novel is a bestseller and every film a potential 'hit'. Nevertheless, where press attention to films and fiction can be located, I have taken pains to include it. This type of press coverage can, after all, occasionally illuminate those themes that were difficult to sell, such as the adolescent love of the girlish heroine, Tess, for the much older Lewis Dodd in Margaret Kennedy's bestselling novel, turned film, *The Constant Nymph* (novel, 1924; film, 1933), discussed in Chapter 4.

Aside from exhibitors' catalogues, the overly enthusiastic reviews of the popular presses, and the challenging absence of reviews in the 'quality' press, how is one to discern what is and is not a bestseller or a hit film in this period? I rely upon studies already conducted by excellent historians who have worked in an area where figures and evidence are clearly difficult, if not impossible, to obtain. Box-office statistics for cinemas in the 1920s and 1930s are largely non-existent and there is limited evidence of either admission figures or film distribution patterns. Figures on bestselling novels are just as scarce, for lists of bestselling novels were not maintained until the 1970s. For the interwar period, as Clive Bloom has noted, 'to discover the actual figures for increased readerships, let alone interpret their real meaning is something of a night-mare'.[80] This nightmare is further exacerbated by the bombing of Paternoster Square in London during World War II, an area that Joseph McAleer identifies as the 'heart of the publishing industry'.[81] The bombing destroyed records of major publishing houses, which may have shed light on audience tastes and preferences.

Cinema records suffered a similar fate, with the BBFC's scenario reports from the 1920s destroyed in World War II and generally poor record keeping on the part of managers. Sue Harper's discovery of the ledger of admission figures for the Regent cinema in Portsmouth remains the only record that clearly links admission figures to the actual titles of feature films in the 1930s. These figures indicate (for one theatre) which films drew the largest number of people, making it a 'hit', and which films did not. The composition of Portsmouth, which was largely working-class, and the Regent itself, which was the largest theatre on the edge of a 'respectable' part of the city, indicates to Harper that it likely catered to the lower middle class. The hit film of the decade, *Snow White and the Seven Dwarfs* (1937), drew 35,761 people during its run at the cinema while the biggest flop of the decade was unfortunately entitled *Determination* and brought in 5,654 people.[82] The 1920s offer no such evidence and the film historian is forced to rely upon a variety of indicators of a film's popularity such as evidence of sequels and informal lists of top films compiled in film magazines.

As difficult as it may be to identify the top films and novels for the interwar period, the historians upon whom I rely have obviously delved into the fray. Clive Bloom, Joseph McAleer, Billie Melman, and Maria Bracco have identified the most popular authors of this period and provide some sense of the hit novels.[83] Bloom in particular took years of his own research into consideration when he compiled a list of the 'bestsellers' of the twentieth century by author. Bloom bases his list on records of Britain's major publisher, Hodder & Stoughton, as well as available evidence from booksellers and libraries. He uses these fragmentary records to discern the popularity of authors whose works were sold in either cheap or expensive editions, and often simultaneously. He notes that a popular author 'could expect his work to sell in half a crown, one shilling and sixpenny editions (and lower) *simultaneously*, gaining the attention of a wider readership'.[84] Libraries offered cheap memberships, and stores including W. H. Smith and Boots operated circulating libraries.[85] Some authors were important enough to garner their own ledger of sales. One example was E. Phillips Oppenheim, who was vastly profitable to Hodder & Stoughton throughout the 1920s and 1930s, a profitability that earned him a life of leisure.[86] Oppenheim continued to be popular into the late 1930s even though he was in his seventies at that point.[87] According to a piece by the *Observer* in 1936, Oppenheim, and a number of the other writers discussed here, were able to weather a publishing slump in the late 1930s.[88] Under the subheading 'Fiction down: facts up' the writer notes that 'Facts are the rage – nicely dressed, pleasantly narrated, entertaining facts', while fiction sales had declined. The piece quotes an editor saying that 'the competent fairly highbrow type' were not popular with readers while authors of 'action or mystery', specifically identifying the author of the Saint series Leslie Charteris, had 'shown considerable increases'. The same article cites an increase in sales for the Collins Crime Club series. Thus certain genres maintained their popularity between the wars, and business was steady for thriller and action writers, even as reviewers occasionally noted that their plots failed to keep up

with the time. The *Observer* in October 1937 described a short story by Oppenheim, called 'An Opportunist in Arms' as 'an epic on the arming of Abyssinia
[by the British] against aggression' but noted that it nevertheless 'comes a little
after the fair'.[89] Still, readers read Oppenheim and others discussed here. Mass
Observation surveys conducted during the war, such as a 1940 survey of the
literature habits of fifty students with an average age of 17 years, provides a
wealth of knowledge about long-time favourite authors. These teenagers identified Oppenheim, Charteris, and Innes as their most popular authors, all of
whom will be discussed here.[90]

For the most part I have focused upon bestsellers regardless of genre or
topic, yet where I have narrowed the field, I have done so in three ways.
First, I have not included works from previous centuries which were reissued
and remained popular with readers, such as those by Charles Dickens and
Jane Austen. While Andrew Higson notes the popularity of 'heritage films' in
the 1980s as a way of reimagining a Britain immune from the political and
economic conflicts of that period, a similar such study could, and it is hoped
will, be done on the way certain classic novels steadily gained in popularity
during the interwar years.[91] Second, and perhaps most significantly, I have
tended to concentrate upon male authors and those novels that were arguably
aimed at a male readership. This leaves women writers as well as romance as a
genre less examined, although these two topics have received significant attention by other historians.[92] Likewise, I have avoided examining the adamantly
American genre of the western. In part I have made these exceptions because
a critical look at the works of lowbrow male authors writing broad thrillers
and adventure stories is needed.[93] Books that do discuss the appeal of *Bulldog
Drummond* and other popular works tend to reminiscence about the innocence
and adventure of boyhood reading.[94] Even Richard Hoggart, whose study
The Uses of Literacy influenced my interest in this subject, tended to view the
works of the interwar period in nostalgic terms, while post-war popular culture
horrified him.[95] For Hoggart, it was the post-war period that ushered in the
sex-and-violence novels that featured pumped-up American male tough guys
and sexually available women. Such polarised comparisons tend to overlook
the efforts of interwar male authors to stabilise masculine roles after World
War I.

I have also concentrated upon the works of male authors because I wish to
demonstrate the pervasiveness of concerns about gender and work in those
works produced by and for men and not only in those by and for women.
Romances were not the only novels that deployed discourses that emphasised

the joys of heterosexual union. Indeed, detective novels by women such as Agatha Christie and Dorothy Sayers are indistinguishable in many ways from similar stories penned by male authors. Yet in order to demonstrate the persistence of gendered labour narratives, and for those that may be interested in questions of audience and authorship, I have chosen to stress masculine novels which indeed may have been read by women such as thrillers, adventure, and detective novels, all of which were incredibly popular in the 1920s and 1930s.[96] It is difficult to gauge the readership of these novels by gender but one can assume that women read these narratives, as did men.

My attention to issues of authorship is limited, although I will note for those who may be interested that no major class, gender, or race discrepancy exists between the lives of popular authors and filmmakers and their subjects in film and fiction. A number of the popular writers featured here, including Philip Gibbs, Michael Arlen, and A. S. M. Hutchinson, had worked as journalists. Gibbs was particularly well known as one of five accredited war correspondents during World War I before writing *The Middle of the Road*.[97] A brief look at the authors reveals that they are not such a haphazard bunch. Most were middle class and few were born of anything that could be identified as the landed gentry. Most of them had received some form of formalised education either at a college or, in Warwick Deeping's case, a short stint at the University of Cambridge.[98] Consequently the middle-class emphasis upon hard work and social mobility in these novels was born of the experience of our authors. Yet their literary ambitions had doubtless acquainted them with the potential poverty that awaits most writers. All were dependent upon employment, but not the employment that defined the working class in this period. In many ways, they possessed the economic and social characteristics of those in the lower middle class.

The background of those involved in producing the hit films of the period are harder to present in a coherent manner. In part this is because of the difficulty of deciding whose role is most instrumental to the final presentation of the story on the screen. An emphasis on the director's vision can often diminish the considerable contribution of the author whose work was adapted, while concentrating on the writer's background can also dismiss the impact of the person who adapts the story for the screen. However, even among directors, screenwriters, and producers one can see a degree of commonality in their backgrounds that put them on a par with the middle-class authors of the bestselling novels. James Hilton, the British novelist whose novels were the basis of hit films such as the American production of *Lost Horizon* (1937) and the British film *Goodbye Mr Chips* (1939), and who also contributed to the screenplay of *Camille* (1936), was the son of a headmaster (on whom Mr Chips was supposedly based). Frank Capra, whose films *Lost Horizon* and *Mr Deeds Goes to Town* (1936) were popular with British and American audiences alike, immigrated to America with his parents from Italy before working his way up from newspaper boy to director. Alfred Hitchcock was the son of a greengrocer. These stories reflect a similar narrative of social mobility that was, in turn, reflected in their work.

In terms of the films I use, the efforts of historians John Sedgwick, Sue Harper, Christine Gledhill, and Annette Kuhn are key in identifying the popular films of this period. Sedgwick's work in particular provides the historian with a thoroughly researched and calculated account of the top films in a number of west-end theatres in London in the 1930s. The formula he has designed is a relative measure of film popularity and is called 'Popstat'. This formula takes into account the earning power of the particular cinema itself, the billing of the film, the number of theatres exhibiting the film, and the duration of the film's exhibition, resulting in a series of appendices listing films by popularity.[99] Sue Harper's concrete admission figures from the Regent cinema in Portsmouth, for the most part, support Sedgwick's works. Yet where there is discrepancy I have looked at hits identified by both scholars. The 1920s, however, are more of a puzzle than the 1930s. Indeed the difference between the two decades in terms of sources is both remarkable and unfortunate. My selection of popular films from the 1920s then are based upon work by Christine Gledhill and are sadly underrepresented here, mostly due to availability.[100] Yet, some hits that generated considerable attention in the developing film press do stand out, such as *The Sheik* (1921 [UK release 1923]) and its sequel *The Son of the Sheik* (1926). Those have been included here.

The number of hit films and their availability make for a somewhat coherent, yet necessarily diverse, category.[101] That said, a study of both film and fiction makes for a dizzying array of stories and the reader will no doubt notice that only a limited number of films and novels are referenced in each chapter and some films and novels may appear in one chapter but not another, while others garner only passing mention in text or footnote. I want to stress that this is not because the stock characteristics I identify in one, particularly among characters and plots, do not exist across the bulk of these stories. For example, it is indeed the case that the features of the love-interest that I discuss here can be found across a wide range of novels and films. To avoid adding to already lengthy chapters on each subject, yet to also illustrate the range of films and novels which audiences saw and read, I have concentrated on a variety of narratives which offer particularly promising opportunities to consider dynamics present in a much broader range of novels and films. I have also tried to narrow my research to films that were in the top ten films of their year of release in Britain, and I have made allowances for bestselling novels that were adapted into films in the same period. Evidence indicates that audiences tended to follow novels into film and vice versa, noting as one respondent to Mayer's survey did, 'It is really interesting to be able to imagine a flesh-and-blood character rather than the shadowy image created by the author's ethereal description'.[102] I should also note that because ranking lists of the top film titles exist, I have not narrowed the field of films towards more 'masculine' films rather than romances.

My work differs from other historians examining the history of popular film in Britain in that I also include American films that were popular.[103] This is a necessary acknowledgement of America's influence over the British film industry and British audiences after World War I.[104] By the 1930s and even in the 1920s, American films predominated in film-goers' tastes. Attempts to rehabilitate the British 'quota quickie' (films produced to meet the requirements of the 1927 Cinematograph Act, which demanded the exhibition of a certain number of British-produced films) from the annals of audience scorn are somewhat dubious on the part of film historians.[105] Within the pages of *Picturegoer* and *Film Weekly* audiences repeatedly expressed their disdain for British films. The Mass Observation survey of film-goers in 1938 demonstrated that 64 per cent of the 559 respondents indicated they preferred American films over British ones; one audience member saying rather bluntly, 'As regards British Pictures candidly I think they are awful. I don't go if I know its British, because the talk is terrible and the people old and ugly.'[106] Even those films that one respondent identified as fine British films such as *Lives of a Bengal Lancer* and *Mutiny on the Bounty* were actually American productions with Britain as a subject and a number of British actors.[107] Indeed, Hollywood demonstrated a fascination with Britain and made numerous films set in Britain, based upon British history, and using British sources and actors.[108] What does one make of Charlie Chaplin's films, which were produced and financed by American companies and were made by a man who experienced a working-class childhood in London but who lived and worked in America? Hitchcock also realised his greatest success when he moved to America and many are unfamiliar with his earlier films made in Britain. The cosmopolitan nature of the film industry in this period makes it difficult to pinpoint either an entirely

British or an entirely American production.

Film studies, using nationality as their point of approach in this period, must engage with the cosmopolitan and global nature of a film industry operating within the confines of global capitalism and also take into account the ability of the audience to transgress national borders. Andrew Higson has written about the false premise upon which many national film-histories are based:

> This traditional concept promoted an ideal version of a national cinema as an entirely self-sufficient cultural and economic institution, financed by local capital, staffed by a native workforce using locally produced technology, and neatly marked off from other national cinemas by borders and customs posts. This ideal cinema is assumed to produce films which express and explore pure, authentic national identities and indigenous cultural traditions.[109]

Higson claims that, 'of course, the ideal cannot exist. Certainly it is far from having existed in Britain – and surely it has never existed in any country.'[110] Studies of cinema within a particular nation must 'acknowledge the representation of cross-cultural, hybrid identities in "national films", rather than some spurious notion of authentic indigeniety'.[111] Even more important for this work than the tangle of national involvements in the production of film was the ability of the interwar British audience to identify with the narratives presented by American films enough to popularise them through attendance.

This premise necessitates moving beyond a tidy equation that conceives of British films (or novels) as reflecting purely British concerns, an equation which ignores what was truly popular as well as the complexities of national identity posed by directors such as Chaplin and later Hitchcock. The limited work on audiences that exists, such as Kuhn's interviews with senior citizens who grew up in the 1930s, indicates that audiences did relate strongly to actors and plots of American films.[112] Thus regardless of the film's geographic ties, we will see that concerns about gender, work, and nation in Britain in the 1920s and 1930s found expression in American films that British audiences paid to see, as well as British novels that were purchased or borrowed. This exchange of culture demonstrates that concerns about capitalism and its relation to gender and the nation took on global dimensions following the war, particularly in the 1930s as both Britain and America experienced large-scale unemployment that chiefly affected male workers.[113] This, at the very least, justifies the inclusion of American film in a study of popular culture in interwar Britain. By including American films, British films where applicable, and the largely British bestseller, this study puts what was truly popular with British audiences at its forefront and examines the messages put forth by these popular narratives.

This book is organised around the characters that dominated the fiction and film narratives of the period: the heroes, villains, and love-interests of popular culture. Additional chapters consider popular culture as part of a larger ideological framework that defined ordinary Britons as interested in the institutions that buttressed interwar Britain. In Chapter 1, I first address the role of the hero as a character who embodies traits collectively valued by readers and the audience. In doing so, I answer Max Jones's invitation to revisit heroic figures as a way of examining the culture of the period.[114] The heroes in these stories did indeed express concerns over the state of Britain after World War I and the viability of a capitalist economy that granted power to unscrupulous businessmen. Ultimately through hard work they nevertheless resituated themselves into this economy, thus promoting a type of moral economy where a breadwinner wage and a commitment to the nation rewards the hallmark traits of the interwar hero. Chapters on the villain and the love-interest further demonstrate the need to not just look at heroes but at those characters around him who were instrumental in defining his traits through their relationships and interactions.

The villain, we will see in Chapter 2, explicitly embodied interwar anxieties about social mobility among both men and women, the acquisition of wealth by businessmen through profiteering, post-war unemployment, and a government that could not entirely be trusted. Central to concerns about the villain, I argue, was a particularly twentieth-century concern about performance and 'knowability', as the hallmark of the villain was his ability to disguise himself as anyone, be it a member of the upper class, government, or even a different race. Yet although the character of the villain expressed concerns about a capitalist economy and the effectiveness of government, the villain in these stories did not triumph; in this way these anxieties were contained and moderated and the moral economy espoused by the hero was endorsed.

Another vital part of this containment of the anxieties outlined above was the role of the female love-interest, which will be visited in Chapter 3. The female love-interest often occupied a fairly dynamic role in bestselling novels and hit films, as her status could radically shift within the narrative. My contention is that concerns about women's roles within the economy and the eroding status of the male breadwinner were moderated by the female love-interest's subscription to love, and only love, at key points in the narrative. Women in these stories gave up their own claims to economic and social mobility for the sake of love and did so repeatedly. This feature became central to modern conceptions of romantic love in the popular culture of the period.

It also soothed concerns about female mobility as women's work was becoming increasingly valuable within emerging industries in the 1920s and 1930s and while traditionally male-dominated areas of work were suffering. These narratives maintained traditional notions of male and female work by emphasising love as an adequate and mutually exclusive substitution for work.

Chapter 4 looks at the British Board of Film Censors and the Home Office's efforts to endorse the above characters through censorship. Although the bestsellers and hit films that form the basis of this study seldom prompted censorship or even comment from the BBFC or the Home Office, I examine the works that did prompt discussion in order to highlight the assumptions at work among censors. Works that did not receive widespread circulation within Britain provide a useful contrast to those that defined 'bestseller' and popular. The process of censorship reveals much about the ideas that these organisations had about the hero, the villain, and the love-interest. Consequently I demonstrate that the government was actively involved in sanctioning a popular culture formula that buttressed the role of the soldier and breadwinner and the role of a capable, upright interwar British government. The government, in this respect, promoted and used the popular culture industry as an ideological tool from its earliest inception.

I end this study by briefly considering the endurance of the breadwinner and soldier ideal beyond the 1920s and 1930s. The media landscape shifted considerably during World War II and beyond, all which would seem to indicate a different life for mass culture and its concerns. I look briefly at the post-war period where heroes and happy endings do take on new meanings, yet I also point to the enduring legacy of a formula that found its footing and an enduring audience within the 1920s and 1930s.

Notes

1 J. Stevenson, *British Society 1914–45* (London: Penguin, 1984), p. 266. Stevenson notes that these official statistics did not encompass agricultural workers or women.

2 N. Hiley, '"Nothing More than a Craze": Cinema Building in Britain from 1909 to 1914', in Andrew Higson (ed.), *Young and Innocent: The Cinema in Britain 1896–1930* (Exeter: University of Exeter Press, 2002), pp. 111–27.

3 Q. D. Leavis, *Fiction and the Reading Public* (London: Chatto & Windus, 1932), p. 70.

4 J. Sedgwick, *Popular Filmgoing in 1930s Britain: A Choice of Pleasures* (Exeter: University of Exeter Press, 2000), p. 270.

5 R. Colls, *Identity of England* (Oxford: Oxford University Press, 2002); W. Webster, *Englishness and Empire 1939–1965* (Oxford: Oxford University Press, 2005); A.

Light, *Forever England: Femininity, Literature and Conservatism between the Wars* (London: Routledge, 1991).

6   T. J. Jackson Lears, 'Making Fun of Popular Culture', *American Historical Review* 97:5 (1992), 1417–26; L. Levine, 'The Folklore of Industrial Society: Popular Culture and Its Audiences', *American Historical Review* 97:5 (1992), 1369–99.

7   D. L. LeMahieu, *A Culture for Democracy: Mass Communication and the Cultivated Mind in England between the Wars* (Oxford: Clarendon Press, 1988).

8   *Ibid.*, pp. 4, 30.

9   *Ibid.*, p. 7. Adrian Bingham also argues that the press catered to women to a greater extent than has generally been acknowledged (*Gender, Modernity and the Popular Press in Interwar Britain* (Oxford: Oxford University Press, 2004)).

10 R. James, *Popular Culture and Working-Class Taste in Britain, 1930–1939: A Round of Cheap Diversions?* (Manchester: Manchester University Press, 2010).

11 M. Horkheimer and T. Adorno, *Dialectic of Enlightenment: Philosophical Fragments*, trans. E. Jephcott (Stanford, CA: Stanford University Press, 1947; reprint, 2002).

12 T. Adorno, 'Culture Industry Reconsidered', *New German Critique* 6 (1975), 12–19, 17.

13 L. Beers, *Your Britain: Media and the Making of the Labour Party* (Cambridge, MA: Harvard University Press, 2010); C. Ross, *Media and the Making of Modern Germany: Mass Communication, Society, and Politics from the Empire to the Third Reich* (Oxford: Oxford University Press, 2008).

14 Adorno, 'Culture Industry Reconsidered', p. 16; M. Foucault, *Discipline and Punish: The Birth of the Prison*, trans. Alan Sheridan (New York: Vintage, 1979).

15 For a discussion of the role of producers of popular culture, see Lears, 'Making Fun of Popular Culture', 1417–26.

16 R. Overy, *The Morbid Age: Britain between the Wars* (London: Allen Lane, Penguin, 2009); S. Kingsley Kent, *Making Peace: The Reconstruction of Gender in Interwar Britain* (Princeton: Princeton University Press, 1993); J. Stevenson and C. Cook, *The Slump: Britain in the Great Depression* (London: Longman, 2009).

17 M. Houlbrook, '"The Man with the Powder Puff" in Interwar London', *Historical Journal* 50:1 (2007), 145–71; Kingsley Kent, *Making Peace*.

18 J. Butler, *Gender Trouble: Feminism and the Subversion of Identity* (New York: Routledge, 1999); M. Foucault, *The History of Sexuality: Volume I: An Introduction*, trans. Robert Hurley (New York: Vintage, 1978; reprint, 1990); M. Foucault, *The Use of Pleasure: The History of Sexuality: Volume II* (New York: Vintage, 1990); E. Kosofsky Sedgwick, *Epistemology of the Closet* (Berkeley, CA: University of California Press, 1990).

19 Foucault, *History of Sexuality: Vol. I*, p. 64.

20 See also M. Foucault, 'Governmentality', in P. Rabinow and N. Rose (eds), *The Essential Foucault: Selections from the Essential Works of Foucault 1954–1984*, pp. 229–45 (New York: New Press, 2003).

21 Matt Houlbrook's exploration of Edith Thompson's intricate relationship to fiction and her 'fashioning of the self' through reading signals both the potential of such an investigation and also its complexity ('"A Pin to See the Peepshow": Culture, Fiction, and Selfhood in Edith Thompson's Letters, 1921–1922', *Past and Present*

207 (2010), 215–49).

22 C. Gledhill (ed.), *Stardom: Industry of Desire* (London: Routledge, 1991).

23 A. Kuhn, *An Everyday Magic: Cinema and Cultural Memory* (London: I. B. Tauris, 2002), pp. 240–8.

24 *Ibid.*, 176.

25 *Ibid.*, 106.

26 A. Davies, 'The Scottish Chicago? From "Hooligans" to "Gangsters" in Inter-War Glasgow', *Cultural and Social History* 4:4 (2007), 511–27.

27 Kuhn, *An Everyday Magic*, p. 107.

28 Mrs J. Holding in J. Richards and D. Sheridan (eds), *Mass-Observation at the Movies* (London: Routledge, 1987), p. 57.

29 Kuhn, *An Everyday Magic*, p. 230.

30 *Landscape for a Good Woman: A Story of Two Lives* (London: Virago, 1986), p. 16.

31 Annie Wright in Kuhn, *An Everyday Magic*, p. 229.

32 *Ibid.*, 230.

33 J. P. Mayer, *Sociology of Film: Studies and Documents* (London: Faber & Faber, 1945), p. 181.

34 *Ibid.*, 190.

35 *Reading the Romance: Women, Patriarchy, and Popular Literature* (Chapel Hill: University of North Carolina Press, 1991); Levine, 'Folklore of Industrial Society', 1369–99.

36 J. Gray, C. Sandvoss, and C. L. Harrington (eds), *Fandom: Identities and Communities in a Mediated World* (New York: New York University Press, 2007); C. Sandvoss, *Fans: The Mirror of Consumption* (Cambridge: Polity, 2005).

37 Ross, *Media and the Making of Modern Germany*; N. J. Cull, *Selling War: The British Propaganda Campaign against American 'Neutrality' in World War II* (Oxford University Press, 1995), pp. 5–32.

38 D. Culbert, 'The Impact of Anti-Semitic Film Propaganda on German Audiences: *Jew Suss* and the *Wandering Jew* (1940)', in R. A. Etlin (ed.), *Art, Culture, and Media under the Third Reich* (University of Chicago Press, 2002), pp. 139–57; M. O'Brien, 'The Celluloid War: Packaging War for Sale in Nazi Home-Front Films', in Etlin (ed.), *Art, Culture, and Media under the Third Reich*, pp. 158–80.

39 N. J. Cull, *Selling War*; James Chapman, *The British at War: Cinema, State, and Propaganda 1939–1945* (London: I. B. Tauris, 1998).

40 E. Shortt, speech to the Conference of the Cinema Exhibitors' Association, 27 June 1935.

41 Harold Perkin notes that the composition of government was increasingly middle class after World War I, due in part to Lloyd George's effort to include businessmen and members of the professionalising class as MPs; H. Perkin, *The Rise of Professional Society: England since 1880* (London: Routledge, 1989).

42 R. McKibbin, 'Class and Conventional Wisdom in Interwar Britain', in *Ideologies of Class: Social Relations in Britain 1880–1950* (Oxford: Oxford University Press, 1990), pp. 259–93.

43 R. McKibbin, *Classes and Cultures: England 1918–1951* (Oxford: Oxford University Press, 1998), p. 49.

44 P. Miles and M. Smith, *Cinema, Literature & Society: Elite and Mass Culture in Interwar Britain* (London: Croom Helm, 1987).

45 McKibbin, *Classes and Culture*, p. 50.

46 *Ibid.*, pp. 44–9.

47 P. Bailey, 'White Collars, Gray Lives? The Lower Middle Class Revisited', *Journal of British Studies* 38:3 (1999), 273–90.

48 Colls, *Identity of England*; Light, *Forever England*.

49 J. Hinton, 'The "Class" Complex: Mass Observation and Cultural Distinction in Pre-War Britain', *Past and Present* 199 (May 2008), 210.

50 A. J. A. Morris, 'Bottomley, Horatio William (1860–1933)', in H. C. G. Mathew and B. Harrison (eds), *Oxford Dictionary of National Biography* (Oxford: Oxford University Press, 2004).

51 M. Arlen, *The Green Hat: A Romance for a Few People* (London: Collins, 1924), p. 15.

52 W. Deeping, *Sorrell and Son* (New York: Alfred A. Knopf, 1925).

53 *Bulldog Drummond* (New York: Doubleday, 1934 [1920]), p. 237.

54 The claims of groups to the title or experience of the 'middle-class' is a subject of considerable debate with historians. See 'Patricians and the Plebs', in E. P. Thompson, *Customs in Common* (London: Merlin Press, 1991); D. Wahrman, '"Middle-Class" Domesticity Goes Public: Gender, Class, and Politics from Queen Caroline to Queen Victoria', *Journal of British Studies* 32:4 (1993), 396–432.

55 B. A. Waites, 'The Effect of the First World War on Class and Status in England, 1910–20', *Journal of Contemporary History* 11:1 (1976), 27–48.

56 M. Glucksmann, *Women Assemble: Women Workers and the New Industries in Inter-War Britain* (London: Routledge, 1990).

57 J. Stevenson, 'Myth and Reality: Britain in the 1930s', in Alan Sked and Chris Cook (eds), *Crisis and Controversy: Essays in Honour of A. J. P. Taylor* (London: Macmillan, 1976).

58 J. Rose notes that the vast majority of working-class readers used subscription and 2d. libraries to procure their reading materials; J. Rose, *The Intellectual Life of the British Working Classes* (New Haven: Yale University Press, 2001), p. 121.

59 S. Harper, 'A Lower Middle-Class Taste-Community in the 1930s: Admissions Figures at the Regent Cinema, Portsmouth, UK' *Historical Journal of Film, Radio and Television* 24:4 (2004), 579–81.

60 *The Uses of Literacy* (London: Essential Books, 1957).

61 See R. Overy, *The Morbid Age*; I. Zweiniger-Bargielowska, *Managing the Body: Beauty, Health, and Fitness in Britain, 1880–1939* (Oxford: Oxford University Press, 2010); J. Walkowitz, *Nights Out: Life in Cosmopolitan London* (New Haven: Yale University Press, 2012); B. Melman, *Women and the Popular Imagination in the Twenties: Flappers and Nymphs* (New York: St Martin's Press, 1988).

62 *The Intellectual Life of the British Working Classes* (New Haven: Yale University Press, 2001), p. 8.

63 See *Cultural and Social History*'s special issue on this subject, and in particular C. Waters's introduction to it, 'Beyond "Americanization": Rethinking Anglo-American Cultural Exchange between the Wars', *Cultural and Social History* 4:4 (2007), 451–9.

64 Stevenson, *British Society 1914–45*, pp. 402–7.

65 *Women and the Popular Imagination in the Twenties*, p. 46.

66 For accounts of changes in the publishing industry and the rise in literacy rates, see J. McAleer, *Popular Reading and Publishing in Britain 1914–1950* (Oxford: Clarendon Press, 1992) and C. Bloom, *Bestsellers: Popular Fiction Since 1900* (New York: Palgrave Macmillan, 2002).

67 Hiley, '"Nothing More than a Craze"'.

68 Lez Cooke, 'British Cinema: From Cottage Industry to Mass Entertainment', in Clive Bloom (ed.), *Literature and Culture in Modern Britain: Volume I, 1900–1929* (London: Longman, 1993), pp. 167–88, 176–7.

69 Kuhn, *An Everyday Magic*, p. 1.

70 *Fiction and the Reading Public*, p. xxxiv.

71 *Ibid.*, 45.

72 *Ibid.*, 7.

73 *Ibid.*, 26.

74 Affable Hawk, 'Book Reviews', *New Statesman*, 18 April 1925.

75 'Review: *The Green Hat* by M. Arlen', *Times Literary Supplement* (19 June 1924).

76 T. E. Welby, 'Review of *Young Men in Love* by M. Arlen', *Times Literary Supplement* (14 May 1927).

77 P. Gibbs's works tended to be reviewed consistently by the *Times Literary Supplement* perhaps in part because of his visibility as a wartime correspondent during World War I. For more on reviews of middlebrow works, see J. S. K. Watson's chapter 'The Soldier's Story: Publishing and the Postwar Years', in *Fighting Different Wars: Experience, Memory, and the First World War in Britain* (Cambridge: Cambridge University Press, 2004).

78 Quoted in Bailey, 'White Collars, Gray Lives?', 287.

79 'Thrilling new "Sapper" story', *Daily Mail* (20 January 1926).

80 *Literature and Culture in Modern Britain: Volume I*, p. 14.

81 *Passion's Fortune: The Story of Mills & Boon* (Oxford: Oxford University Press, 1999), p. 7.

82 Harper, 'Lower Middle-Class Taste-Community in the 1930s', 565–87; S. Harper, 'Fragmentation and Crisis: 1940s Admissions Figures at the Regent Cinema, Portsmouth, UK', *Historical Journal of Film, Radio and Television* 26:3 (2006), 361–94.

83 Bloom, *Bestsellers*; Bloom (ed.), *Literature and Culture in Modern Britain: Volume I: 1900–1929*; C. Bloom (ed.), *Spy Thrillers: From Buchan to Le Carré* (New York: St Martin's Press, 1990); R. M. Bracco, *Merchants of Hope: British Middlebrow Writers and the First World War, 1919–1939* (Oxford: Berg, 1993); McAleer, *Passion's Fortune*; McAleer, *Popular Reading and Publishing in Britain*; Melman, *Women and the Popular Imagination in the Twenties*.

84 Original emphasis in Bloom (ed.), *Literature and Culture in Modern Britain: Volume I*, p. 15.

85 G. Orwell, 'Bookshop Memories', in S. Orwell and I. Angus (eds), *The Collected Essays, Journalism and Letters of George Orwell: Volume I: An Age Like This 1920–1940* (London: Penguin, 1968), pp. 273–7.

86 Bloom (ed.), *Literature and Culture in Modern Britain: Volume I*, p. 16.

87   R. Standish, *The Prince of Storytellers: The Life of E. Phillips Oppenheim* (London: P. Davies, 1957).

88   'What people are reading', *Observer* (28 June 1936), p. 11.

89   'Thorndyke and others' by 'Torquemada' *Observer* (10 October 1937), p. 7.

90   H. P. Elderton and G. L. Wallace, 'Literary Questionnaire' (March 1940) Mass Observation Report 62, File Reports 1937–72.

91   A. Higson, 'Re-Presenting the National Past: Nostalgia and Pastiche in the Heritage Film', in L. Friedman (ed.), *Fires Were Started: British Cinema and Thatcherism* (Minneapolis: University of Minnesota Press, 1993), pp. 109–29.

92   N. Humble, *The Feminine Middlebrow Novel, 1920s to 1950s: Class, Domesticity, and Bohemianism* (Oxford: Oxford University Press, 2001); H. Ingman, *Women's Fiction between the Wars: Mothers, Daughters, and Writing* (New York: St Martin's Press, 1998); M. Joannou (ed.), *Women Writers of the 1930s: Gender, Politics, and History* (Edinburgh: Edinburgh University Press, 1999); Light, *Forever England*.

93   An important exception to this is Melman's chapter on the so-called 'masculine' novels, although she does not concentrate upon popular thrillers (*Women and the Popular Imagination in the Twenties*).

94   R. Usborne, *Clubland Heroes: A Nostalgic Study of Some Recurrent Characters in the Romantic Fiction of Dornford Yates, John Buchan and Sapper* (London: Constable, 1953); J. Chapman, *Licence to Thrill: A Cultural History of the James Bond Films* (New York: Columbia University Press, 2000).

95   Hoggart, *Uses of Literacy*, p. 258.

96   See ch. 3 'Genre: History and Form', in Bloom, *Bestsellers*.

97   Melman, *Women and the Popular Imagination in the Twenties*.

98   H. C. G. Matthew and B. Harrison (eds), *Oxford Dictionary of National Biography: In Association with the British Academy: From the Earliest Times to the Year 2000*, 62 vols (Oxford: Oxford University Press, 2004).

99   The result of this calculation is a formula that Sedgwick discusses in detail in his chapter 'Measuring Popularity' (*Popular Filmgoing in 1930s Britain*).

100   C. Gledhill, *Reframing British Cinema 1918–1928: Between Restraint and Passion* (London: BFI, 2003).

101   Availability of films is further affected by efforts of production companies and archivists to recognise the value of and to save the highly combustible nitrate stock on which films were made prior to 1951.

102   *Sociology of Film*, p. 200.

103   S. C. Shafer, *British Popular Films, 1929–1939: The Cinema of Reassurance* (London: Routledge, 1997); A. Spicer, *Typical Men: The Representation of Masculinity in Popular British Cinema* (London: I. B. Tauris, 2001).

104   K. Thompson, 'The Rise and Fall of Film Europe', in A. Higson and R. Maltby (eds), *'Film Europe' and 'Film America': Cinema, Commerce and Cultural Exchange 1920–1939* (Exeter: Exeter University Press, 1999), pp. 56–81, 64.

105   L. Napper, 'A Despicable Tradition? Quota Quickies in the 1930s', in R. Murphy (ed.), *The British Cinema Book* (London: BFI, 1997), pp. 37–47. Napper tries to write against Rachael Low's dismissal of the quota quickies that she presented in volume seven on the history of the British film (*The History of the British Film:*

Filmmaking in 1930s Britain, vol. VII (London: Allen & Unwin, 1948–)).

106 *Mass-Observation at the Movies*, p. 58.

107 Comments of Edgar F. Andrews (*ibid.*, 50).

108 Mark Glancy states that 'between 1930 and 1945, over 150 "British" films were made in Hollywood'. He also examines the convergence of British actors, directors, screenwriters, and literary sources for many Hollywood films (*When Hollywood Loved Britain: The Hollywood 'British' Film 1939–45* (Manchester: Manchester University Press, 1999), p. 1).

109 'National Cinema(s), International Markets and Cross-cultural Identities', in Ib Bondebjerg (ed.), *Moving Images, Culture and the Mind* (Luton: University of Luton Press, 2000), pp. 205–14.

110 *Ibid.*

111 *Ibid.*

112 Kuhn, *An Everyday Magic.*

113 A. Bergman, *We're in the Money: Depression America and Its Films* (New York: Harper & Row, 1972); B. Melosh, *Engendering Culture: Manhood and Womanhood in New Deal Public Art and Theater* (Washington, DC: Smithsonian Institution Press, 1991).

114 M. Jones, 'What Should Historians Do with Heroes? Reflections on Nineteenth- and Twentieth-Century Britain', *History Compass* 5:2 (2007), 439–54.

A man imagined:
heroes, work, and nation

For the last three years, ever since his demobilization, life had been to Sorrell like some huge trampling beast, and he – a furtive thing down in the mud, panting, dodging, bewildered, resentful and afraid.

Warwick Deeping, *Sorrell and Son* (1925)

On 30 May 1919, the *Daily Express*, one of Britain's largest circulating newspapers, quoted the Prince of Wales saying, 'I shall never regret my period of service overseas. In those four years I mixed with men. In those four years I found my manhood.' The article further documented the tributes granted to the Prince for his service in World War I, not the least of which was an informal parade through London featuring 'the acclamations of the citizens, who gathered in the thousands to greet him'.[1]

This hero's welcome, as historians have noted, was what many soldiers expected upon their return to Britain after the war. Yet even as the Prince celebrated the discovery of his masculinity in war, it was clear that numerous soldiers did not feel the same way. That same May had witnessed a number of demonstrations by recently demobilised and unemployed soldiers and those soldiers still enlisted. On 27 May, a demonstration near Westminster Abbey turned violent. A police officer was pulled from his horse in the fray and hospitalised, while others were hit with 'wooden paving blocks' thrown by the ex-soldiers.[2] The government seemed to be largely sympathetic to the protesters, declaring to the press that, 'If, after a reasonable time trade did not reassert itself and absorb the unemployed ex-servicemen, steps would be taken to introduce schemes to deal effectively with the whole problem.'[3] But, by 1925, when Warwick Deeping's bestselling novel *Sorrell and Son* was published, it was clear that the market had been unable to 'deal effectively' with the unemployment of ex-soldiers. In the winter of 1920 there were over two million men out of work and this figure did not drop below one million for the entirety of the interwar period.[4]

The experience of men who did not receive a parade of welcome upon their return from the war contributed to the success of a number of interwar novels and films that engaged with the plight of the soldier. Deeping's description in *Sorrell and Son* of Stephen Sorrell's experience following demobilisation emphasised a process of dehumanisation and emasculation. The 'panting' and 'dodging' in the mud symbolised the protagonist's exposure to unemployment, thereby highlighting similarities between unemployment and the dehuman-isation of war. As Billie Melman points out, the trials of the ex-soldier as he returned to civilian life was a common theme in popular novels of the 1920s.[5] This theme continued to resonate beyond the 1920s and throughout the interwar period in both novels and films. Numerous bestsellers of the first half of the 1920s dealt directly with the unemployment and disillusionment of the ex-soldier, and many other novels and films beyond that period included characters indelibly marked by their service to their country. Deeping, Philip Gibb, A. S. M Hutchinson, Michael Arlen, E. Philips Oppenheim, and H. C. McNeile were just a few of the bestselling novelists who profited from a focus upon the ex-soldier. Films such as *Lives of a Bengal Lancer*, *Bulldog Drummond* (1929), *Cavalcade*, and *Mutiny on the Bounty*, among others, either emphasised the role of the World War I soldier or strove to situate their hero within a combat situation. These films did extremely well at the box office. The soldier became a key figure in the popular formula of a hit film or bestseller. It was his story that was most in need of the stabilising influence offered by popular culture's ideological framework.

This fictional presentation of the soldier must be evaluated alongside the numerous non-fiction biographies published at the end of the 1920s by upper-class writers such as Robert Graves and Siegfried Sassoon.[6] These works by the 'soldier poets' have long been used both within the classroom and within seminal works such as Paul Fussell's *The Great War and Modern Memory* to illustrate the effect of World War I upon ex-soldiers and, by an extension that is often taken for granted, British society.[7] Yet Janet S. K. Watson notes that the period from 1928 to 1930 witnessed a veritable boom in 'war novels' that made the war and its soldiers their subjects, along with those works by the 'soldier poets'. I would argue that the boom in war novels occurred over a much longer period and that the boom in war narratives should take into account the popularity of film. It is only by looking at the interwar period as a whole and examining both novels and films from a range of producers that the extent of the war's impact upon a generation can be gauged.

Common to lowbrow and middlebrow novels and films was the display and recuperation of a particular type of British manhood that was under threat. In these narratives British masculinity rooted in ideas of work and nation was destabilised at the outset and was largely restored by the end. The aim here is not to discount the feelings of disillusionment presented by the soldier poets but rather to broaden the perspective on the war's impact in order to address the middle and working classes as consumers of popular culture and to more accurately gauge the extent of disillusionment with ideals of work and nation across these classes. As Graham Dawson has said in his discussion of the appeal of Lawrence of Arabia to post-World War I audiences, 'The history of masculinities must therefore include within its scope the tracing of those many and varied historical imaginings which have given shape, purpose and direction to the lives of men.'[8] We shall see that the post-World War I disillusionment of Graves and Sassoon in 1930 was evident throughout the entirety of the interwar period and encompassed much more than the upper middle and upper-class ex-soldiers of Oxford and Cambridge. It also included the decidedly more middle, lower middle-class, and working-class men and women who bought or borrowed low and middlebrow novels and visited the cinema.

In examining the wider impact of the war upon the working and middle classes, this study also moves beyond a focus on interwar disillusionment with concepts such as valour and honour to include the much more tangible and equally disillusioning experience of finding work in a period of depression. In this chapter I argue that the common characteristics of the hero in these popular novels and films constituted a type of masculinity that was destabilised by specific concerns in two areas following World War I – work and nation. Central to the concerns of these bestsellers and films were male anxieties about the position of men within the economy and the nation.[9] The 'culture industry' catered to these specific concerns about class, nation, and masculinity. Adorno notes the repetitive pattern endorsed for heroes within the culture industry, arguing that by the end of the narrative, and 'in empty harmony, they are reconciled with the general, whose demands they had experienced at the outset as irreconcilable with their interests'.[10] Heroes are thus returned to the collective and fashioned as central to this 'empty harmony' necessary for the narrative. What is clear from popular fiction and films is that post-war harmony included a reassertion of the masculine soldier as employed and re-dedicated to broad notions of British nationalism. The widespread popularity with British audiences of bestselling novels and films that featured a soldier figure is a testament to the impact of war and unemployment upon British conceptions of masculinity. These popular narratives indicate the management and rejection of this impact, for they ultimately worked to recuperate conventional pre-war notions of work, nation, and masculinity.

Soldiers, World War I, and the aftermath

The end of World War I marked the beginning of a particularly turbulent time in Britain for soldiers, workers, and Parliament. The confusion and anger surrounding the uneven demobilisation of almost four million soldiers was just a sign of things to come. The protests by ex-soldiers that occurred in 1919 continued into 1920, and the government appeared to be ineffective at addressing the concerns of ex-soldiers regarding employment. The *Daily Express* reported on a riot in London in 1920 that a medical staff member said 'was almost like being in France', and the paper called throughout the interwar period for Parliament to do something about unemployment.[11] Instead of experiencing one decade of acute economic problems in the 1930s as the United States did, Britain suffered two decades of relatively constant unemployment, with unemployment figures consistently showing at least a million men out of work and peaking at three million unemployed men in 1932.[12] Not surprisingly, the government was forced to expand the 'dole' as the decade wore on, through a modified Unemployment Insurance Act.[13] The interwar economy remained weak, with periods of high inflation worsening the effects of unemployment. The headline that the *Daily Express* ran in June 1919, 'The appalling cost of everything', was followed by a list of prices of various goods in 1914 and 1919. The subtitle that said 'When will it stop?' was still relevant at the close of the 1920s.[14] The ultimate price of this turbulence was strained relations between soldiers and the nation they were meant to represent during and after the war.

Much speculation resulted about what and who was at the root of the depression that plagued the interwar period – everyone from Bolsheviks to women workers were identified by the press, the bestsellers, and films as culprits – but Parliament was a particularly compelling target immediately following the war. The disastrous post-World War I coalition government under Lloyd George took much of the initial blame, but even with a change in government to the conservatives in 1922 and again in 1924 to the relatively new Labour party, these types of complaints continued. Distinctions between parties were blurred in the press as well as popular culture, no doubt aided by the dominance of the conservatives throughout the interwar period.[15] The

New Statesman declared in 1920, 'Behind every failure and every muddle of the last two years it is possible to perceive the same fundamental cause. It is not that the British Government has pursued wrong policies, but that is has had no policy and kept no faith … Everywhere it cheats.'[16] Indeed, the dishonest dealings of politicians were a preoccupation of interwar popular culture, as will be illustrated in Chapter 2. Popular culture developed its own particular blend of 'reality' and fiction in this period, just as British society as a whole became concerned with the fictions and realities of politicians. Politics was increasingly seen by some as an elaborate performance conducted in order to hide the 'truth' from the people, a feeling very much in evidence even at the eve of World War II, as we shall see. Political disillusionment and attention to performance and truth were important aspects of film and fiction in the 1920s and 1930s.

The character whose job it was to see through the corrupt performances of politicians and dishonest businessmen was the hero – often an ex-soldier whose role was actively equated with 'Englishness' in these novels and films. Philip Dodd argues that 'Englishness' in the late nineteenth and early twentieth centuries was located in Britain's public institutions such as the universities as well as within the teaching of subjects like history that were increasingly organised to serve what were deemed national and imperial needs.[17] He goes on to note that this portrayal of the past privileged a type of masculinity that was primarily middle or upper class, thus making the incorporation of other groups such as women and the working class a significant challenge to 'Englishness' after 1920. Dodd's argument can be extended to include the military as another masculine institution that served the interests of Britain in its wider sense, an approach that Michael Paris has drawn upon in his conceptualisation of Britain as a 'Warrior Nation'.[18] Characters within interwar mass culture tended to speak of 'England' far more often than they did of Britain, seemingly offering support for Alison Light's assertion that the interwar period saw the development of a 'little England' rather than a Great Britain.[19] Yet they spoke of England and Englishmen and acted for Britain in ways that defied Light's notion of a little England. These were ex-soldiers protecting Britain from domestic and foreign plots. Englishness was thus defined in low and middlebrow works as virtually synonymous with a protection of Britain's dominant institutions.

The concept of heroic masculinity rooted in nationalist glory is not new in British history. Michael Paris, much like George Mosse before him, argues that little separation existed between masculinity and the nation in the nineteenth century.[20] This rhetoric was particularly compelling in the late Victorian and Edwardian period when love of one's nation and action upon this love coincided with British ideals of manliness, as well as Britain's imperial mission.[21] Colonial warfare was represented as an adventure, and Englishness and the British institution of warfare were very much related.[22] Newspaper reporting also participated in the rhetoric of adventure stories by equating the colonial soldier with Britain abroad and emphasising the thrilling aspects of colonial warfare rather than tangible experiences of death and destruction.[23] Such representations in fiction and journalism were key in equating the soldier with the nation. The type of narrative framework that conflated the soldier with the nation was central to the ideology of popular culture in the late nineteenth and early twentieth centuries.

What is significant to the novels and films of the 1920s and the 1930s is how defensive the relationship between the soldier and the nation was in the aftermath of World War I and how much work had to be done within popular narratives to maintain this connection. By the end of World War I, the relationship between masculinity and the nation was clearly under strain if not entirely altered. The experience of trench warfare, the conscription of soldiers halfway through the war, press censorship that fostered a divide between the fighting front and the home front, and unemployment all contributed to an increased inability of many soldiers to identify with and represent Englishness. A dominant narrative arc in the films and novels I examine here is the initial exile from, and then the return of, the soldier hero to the centre of the economy and the nation by the work's end. This aggressive fostering of a relationship between man and nation seems strategic in light of the general unease following the war. The clear and often belaboured links that were established in these post-World War I narratives between the soldier and the nation were attempts to rehabilitate a type of masculinity believed to be under threat following the war, and because the relationship between the soldier, the nation, and the economy was in danger. The aggressive articulation of this relationship continued up to the outbreak of World War II as authors such as E. Phillips Oppenheim, Leslie Charteris, and Eric Ambler awkwardly positioned their action heroes as peacekeepers.

By the outset of World War II, popular authors and filmmakers had worked hard to distance the soldier from the horrors of trench warfare that had come to characterise World War I. The disorienting and dehumanising experience of trench warfare has been well documented by British writers such as Graves and Sassoon, and German writers such as Erich Maria Remarque in *All Quiet on the Western Front* (1929). Kelly Boyd argues that this vision of warfare was seldom represented within boys' story papers. World War I's type of warfare was not suitable for young British boys, nor did it communicate proper ideals of either Englishness or manliness.[24] The popular novels and films examined here, which did directly address the impact of the war upon men, also did not engage with descriptions of the war itself. A poorly equipped soldier often insensible of what was happening around him did not make for the stuff of adventure stories, which were dependent on the easy equation between soldiering and Englishness. As Jim Reilly has noted about fictional works from this period by D. H. Lawrence and Virginia Woolf, 'The war is characteristically circled rather than represented'.[25] The war enters the novel as an event too large and too traumatising to be represented, so the focus instead is on developments 'before the war' and 'after the war'.

The same narrative absence exists in bestselling works, but for different reasons. When Hugh, otherwise known as 'Bulldog', Drummond mentions the war in H. C. McNeile's action novel *Bulldog Drummond*, it is only to describe how it honed his abilities to kill with nerves of steel. Bulldog Drummond spends the entirety of the story foiling the plans of the evil Carl Peterson to introduce Bolshevism to Britain. His training as a soldier is referenced throughout the novel while he battles a gorilla, a mad scientist, and a pygmy with poison darts, yet his only negative reference to the war itself is a flippant one to his comrades: '"Has it struck you fellows", remarked Hugh, at the conclusion of lunch, "that seated around this table are four officers who fought with some distinction and much discomfort in the recent historic struggle?" "How beautifully you put it, old flick!" said Darrell'. This offhand mention of the war and the cheerful response of a fellow soldier are as close to a discussion about the war as the novel gets. In *If Winter Comes* by A. S. M. Hutchinson, a novel which examines the life of Mark Sabre both before and after the war as he endures an increasingly uncomfortable marriage and job, his experience in the war is summed up over three pages in vague terms that do not describe the actual experience of trench warfare but rather his own feelings of confusion. Even Bertram Pollard, hero of Philip Gibbs's *Middle of the Road*, an ex-soldier experiencing disillusionment with the home front on his return from the war and who spends the novel writing what is presumably *the* definitive novel of the war, rarely addresses the war itself. Popular films, as I will elaborate, tended to avoid it altogether. The silence in this case does not simply represent the death of an aestheticised British culture but rather seems to work as a strategy within popular culture against the representation of a new type of warfare that strained the bonds between soldier and nation that had been so central to the character of the hero.

Along with trench warfare, conscription and press censorship also taxed the relationship between the soldier and the nation. Nicoletta Gullace sees the British introduction of conscription in 1916 as a key moment in unravelling the relationship between man and nation. The idea of a large body of men in Britain who were able to participate in the war but unwilling to do so severely disrupted the previously stable relationship between the nation and man, a disruption that Gullace argues allowed women to articulate their own patriotism.[26] Indeed, shirkers had a prominent role in some of the novels and films discussed in this chapter, and will be further examined in my chapter on villainy. Mark Sabre, in *If Winter Comes*, feels very deeply his initial inability to join the ranks because of a poor heart and rejoices when the requirements are lessened as the war progresses. Not serving one's country remained problematic for British society at large both during the war and after it, as demonstrated within popular narratives. Conscription and shirking demonstrated to the government that the relationship between man and the nation was not so stable that automatic enlistment could be counted upon.

While conscription during the course of the war may have demonstrated to Parliament that British male patriotism could not be trusted, press censorship illustrated a similar point to soldiers about the government's lack of concern for them. Heavy press censorship contributed greatly to the disassociation soldiers felt with the home front when they returned from the war. Press censorship did not tolerate anti-war dissent. At the outset of the war, the coalition government ushered in unprecedented emergency measures in the form of the Defence of the Realm Act, widely known as DORA. Along with a variety of uses extending to the home front, DORA allowed the War Office to monitor cables and the press in general. Foreign correspondents had to submit their stories to the Official Press Bureau and could be subject to prosecution and even death if they did not. Philip Gibbs, working as a war correspondent, felt this keenly. He saw the editing of his wartime reporting as a distortion of the experiences of trench warfare. In his non-fiction work released after the war, *Now It Can Be Told* (1920), he condemned the role of censorship in the war, perhaps in an attempt to justify his patriotic yet somewhat uninformative reports from the front. In so doing, he caricatured Sir Douglas Haig, the much-maligned British Commander-in-Chief during the war. Although a woman popularly symbolised DORA at home, for Gibbs DORA was embodied by Haig. In response to Haig's continued belittlement of war correspondents, Gibbs wrote:

> We took occasion to point out to him that the British Empire, which had sent
> its men into this war, yearned to know what they were doing and how they were
> doing, and that their patience and loyalty depended upon closer knowledge of
> what was happening than what was told them in the communiqués issued by the
> Commander-in-Chief himself.[27]

For Gibbs, the censorship of the war correspondents belittled the experiences
of the soldiers in the field and created a significant gap of experience between
the soldiers and the public at home. The sense of betrayal that resulted from
the war was not simply based on a clear distinction between the soldier and
civilians, a process that has been somewhat simplified by Samuel Hynes, but
instead also involved a government that seemed content to create distinctions
between soldiers and the home front.[28] Such distinctions worked to further
alienate soldiers from their previous positions of embodying both the nation
and the home front.

Soldiers were not only alienated in regard to their centrality to the nation,
but also through their position within Britain's economy. While the rupture
between soldier and nation had been articulated during the war itself, the
fissure between soldiers and the economy was realised following the war when
the job of soldiering came to an end and unemployment numbers steadily
increased. This scale of unemployment was unprecedented as the pre-war period
had witnessed an increased standard of living for most workers, while war
itself had ushered in substantial wage increases for those fuelling the wartime
manufacturing industry.[29] Following the war, Britain's role as a pre-eminent
producer of manufactured goods was supplanted by the United States, which
then experienced its own economic crisis in 1929 with the Wall Street crash.
These circumstances all contributed greatly to a widespread, although uneven,
experience of unemployment that had never been felt before.

Historians of the interwar period have noted that the experience of unemployment in Britain was regional, yet popular culture and the press emphasised
a crisis of unemployment that affected middle-class men as a whole.[30] The
unemployment of the protagonists in *Middle of the Road*, *Sorrell and Son*, and
If Winter Comes or films like *Grand Hotel* is portrayed as remarkable in light of
their identities as members of the middle classes and as ex-soldiers. That men
who exuded Englishness in every way and who cared about the nation and
the creases in their trousers could be undone by unemployment was depicted
as wholly unnatural, for their relationship to the economy was similar to their
relationship to the nation; it was assumed and emphasised through a variety
of British institutions. The freeborn Englishman that historians such as E. P.

Thompson and Anna Clark discuss was employed, male, and self-consciously British; seldom were the roles separated.[31] The widespread unemployment of not just the working class, but the middle class and ex-soldiers was what made unemployment in the post-war period so startling for many, because it indicated the extent of the crisis in masculinity, work, and nation. The *Daily Express* emphasised as much when it differentiated between 'unskilled workers' and 'genuine workers', complaining that 'large numbers of unskilled workers, particularly women, girls, and lads whose earning capacity is small, are making no effort to obtain employment while the state donation continues. Thousands of genuine workers find that employment exchange as a medium for obtaining work useless.' It went on to argue that 'no sane person objects to a State allowance during unemployment to the demobilised soldier or sailor or the genuine worker who has lost his job owing to the change from war to peace industry: but the whole country is crying out against the system as at present administered'.[32] Genuine workers would no doubt have included our fictional protagonists and any other middle-class, educated worker. The *New Statesmen* expressed a similar sentiment: 'The present unemployment is altogether abnormal. Those who are out of work to-day are no mere "reserve of labour" whose reemployment may be expected with confidence as soon as another turn is given to the wheel of trade. They are a large section of the normal labour force of industry.'[33] These were men, in other words, who should have a central place within the economy as well as the nation.

Such a crisis that affected the middle-class male ex-soldier created a climate within popular film and fiction narratives that made the expressions of socialism marginally more acceptable for a short period of time. Ronald C. Davison, an economist, in interpreting investigations made by the Ministry of Labour in the 1920s, noted:

> According to the official analysis in November 1924, as many as 63 per cent of the males and 77 per cent of the females were, in the opinion of Exchange officials, persons who in normal times would have been in steady employment. The figures appear to be very creditable to the personal quality of the unemployed as a whole … The depression was so severe that men of the highest qualifications were continuously deprived of work.[34]

Davison also saw the unemployment of those of such high personal quality and qualifications as not 'normal'. Thus the war had ushered in abnormal times, rupturing the steady workings of the nation and a capitalist economy which had previously employed such upstanding British citizens. G. D. H. Cole, the Fabian economist and detective fiction writer, argued in 1923 that this unemployment was likely to remain as long as Britain was entrenched in a capitalist economy. For Cole, the intersection of a world war with a capitalist economy was devastating, and his book *Out of Work: An Introduction to the Study of Unemployment* documented the economic corner in which Britain had trapped itself: 'There is no evidence that that even the coming "boom" will be enough to absorb anything like the whole number of the unemployed … It may well be that heavy and chronic unemployment has become a permanent thing as a result of the triumphs of Imperialism, and the fuller working out, in consequence of the war, of the vicious tendencies inherent in the capitalist system.'[35] Cole's published works and his writings for the *New Statesman* promoted socialism as an alternative to capitalism, and a number of the authors considered here had some sympathies with the socialist movement in the 1920s, and then later somewhat confused interpretations of fascism as it grew in Europe.

In *Now It Can Be Told* and *The Middle of the Road*, Gibbs had stated the appeal of socialism to Britain's workers, echoing the fears of many within the Lloyd George coalition government. Gibbs, claiming to echo the thoughts of ordinary Germans, wrote: 'The rich, the gilded ones, the bloated aristocrats gobble everything in front of our very eyes … All soldiers – friends and foe – ought to throw down their weapons and go on strikes, so that this war, which enslaves more people than ever, may cease.' Gibbs went on:

> It was that view, terribly in its simplicity, which may cause a more passionate revolution in Germany when the people awaken from their stupor. It was that view which led to the Russian Revolution and to Bolshevism. It is the suspicion which is creeping into the brains of British working-men and making them threaten to strike against any adventures of war, like that in Russia, which seems to them (unless proved otherwise) on behalf of the 'gilded ones' and for the enslavement of the peoples.[36]

For Gibbs, the British working men may well identify with the 'people' or Germany or Russia and sympathise with their desire for action against their governments. Lloyd George had voiced concerns in his Fontainebleau Memorandum (1919) that a desire for revolution on Germany's part would mean a commitment to Bolshevism: 'The greatest danger that I see in the present situation is that Germany may throw in her lot with Bolshevism and place her resources, her brains, her vast organising power at the disposal of the revolutionary fanatics whose dream it is to conquer the world for Bolshevism by force of arms.'[37] The implicit threat here was that Bolshevism would appeal not only to Germany, but to Britain's vast working force, thereby contributing to Bolshevism conquering the world.

This fear initially justified the government's involvement of British troops in the Russian civil war, an endeavour that Gibbs expressed scepticism about in his discussion of the 'adventures of war' in Russia. Britain's troops were enlisted to the cause of the loose coalition of rebels, known as the 'White Russians', fighting against the Bolshevik Red Army. Although Lloyd George himself, as Kenneth Morgan has pointed out, believed that the threat of Bolshevism would be undermined by the appeals of free trade and advocated for the removal of the troops from the conflict, others in Lloyd George's Cabinet, most notably Churchill, were less optimistic.[38] Morgan notes that Churchill's rhetoric on this issue was pointed. Indeed in a *Times* report of his speech at the Oxford Union, Churchill stated:

> My view has been that all the harm and misery in Russia have arisen out of the wickedness and folly of the Bolshevists, and that there will be no recovery of any kind in Russia or in Eastern Europe while these wicked men, this vile group of cosmopolitan fanatics, hold the Russian nation by the hair of its head and tyrannise over its great population. The policy I will always advocate is the overthrow and destruction of that criminal *regime*.[39]

Churchill's description of these groups of 'wicked men' and 'criminal regimes' may have drawn on a familiar language to producers and consumers of mass culture, even while some authors such as Gibbs accounted for the appeal of socialism to British workers. Despite Churchill's rhetoric, the involvement of troops in Russia was nevertheless limited and British troops were removed by the end of 1919. Gibbs's complaints about the civil war did seem to reflect the concerns of a number of the British public about yet another armed mission for British troops at the end of the Great War, and coming in a period of considerable economic instability.[40]

At first glance some of the novels examined here seem to address leftist sympathies with the Bolsheviks as another potential reason for the unpopularity of Britain's involvement in the Russian civil war. Certainly the hero of Gibbs's *Middle of the Road* flirted with socialism as a solution to Britain's social and economic crisis. Leslie Charteris, who penned the popular Saint series, has his hero, the Saint, otherwise known as Simon Templar, exhibit pronounced sympathies for the young socialist killed by a fictional fascist group called the 'Sons of France' in his 1938 novel, *Prelude for War*.[41] While films were constrained in what they could show of politics on screen by the BBFC in Britain and the Hays Code after 1934 in the United State, the economic crisis in both Britain and the United States accounts for the popularity with British audiences of certain American films such as *Roman Scandals* (1933 [UK 1934]), which John Sedgwick identifies as the third most popular film in Britain in 1934. It featured the comedian Eddie Cantor as a charismatic drifter who works piecemeal jobs and is chastised for giving food away for free at the local grocers.[42] When most of the town is turned out of their homes so that businessmen can sell the land for a profit, Eddie advises them, through song, to build houses in the streets and take back their lives from the wealthy and corrupt politicians in the town. The chorus of the song celebrates communal and free living: 'It's not a palace or a poorhouse/But the rent is absolutely free/ It's not my house/but it's our house'. The 'town' that the city's citizens make on the streets is one that is nevertheless idyllic and middle class in appearance, with clean rugs, proper furniture, and family dinners. This view of socialism was decidedly comfortable and community oriented and not particularly provocative. Likewise another American film, Capra's popular *Mr Deeds Goes to Town* (1936), featured the naive but honest Longfellow Deeds giving his inherited fortune away to poor farmers affected by the depression after he is made cynical by the power-hungry business and literary elite of New York. *Mr Deeds* was the fourth most popular film in 1936 according to Sedgwick.[43] Deeds is arrested for this redistribution of wealth, which involves parcelling a section of land into equipped 10-acre farms, until he is triumphantly exonerated at a sensational trial.

Sympathies towards socialism as a viable alternative to capitalism, for the most part, were nevertheless short-lived in popular fiction and film and the all-important endings of the narratives tend to convey their conservatism. The bulk of narratives popular with middle-class readers and attendees of the cinema were those that showed heroes working to reform a capitalist system rather than reject it, a process that had defined British constitutional history for centuries. The heroes righted certain inequalities within capitalism such as unfair monopolies, but ultimately were rewarded in ways that affirmed the benefits of a liberal capitalist society. Consequently, believers in socialism, particularly Bolsheviks, were demonised in a number of popular works. Bulldog Drummond's enemy, Peterson, is vilified by his association with a motley group of hysterical Bolsheviks. Even Gibbs's early sympathies towards socialism gave way in later works such as *Young Anarchy*, which provided an unsympathetic portrayal of socialism through an angry young Bolshevik when it was published in 1926 during a minor upsurge in the economy before the devastating 1929 stock market crash in America.[44] Charteris's *Prelude for War*, while relatively sympathetic to socialism in 1938, still characterised it as the idealistic domain of the young in the Saint's description of the young ill-fated follower: 'young Kennet was a pacifist, an anti-blood-sporter, an anti-capitalist, an anti-fascist, and the Lord knows what not; and he once said publicly that his father had proved to be the arch-Judas of the working classes'.[45] Kennet's socialism was treated by Charteris's hero as part of a string of ideologies the young man engaged in, to be tolerated and amused by, rather than seriously engaged with.

By 1938, when the Pilgrim Trust published *Men without Work*, Cole's earlier predictions had been realised and unemployment was no longer so abnormal and was situated more clearly within the working class who had not seriously been tempted by either socialism or fascism in Britain. The Trust, looking backwards, briefly surveyed the economic history of the 1920s and commented that 'this state of affairs, though puzzling to the mind of those used to the "good old times" before the War (and incidentally before disturbing figures of unemployment began to be officially published), had gradually come to be accepted as a normal state'.[46] The Pilgrim Trust, as McKibbin argues, itself contributed to the normalcy of unemployment with this study, placing it squarely within the working class.[47] The middle class was no longer at risk, circumstances that were mirrored in popular fiction and film, which showed middle-class heroes resituated at the centre of a capitalist economy by the narrative's end and which ultimately rejected socialism as a viable alternative.

The hero as breadwinner

Concerns about men's uncertain place within the interwar economy were expressed, in part, through the popularity of fiction and film that featured a hero struggling to maintain his role as a breadwinner. The man who worked to support himself and those attached to him was idealised, and the idle non-working hero was simply not a character option. This was particularly notable in film, where unemployed heroes were rare to non-existent. Instead heroes were working constantly to find employment or were working for the good of the nation in a variety of ways. In this way the masculine independent breadwinner ideal that had been articulated in the eighteenth and nineteenth centuries continued to be buttressed in popular narratives.[48] Hard work continued to define a predominantly middle-class hero. Yet the breadwinner ideal was bolstered within a climate that had to acknowledge the presence of unemployment and indeed the strained relationship between man and work was central to a number of bestsellers and hit films. Unemployment was the abnormal tragedy beyond the hero's control and drove much of the plot. This aberration in popular narratives either resulted in tragedy, as a caution to audiences of the dangers of men out of work, or was righted by the end of the narrative as the efforts of the hero were recognised and he was brought within the confines of a capitalist system. The endings of many of these narratives will be discussed further in Chapter 3, where I argue that an important part of the rehabilitation of the soldier within capitalism was dependent upon a shift in the female love-interest's own role in that system.

Work within the narratives discussed here was equated with manliness and economic independence. Mark Sabre in the novel, *If Winter Comes*, expresses this ideal when arguing with his wife Mabel about the National Insurance stamps, the scheme introduced before World War I where workers contributed part of their wages to a fund that could later be used to support them in unemployment. Upon discovering that Mabel had been paying the servants' contribution instead of taking it out of their wages (uncharacteristically nice for the dreadful Mabel), Sabre objects: 'Don't you see half the idea of the Act is to help these people to learn thrift and forethought – to learn the wisdom of putting by for a rainy day. And to encourage their independence. When you go and pay what they ought to pay, you're simply taking away their independence.'[49] Although the logic is arguable, it is clear that Sabre sees economic independence as fundamental to one's self-worth. The 'dole', which was introduced after the war and expanded the original National Insurance Act, offered up payment from government without the prior culling from wages. This was largely due to the numbers of unemployed now drawing on it and because many had simply exhausted what little they had paid into it before the war. Nevertheless, the dole, while privileging the economic role of men, as Susan Pedersen has pointed out, also highlighted their economic dependence upon the government and undermined their roles as independent breadwinners. Gibbs's narrator in a later bestseller, *Young Anarchy* (1926), commented: 'I had written articles against the dole, and still believed – and believe – that it was a tragic and demoralizing system which would sap the moral fibre of our manhood.'[50] The popular hit of 1933, *Cavalcade*, which critiqued the impact of war while extolling the virtues of one upper middle-class British family during wartime, featured a scene that indicated that the soldier's inability to work after the war was its greatest tragedy. The film was based on a popular play by Noel Coward and was Britain's top film in 1933 according to the study conducted by Sedgwick. Harper identifies 31,824 viewers in ticket sales at the Portsmouth cinema, making it a tremendous success.[51] One of the most startling scenes of the film is of wounded and blind soldiers basket-weaving at a table presumably within a hospital.[52] The insensible looks on their faces, captured in a frontal medium shot, both emphasises the futility of their work and the undoing of their manhood following the war. The scene's dramatic impact is stressed further in the film as the first in a montage depicting the effect of war upon soldiers during the Great War, and when it is shown again as one of the last images of the film. As one of the last shots, the futile work of an ex-soldier is granted significant gravity as a ghostly reminder on screen of the tragedy of the war.

Philip Gibbs's *Middle of the Road* also made it clear that the charity offered to soldiers following the war was not acceptable to soldiers and their notions of independence. It is quickly apparent to the reader of *The Middle of the Road* that the ex-soldier, Bertram, with no titles to his family, is less well off than his wife. Upon his return to his life with his young aristocratic wife, he is disillusioned by his reception at home and is also unemployed. His own unemployment and that of many other soldiers fills Bertram with concern, and much of the first part of the novel provides descriptions of the state of the returning soldier. Everywhere Bertram looks he is troubled by their existence:

> They carried banners with the proclamation, 'We want Work, not Charity'. They were men whom he'd seen marching up the Albert-Bapaume road, the Arras-Lens road, and the Ypres-Menin road, when England and the world had needed them. They were the heroes who were fighting in a war to end war, the boys in the trenches for whom nothing was too good. Now they were shabby and down at the heel, some of them in the old khaki with buttons and shoulder-straps torn off, all of them downcast and wretched-looking.[53]

Bertram does not immediately count himself as one of these men. He is, after all, by proxy part of a relatively wealthy family and is well educated. Gibbs makes Bertram's realisation of the connection between the masses of unemployed soldiers and his own situation a somewhat slow process, developed it seems over a matter of weeks in the narrative. Gibbs writes, 'Bertram could never pass one of these boxes [held by ex-soldiers] without putting a few coppers inside, until one day he remembered that it was his wife's money, not his own, that he was giving away. The thought made him flush in the street, and walk on with a quicker, restless pace as far as Upper Tooting.'[54] The shame of this economic dependency becomes central to the novel and Bertram takes to spending his time with his friends Luke Christy, Janet Welford, and their socialist circle while fretting about finding work. This inspires Bertram to write an honest book about the war as his marriage declines. Hurt but still faithful to Joyce, Bertram heads to Europe where he documents the plight of those in Germany and Russia for a leftist weekly. Bertram believes his book will be a means of escaping this economic situation and indeed he is employed as a journalist at the end of the narrative, while Joyce herself has experienced financial difficulties. Thus Bertram presumably becomes breadwinner for the family as Joyce's aristocratic heritage amounts to little.

Bertram's initial inability to connect his own economic position with that of the masses of unemployed men is mirrored by other heroes examined here. *Sorrell and Son* by Warwick Deeping also begins with an unemployed ex-serviceman. In both the novel and film Sorrell returns from the war with few prospects, as well as the burden of his son after his wife leaves him. He is in sole charge of his young son Christopher, or 'Kit'. Both film and novel follow Sorrell's degradation as he is forced to take a job as porter in a seedy hotel with a domineering and cruel female owner. This degradation is captured most dramatically on film in the 1927 version as Sorrell, played by the stately actor H. B. Warner, washes the floor of the hotel on his hands and knees. (See Figure 1.1.) Yet Sorrell eventually, through thrift and hard work, is able to impress

1.1   Captain Stephen Sorrell washing the floor of the Angel Hotel under the supervision of his female employer. Her husband looks on in the background.

himself into the service of a relatively well-off gentleman and ex-soldier, Mr Roland, who hires him at his hotel. From there Sorrell works diligently until he is made a partner in the expansion of Roland's hotel holdings, all the while saving so that Kit can have a better chance at gaining his economic independence. Kit, in gratitude for this help, takes up medical studies. Sorrell, after years of poor health and hard work, eventually dies with the help of Kit, who administers enough medicine to take the pain away permanently. Yet at the outset of the novel in particular Sorrell is constructed, like Bertram, as slow to recognise himself among the unemployed:

> For Sorrell still kept his trousers creased, not had he reached that state of mind when a man can contemplate with unaffected naturalness the handling of his own luggage. There was still things he did and did not do. He was a gentleman. True, society had come near to pushing him off the shelf of his class-consciousness into the welter of the casual and the unemployed, but though hanging by his hands, he had refused to drop.[55]

Sorrell expects the same type of behaviour from his son, Kit. Both Sorrell and son are grieved by Kit's attendance at a local council school, rather than a private school. Deeping writes of the shame of it: 'With the man it had been a matter of resentful pride, but for the boy it meant contact with common children, and Kit was not a common child. He had all the fastidious nausea of a boy who has learnt to wash and to use a handkerchief, and not to yell "cheat" at everybody in the heat of the game.'[56] Kit had clearly incorporated some of his father's class-consciousness. From here things rapidly change and Sorrell in fact 'drops'. An antiques dealer, with whom Sorrell had expected to take a job, dies on the day of Sorrell's arrival. Faced with not enough money to pay either lodging for another night or transportation home, Sorrel says to his son 'I'm not going to bother about the crease in my trousers, my son. Keeping up appearances. I don't care what the job is, but I am going to get it.' Kit assures his father, 'But you will still be Captain Sorrell, M.C., to me, Daddy'.[57] This sentimental scene is one where Sorrell abandons a specific class identity yet retains a British identity through his war service in the eyes of his son. Although socially Sorrell and his son lose a degree of status, Kit still acknowledges his father's considerable work in the war, even if the rest of Britain does not. It is only later on in the novel that Sorrell is rewarded for his soldierly approach to work by the wealthy ex-officer Mr Roland. At the outset, both novels take pains to construct the unemployment of these soldiers as a painful revelation, an abnormality to be exposed and then addressed in the rest of the narrative.

For Mark Sabre, the protagonist of *If Winter Comes* by A. S. M. Hutchinson, economic circumstances are generally more comfortable, even if the atmosphere of his work environment is not. Before the war, Sabre is employed in his father's company Fortune, East, and Sabre. He works on the publishing of scholastic textbooks, most of which are distilled histories of Britain and the world. The story opens with Sabre's marriage to Mabel and his misgivings about the match. Mabel proves to be the antithesis of everything that Sabre believes in and their life together is, for the most part, miserable. Sabre is constantly reminded of this through the presence of his adolescent love, Nona, now Lady Tybar, who has also chosen wrongly in marriage. Sabre eventually goes off to the war and jeopardises his job in the process. His fortunes decline upon his return home as he is let go by Fortune and his kindness to an unwed young mother plunges him into social scandal that eventually leads to the death of the young woman and her baby. Sabre is wrongly held responsible, suffers through an inquest and then, remarkably, a 'brain haemorrhage' before being divorced by Mabel and reconciling with Nona.

Sabre's economic fortunes throughout the novel are subject to the will of the firm's elderly partner, aptly named Reverend Sebastian Fortune, who 'bore a certain resemblance to a stunted whale'.[58] Fortune is immensely fat and sits moored behind his desk in most of his dealings with Sabre, a characterisation of villainy that will be discussed in detail in the next chapter. Sabre himself had inherited his father's fifth share in the firm, a share that had been diminished by Fortune in his political manoeuvrings. Sabre has no stake in the company that bears his name but is continuously assured by Fortune that he will be brought into official partnership in the firm. Yet this honour goes not to him, but to his scheming co-worker, Twyning. This slight is felt deeply by Sabre and marks the beginning of his increasingly attenuated role at work. When Sabre finally joins the war, the two partners use this as an excuse to further marginalise Sabre's position within the firm. On a visit to the firm during his leave, Sabre is well aware of the process: 'It was only what he had expected; a trifle pronounced, perhaps, but the obvious sequel to their latter-day matter towards him: they had wanted to get him out; he was out and they desired to keep him out.'[59] Sabre's despair is offset somewhat by the satisfaction he feels at working for the army, even at less than astronomical pay. The narrative makes a point of emphasising Sabre's pride at earning these wages: 'in the breast pocket of his waistcoat, specially cleared to give private accommodation to so glorious a prize, were a half-crown and two pennies, the most thrilling magnificent sum he had ever earned – his army pay'.[60] Sabre's work for his nation is especially meaningful for him and the payment he receives as recognition for this stands in stark contrast to the lack of recognition offered by Fortune for his hard work. When Sabre is embroiled in the scandal with the unwed mother, whom is later revealed in the novel to have been impregnated by Twyning's son Harold, the firm completes Sabre's removal. This event is constructed in the narrative as a profound betrayal in light of Sabre's war service and the non-service of both Fortune and Twyning. Unemployment and Sabre's wrongful dismissal is contrasted with his work for the nation in the war and Fortune's lack of similar work. Sabre is vindicated, but only after the terrors of unemployment are spelled out.

Even Bulldog Drummond in H. C. McNeile's 1920 novel and the 1929 film version is subject to unemployment following the war and it is his boredom, if not the economic necessity of work, that propels him into his first of many adventures. Captain Hugh Drummond, DSO, MC possesses a large enough fortune to justify the hiring of his trusty servant Denny and maintain his club membership, yet Drummond first courts excitement by taking out an ad in the paper including the following: 'Demobilised officer ... finding peace incredibly tedious, would welcome diversion. Legitimate, if possible; but crime, if of comparatively humorous description, no objection. Excitement essential.' Inactivity is not ideal for Drummond, who wishes to put to use his considerable skill set from the war. This plea sets up the plot of the story and keeps Drummond admirably involved throughout, even while small references to other unemployed soldiers are made here and there, as when Drummond pays an unemployed ex-soldier to act as odd man in his dealings with the book's villain. Even the ex-soldier, Mullings, eventually tells Drummond he would help without pay: 'any time, sir, as you wants me, I'd like to come just for the sport of the thing'.[61] As an ex-soldier, Mullings's unemployment is de-emphasised in his willingness to work against the villain and for the good of Britain.

Other novels and films illustrate the desire of the hero to be engaged in work while also showing the pitfalls of unemployment. *Captain Blood* (1922), the bestseller by Rafael Sabatini and the slightly less popular 1935 film starring Errol Flynn, both dealt rather delicately with the Captain's foray into piracy during the seventeenth century.[62] Peter Blood begins both novel and film as a British doctor whose soldiering background is impeccable. In the 1935 film, this is dealt with in the first scene where Blood's affectionate and elderly maid chastises him while dressing him in his chambers for not being involved in the fight against James II's tumultuous occupation of the throne by saying that the town gossips about his lack of a role. Blood responds with spirit in this amicable exchange:

> You can tell them if you like that I've been most anywhere that fighting's been in evidence. I fought for the French against the Spanish and the Spanish against the French and I learned my seamanship in the Dutch Navy. But having had adventure enough in six years to last me six lives, I came here, hung up the sword and picked up the lancet – became a man of peace and not war, a healer, not a slayer.[63]

Blood is nevertheless forced to abandon his profession, his peaceful stance, and his luxurious chambers after his ministrations to a wounded rebel lands him in jail and sentenced to hanging during a farce of a trial by the King's magistrate. But through a twist of fate, Blood's sentencing coincides with the King's need for workers in the West Indies and Blood and some compatriots are shown being shipped as slaves to the British colony Port Royal. The film dwells upon the injustice of a white man enslaved by having the men evaluated roughly like cattle and sold at a slave market in the colonies. Blood, played by Flynn, looks out a porthole in the belly of the ship and comments pensively on their slavery by the king: 'He grants us our lives in exchange for living death'. Blood is able to utter such things when the film's setting is the Glorious Revolution. Blood is quickly elevated from his position as slave to one of doctor to the Governor, who suffers from gout. He then makes it his mission to rescue his fellow Englishmen from their bonds of slavery and in doing so casts them into the practice of piracy in order to make their living. Yet when outlining the articles that will govern his ship, Blood makes it clear that he is both forced into this position and interested in maintaining a type of moral economy that grants the men fair profit:

> We the undersigned are men without a country, outlaws now in our own land and homeless outcasts in any other. Desperate men we go to seek a desperate fortune … All moneys and valuables which may come into our possession should be lumped together into a common fund. And from this fund shall first be taken the money to fit, rig, and provision the ship. After that the recompense each will receive who is wounded shall be as follows, for the loss of the right arm 600 pieces of eight, left arm 500.[64]

According to the moral economy established by Blood, a man's service in battle is recognised to the extent that limbs are valued with cash, and much time is devoted in the film to showing Blood doling out the bounty in an organised and fair way from behind a desk on the ship's prow. He is presented on film as the true judge and jury of a man's ability and the atmosphere of the ship is presented as positive and industrious. More importantly Blood is happy to abandon his life of pirating once he discovers that King James has been ousted by the 'good King William'. This allows him and his crew to wage war against the French, who are attacking Port Royal. For his bravery, Blood is rewarded politically and economically by being made Governor of the colony.

The hero frustrated in his work was a familiar trope across a range of films in the interwar period. The popular empire film by Alexander Korda, *The Four Feathers*, showed the long journey of a hero realising the work he is meant to do for empire and empire alone. Frank Capra, the popular American film director often showcased the everyman frustrated in his attempt to complete his work; in the case of *Mr Smith Goes to Washington*, for the boy scouts he wishes to build a camp for, or in the case of Longfellow Deeds in *Mr Deeds Goes to Town*, Deeds's effort to allot land to poor farmers. Even in slightly more trivial occupations, a man's inability to work is showcased as a tragedy. Norman Maine, tragic protagonist of the third most popular film in Britain in 1937, *A Star Is Born*, is tragic for the very reason that his work as a film star is supplanted by his wife's own success. His unemployment is captured on film in silent scenes of him playing indoor golf, juxtaposed against spectacular scenes of drinking and bar-room violence. Mr Deeds also reacts to the court's attempt to stop his work of doling out his fortune with dejected silence. Film narratives in this period often convey the tragedy of unemployment through a virtual silencing of male characters.

Heroes in interwar mass culture unable to escape unemployment, made for a tragic and poignant ending to the soldierly ideals constructed in these novels and films. The movie *Grand Hotel* (1932), directed by British director Edmund Goulding, was the second most popular film of 1932 in Britain and starred audience favourites Greta Garbo and John Barrymore along with a varied cast that included popular film villain Wallace Beery as well as Joan Crawford. The movie centres on two days in the lives of a number of guests at the luxurious Grand Hotel in Berlin, making ample visual use of the revolving doors at the entrance of the hotel. The film begins and ends with the introduction and then death of Garbo's love-interest the Baron Felix von Geigern, played by the charismatic Barrymore. He is introduced to the audience first in a montage of guests placing calls from phone boxes in the hotel lobby. The Baron is in need of money, saying into the phone, 'I don't need advice thanks very much. I need money.'[65] Soon after this scene the audience is informed that he is not only in need of money but was also in World War I. When the Baron comments to a man at the hotel desk about a doctor with an obvious scar on his face that 'He always seems to be waiting for something but it never happens', the desk man responds, 'The war dropped him here and forgot him'. Baron looks at the scarred doctor with sympathy and says solemnly, 'Yes, I was in the war', and falls quiet. War trauma, like unemployment, is unspoken. The Baron's role as a soldier is emphasised throughout the film as he courts the troubled ballerina Grusinskaya. Her maid tells her after receiving flowers from him, 'I think they are perhaps from the same young man. He is at the end of the corridor. Tall. He walks like a soldier.' This identity is at the root of von Geigern's honourable behaviour in the film, even as the audience discovers he is at the hotel to steal Grusinskaya's pearls in order to satisfy a large gambling debt. The Baron is reluctant to perform the crime and when the thug who is sent to keep an eye on him suggests they chloroform the maid outside Grusinskaya's room, the Baron rejects the plan, responding, 'Poor kid. In the first place, it would give her a rotten headache. I know all about chloroform. I had it in the war.' The thug replies angrily, 'You're too much of a gentleman; that's the trouble with you'. Being a gentleman and a soldier are firmly linked in the film through the Baron.

The Baron is ultimately unable to go through with his plan of robbing Grusinskaya when after hiding in her room he sees her contemplating suicide. He reveals himself and declares his admiration of her and they spend the night together talking, after which he confesses his real reason for being in her room. He explains, 'I was threatened. I was desperately in need of a big sum of money', as he gives back her pearls. She forgives him, is transformed by his declaration of love, and asks that he come to Vienna with her the next night. He seems uncertain and they discuss his financial situation briefly:

GRUSINSKAYA: Flix [the Baron's nickname] is it money?
BARON: Of course.
GRUSINSKAYA: But I have money. I have money enough for both of us.
BARON: No. That would spoil everything. I'll manage somehow. I'll get it. I have a whole day. I'll be on the train.

They embrace and then, wildly, the last thing he says to her is, 'I'll be on the train. I'll get the money.' The Baron spends the day trying to procure the money first through gambling, then by stealing the pocketbook of his friend Kringelein, which he returns, and then finally by stealing into the room of a wealthy industrial magnate named Preysing. Preysing, the only actor exhibiting a German accent in a film set in Berlin, is easily the most unlikeable character, and when he discovers the Baron in his room he beats him to death before being arrested. This sends waves of shock throughout the hotel. The head porter discusses the events with some of the clerks at the hotel. 'They say he's a thief', says one, to which the head porter responds, 'I don't believe that.

He was a real gentleman.' Throughout the film the Baron's role as a gentlemen is emphasised first through his service in the war, his education and manners, and his duty to friends, and then in his refusal to take the charity of his female love-interest and consequently his adherence to a male breadwinner role. His inability to fulfil a masculine breadwinner ideal through his terrible death, rather than the crimes he planned against others, was the real tragedy of the film.

By the late 1930s we see heroes in both fiction and film who were less tied to the war. The depression instead acted as the catalyst that had thrown good men out of work. Eric Ambler was a relatively new author when he published 1938's *Cause for Alarm* and sketched out a good man dismissed from a job because of the depression. His lead character, Nicholas Marlow is described by his fiancé as 'thirty-five, five foot ten in your socks, and handsome to boot' as well as 'a very clever engineer' thrown out of work. Marlow remarks on the economic climate, 'As far as I could see there wasn't a great deal of difference between a trade recession and a good old-fashioned slump.'[66] Marlow's unemployment is also cast as abnormal for the period and the protagonist remarks, 'the girls would be quickly absorbed by neighbouring factories. Girl labour was at a premium in the Barnton district. The skilled men would not have much trouble either.' Women and working-class men would bounce back, but for Marlow as a middle-class professional it is a different situation. For Marlow, 'production engineers might not grow on trees, but then nor did jobs'.[67] Too young to participate in World War I, Marlow is nevertheless associated with a job central to building Britain and is ultimately engaged in efforts to thwart Italy from maintaining a solid alliance with Germany, a type of anticipatory warfare on behalf of Britain in the age of appeasement. The tragedy of his unemployment pushes him to take a job with an armaments company in Italy, where he discovers the extent of Italy's preparedness for war. He is soon embroiled with numerous spies and is able to smuggle out information that single-handedly contributes to an 'unexpected coolness which has developed lately between the two partners of the Axis', thereby avoiding the possibility of World War II. The novel ends by addressing Marlow's job status as newly secure. On his return to Britain he is met with a job offer, which he immediately takes up.[68] In this case Ambler's hero is able to turn his unemployment into service for his country and a job, avoiding the fate of the Baron.

Interwar film and fiction that featured a man exiled from a central role within the economy are featured again and again throughout this study, as it was a central trope in film and fiction popular with British audiences. The centrality of this trope says much about the importance of the male bread-winner to the dominant ideology in Britain before the war. The war ushered in what was an active discussion and rehabilitation of this role by audiences, producers, and censors. Yet in order to fully appreciate the extent of the exile of the male hero, as well as his place within the ideology of popular culture, we must first turn to his role within the nation. For to be exiled from the economy and the breadwinner role in the interwar period also indicated an exile from notions of 'Englishness' that were central to conceptions of the nation.

A man and his country

The heroes most popular with British readers and audiences in the 1920s and 1930s demonstrated not only their commitment to a role as breadwinner, but also their devotion to the nation, often at the same time. Love of one's country was usually established at the outset of the narrative seemingly to temper the radical positions of some of the heroes discussed here. The narratives that were most popular with British audiences eventually rewarded the hero's type of loyalty to the nation by placing him back at the centre of the nation. Conse-quently throughout the interwar years the Englishness on display in popular film and fiction was even more middle class than in the period studied by Dodd. An Oxford education was no longer deemed necessary as a credential of Englishness, but the hero usually displayed some sort of vague learnedness, often indicated by the overwhelmingly upper-class accent of the British actors on the screen in both British and American productions. The hero's link to the military as an institution, as mentioned, was also exhibited early on in the narrative and he could be further linked to other vital institutions such as the law or the medical profession.

Regardless of the institution the soldier was affiliated with, soldiers all displayed remarkably similar qualities that came to constitute Englishness. For Bertram, from Gibbs's *Middle of the Road*, one particular soldier he met, Huggett, embodied the ideal of British masculinity. Bertram 'believed that Huggett knew the truth of things about the spirit of the men. He marvelled at this fellow's common sense, his soundness of judgment, his sense of humour, his patience. Those had been the qualities of the men in the war. They were still there. If all the men were like Huggett, or most of them, England was safe.'[69] Here Bertram makes the connection between soldiering and English-ness explicit, arguing that the safety of the nation relied upon the masculinity embodied by the soldier figure yet also implying that men like Huggett were becoming harder to come by.

Bertram himself, for all his socialist leanings, clearly displays a love of Britain through his participation in the war. Gibbs, in the first pages of *The Middle of the Road*, makes it clear that Bertram is firmly anchored by his love of Britain, particularly of London, to which he returns after the war. Bertram's description of London borders on romantic: 'Every dimly lighted lamp was a beacon of delight; the smell of the streets, the rushing swirl of taxis … The wet crowds outside of the theatre, the dear damned dismalness of London, drugged him, made his senses drunk with gladness.'[70] Rarely has the smell of London streets been described with such passion. As Bertram enters the socialist circles of his friend Christy, he finds himself drawn into revolutionary talk with the writers and artists who surround him. Yet he still remains loyal to ideas of service to Britain, claiming passionately after a night of arguing that, 'if you deny patriotism, you rule out human nature and one of its strongest instincts'.[71] For Bertram, nationalist loyalty is not an act or a decision; it is something much more essential than that, and something that he possesses in spades. Bertram's desire in the narrative to write a novel about the war is in part fuelled by his desire to tell Britain how it really was: 'He was telling it all, nothing left out, nothing shirked, in horror, courage, boredom, fear, filth, laughter, madness.'[72] He has an infinite faith in the ability of the British to respond to reasoning, truth, and justice; all which he thinks will be captured by his novel, produced as the truth told by a soldier. For him, being a soldier was synonymous with expressing a love of Britain and England in particular:

> Lying in the earth of France, he had thought back to England, yearned for it. Not only and always for London, its mighty heart, which he'd loved, but for the smell of fields like this, for the sight again – once again – of an old village like one of those, with a square church tower and walled gardens and orchards white, as now, with blossom. He had tried to get something of that into his book – the inarticulate, half-conscious love of England which had come to country boys, cockneys, young louts in khaki, so that some instinct in them, some strain of blood, some heritage of spirit, had steeled them to stand fast in the dirty ditches of death, whatever their fear.[73]

Bertram, as much as he criticises the impact of the war and the society to which the soldiers return to, also argues for a recognition of the 'heritage of spirit' that lay within the fighting soldiers, a spirit so integral it resisted articulation.

Similar sentiments towards the nation are evident in Hutchinson's works. In *If Winter Comes* Sabre's devotion to the nation is signified through his dream to write a primer called 'England' with mildly leftist leanings, that sounds like an early foray into social history. According to Sabre, 'Kings were to enter this history but incidentally, as kings have in fact ever been but incidental to England's history.' Sabre describes the introduction to the text: 'This England' (it said) 'is *yours*. It belongs to *you* [original emphasis]. Many enemies have desired to take it because it is the most glorious and splendid country in the world.'[74] Sabre's love of Britain is demonstrated not only through his participation in the war effort but also through his tangible love of the textbooks that he has created which offer a democratic vision of community. Textbook publishing is only one aspect of Fortune, East, and Sabre, as they deal in all things relating to schools and churches, including the production of school desks and supplies. Of the company, 'It is said that if you loitered long enough in Fortune, East and Sabre's you would meet every dignitary of the Church and of education in the United Kingdom; and it was added that you would not have to wait long.'[75] The worthiness of this enterprise is never criticised in the book, even if Fortune's management is. Sabre's particular branch is one that he himself developed and he often touches the books dotingly and refers to them as his children. The books with their histories become symbolic of Britain. Sabre, not surprisingly, is passionately ready to defend this 'glorious and splendid country' once Britain declares war. The day after war is declared Sabre learns that his bad heart will prevent him from enlisting. Nevertheless, as the war wears on and the recruitment standards drop, Sabre finally passes in 1916. His joy is expressed through his racing heart and his 'bursting emotions'. Upon Sabre's official enlistment and his return home to Penny Green to spread the news to an unimpressed Mabel, Hutchinson writes, 'The most stupendously elated man in all England was presently riding to Penny Green on Sabre's bicycle.'[76]

Sorrell in *Sorrell and Son*, like Mark Sabre, expresses his nationalist devotion through his service to Britain during the war. Sorrell's rank and title in the war is a matter of utmost pride. Indeed, rank and title offered Sorrell specific ways of coping with shameful moments in front of his son: 'There were times when Sorrell felt very self-conscious in the presence of the boy. The pose he had adopted before Christopher dated from the war, and it had survived various humiliations, hunger, shabbiness, and the melodramatic disappearance of Christopher's mother ... To Christopher he wished to remain Captain Sorrell, M.C.'[77] This identification with a medal awarded for bravery in the field, is portrayed as Sorrell's defining characteristic early in the book. It provides a framework for the reader's understanding of him, as does his middle-class respectability. The trade magazine *Bioscope* also recognised that it was Sorrell's service to his country that made him such a gripping figure, advising exhibitors of the 1927 silent film version:

The picture has the curious effect of reality, and as it appeals directly to the heart, should interest any audience. To mere pleasure lovers the sentimentality may at times seem overstrained, but the chequered life story of a man who has nobly served his country and remains a gentleman in the strict sense of the term and devotes himself to the upbringing of his boy, commands respect.[78]

Sorrell's work in the war, nobly serving his country, eventually puts him in contact with Mr Roland, the ex-serviceman. Sorrell's soldierly commitment to work convinces Roland to hire him. Sorrell works for him diligently, coming up with new ideas to promote their hotel chain and through hard work, becoming a self-made man and ensuring his son's upward social mobility.[79] The London-born actor H. B. Warner, starring as Captain Sorrell in the 1933 movie made a tremendous impact on our aforementioned 50-year-old housewife with 'Domestic Trouble'. She wrote about Sorrell's attributes to Mayer, stating 'The part of "Sorrell" impressed me so much – such a strong character he had – noble and self sacrificing in spite of his continuous ups and downs and not troubling about false Pride which enabled him to rise above all obstacles.' She goes on to write 'I tried to do the same – in fact did and found my many vicissitudes gradually disappearing and so feel grateful to the film *Sorrell and Son* and the actors who made it possible to impress an individual.'[80] Warner's depiction of Sorrell emphasised his gentle and upright perseverance and the same actor would go on to embody those very traits in a number of Frank Capra's films, including as the kind-hearted judge in *Mr Deeds Goes to Town*. For the British housewife impressed by the film, Sorrel's strength and stoicism ultimately lead to his success in the film, and seemingly her own success at home.

In *Bulldog Drummond*, Drummond's service to Britain during the war is continuously stressed throughout the novel. Drummond's identity is often reduced to 'soldier': 'Not a muscle on the soldier's face twitched; not by the hint of a look did he show the keenly watching audience that he realised his danger.'[81] Moments like these emphasise that soldiering was an ongoing duty for Drummond. His mission of saving Britain makes his commitment glaringly obvious. Indeed, much of Drummond's nationalism is proved through his actions against the villain Peterson, who proposes to his evil coalition at the novel's outset, 'the defeat of England … a defeat more utter and complete than if she had lost the war'. Peterson promises them that 'not only will you humble that cursed country to the dirt, but you will taste power such as few men have tasted before'.[82] Drummond spends his time battling, with the help of a number of other ex-soldiers, against the coalition of Bolsheviks and 'filthy boches' that Peterson has mobilised. Drummond's ex-soldiers constitute a gang, renamed 'The Black Gang' in a sequel, with a collection of skills that is familiar to viewers of contemporary action movies. Ted Jerningham had 'an ability to hit anything at any range with every conceivable type of firearm', and Jerry Seymour is included because it's 'not a bad thing to have a flying man – up one's sleeve … And possibly some one versed in the ways of tanks might come in handy.'[83] The group unfailingly exhibits chivalry towards Phyllis (the future Mrs Drummond), defends Britain, and maintains Drummond's life of bacon and kidney for breakfast and drives through the British countryside. The novel also draws direct links between the group's loyalty to Drummond during the war and loyalty to Britain:

> Perhaps a patrol coming back would report a German, lying huddled in a shell-hole, with no trace of a wound, but only a broken neck; perhaps the patrol never found anything. But whatever the report, Hugh Drummond only grinned and saw to his men's breakfasts. Which is why there is in England to-day quite a number of civilians who acknowledge only two rulers – the King and Hugh Drummond. And they would die for either.[84]

The equation between soldier and country is explicit. Drummond goes on to defend Britain throughout the novel even while allowing some doubts about its state following the war to be voiced. Drummond assures his audience in the novel, 'There are many things, we know, which are wrong in this jolly old country of ours; but given time and the right methods I am sufficiently optimistic to believe that could be put right.' While acknowledging that there are reasons for the common man to feel disillusioned, Drummond is positive that socialism is not the answer. Drummond makes his position clear when addressing the Bolsheviks that Peterson has mobilised:

> Not by revolution and direct action will you make this island of ours right – though I am fully aware that this is the last thing you would wish to see happen. But with your brains, and for your own unscrupulous ends, you gull the working-man into believing it. And he, because you can talk with your tongues in your cheeks, is led away. He believes you will give him Utopia, whereas, in reality, you are leading him to hell. And you know it. Evolution is our only chance – not revolution.[85]

For Drummond, socialism is worse than capitalism and his cry of evolution, not revolution, is one that argues that capitalism must be maintained. In addition, his rather condescending discussion of the working man makes it clear that those of the middling classes must prevent the working class from being misled towards socialism. Drummond's role as a soldier, his bravery in

World War I, and his unswerving loyalty to king and country grant him the authority to make such statements about the condition of Britain.

Popular films generally chose to concentrate on the soldier in a war, but not any one war in particular. The films most popular in Britain in the interwar period were often American and were perhaps less invested in explicitly identifying the World War I soldier as hero. Certainly the avoidance of the war was supported by the activities of the British Board of Film Censors, which had strict ideas about how the soldier was to be presented and was uncomfortable with representations of World War I in general, a topic which is explored further in Chapter 4. As well, producers of films were concerned with presenting a war to an audience that was often envisioned, not always inaccurately, as tired of the war. The relative lack of success of films like *All Quiet on the Western Front* (1930) acted as a caution to studios; Harper notes that only 9,711 people viewed it in Portsmouth.[86] Audience fatigue with the war is difficult to gauge, yet the response to the Mass Observation survey of film-goers in 1938 recorded the thoughts of a Mr J. Smith who wrote, 'War pictures keep many patrons away because it brings back many sad and unpleasant memories.'[87] Yet war-like adventure stories like *Captain Blood* and *Lives of a Bengal Lancer* remained popular on the screen, proving that war presented in different guises made for popular viewing and that the hero in combat still resonated with interwar audiences.

An important exception to the tendency in film to disassociate the hero from World War I was the British film *Cavalcade*. The popularity of *Cavalcade* in part depended upon its mobilisation of key institutions of Englishness and a carefully balanced message that gently critiqued war in general, not just World War I, while also praising the sacrifice of British soldiers. *All Quiet on the Western Front* (1930) criticised not only war but also the institutions that supported war such as schools, in a memorable scene of a schoolmaster whipping his students into naive enthusiasm and enlistment at the outset of the war. *Cavalcade*, in contrast, documented the plight of the Marryots from 1899 to 1933 as they endured, rather melodramatically, the Boer War, the death of Queen Victoria, the sinking of the Titanic, and then World War I. Through it all, institutions of Englishness are represented by the man and wife at its centre, Robert and Jane Marryot. Robert is seen heading off to the Boer War in the first moments of the film, where his brave service earns him a type of upward mobility, a knighthood, and their son later fights in World War I. Lady Jane remains sad but stoic throughout, as she loses both sons, one on the Titanic and the other in World War I, all the while keeping genial relations with her servants and mourning the passing of another British institution, Queen Victoria, saying, 'I feel listless and sad, as though her death is a personal loss'. The Marryots' embodiment of Englishness overcomes the tragedy of the war as Lady Jane makes a toast to the New Year of 1933 at the end of the film: 'Let us drink to the spirit of gallantry and courage that made a strange heaven out of an unbelievable hell. Let us drink to the hope that one day this country of ours that we love so much will find dignity and greatness and peace again.' Country above all is the message of the film, one that Reginald Berkeley recognised when he wrote for *Picturegoer Weekly* about his adaptation of the play for the screen: 'The pure unboastful [*sic*] love of country which leads people to sacrifice themselves uncomplainingly in the hour of that country's need is common to us all.'[88] The film, instead of making one man a hero through his actions, instead made the upper middle-class couple of Robert and Jane the heroes of the new age by simply surviving and serving. By addressing the war directly *Cavalcade* was exceptional, yet it was not exceptional in promoting love of and service to country as vital traits of heroic Englishness.

Other popular films portrayed soldiers in various types of warfare and affiliated the hero with institutions that embodied the nation. An example of an American film that made this association was *Arrowsmith* (1931 [UK, 1935]). *Arrowsmith*, based on the novel by Sinclair Lewis, was the fifth most popular film in Britain in 1935, according to Sedgwick, and brought in 15,277 filmgoers at the Portsmouth cinema.[89] It starts out with a picturesque scene of pioneers going west in a covered wagon in the late nineteenth century and full of enthusiasm to settle the new frontier. We are led to understand these are the grandparents of the story's hero, Arrowsmith, even as he himself is played by the quintessential British actor, Ronald Colman, complete with an upper-class accent that is never accounted for. In the film, Arrowsmith is a country doctor married to a devoted nurse who eventually creates a vaccine that prevents a plague infecting ships across the world. Early on an attachment of the medical profession to that of the soldier is established. Arrowsmith is seen attending a lecture in which a 'Member of the Royal Swedish Medical Academy will Deliver His Inspiring Talk on Heroes of Health'.[90] Arrowsmith listens raptly to the doctor's lecture as the doctor declares in his imperfect English, 'I tell you we don't want no more old style soldiers. We want new style. Doctor soldiers! Scientific soldiers!' This lecture inspires Arrowsmith to greater heights and the eventual discovery of the serum that 'saves the world'. It also makes the connection between heroic institutions such as medicine and the military explicit. Arrowsmith's noble profession as a doctor is equated with the noble profession of the soldier.

In the case of *Mr Deeds Goes to Town*, the protagonist demonstrates his love of the nation by affiliating himself with a past hero from the American Civil War, Ulysses S. Grant. Deeds is doubtful about relocating to New York to take up his enormous inheritance but does express interest in seeing Grant's Tomb, the monument to Ulysses S. Grant. He repeatedly expresses interest in seeing this even as he is overwhelmed by a variety of people clamouring for his attention and his pocketbook in New York. Babe Bennett, the cynical journalist posing as an innocent down-on-her-luck girl in order to gain an exclusive on Deeds, finally takes him there. As they arrive at night-time at the Tomb, the audience is invited to dwell on its majestic grandness. Bennett says, 'There you are. Grant's Tomb. I hope you're not disappointed.' Her performance of authenticity makes her cynical about this display of devotion to the nation. Longfellow murmurs, as they stand dwarfed by the tomb, 'It's wonderful'. When Bennett says that 'to most people it's a washout', Deeds responds by explaining what he sees in the monument:

> Oh, I see a small Ohio farm boy becoming a great soldier. I see thousands of marching men. I see General Lee with a broken heart, surrendering, and I can see the beginning of a new nation, like Abraham Lincoln said. And I can see that Ohio boy being inaugurated as President. Things like that can only happen in a country like America.[91]

His voice full of emotion, Deeds honours the role of soldiers and heroes that forged the nation. This identification with a historical soldier hero sets his character up for a similar claim to the hearts of the people.

Yet even as Mr Deeds's actions in regard to his inheritance favour the small farmers in the story and his division of land ownership would indicate some affinity for socialist leanings, the film is careful to explain that this is not a new type of socialism but a simple hand up from within a system that is still working. During his trial when his sanity is questioned for giving away his fortune, Deeds sits quietly until he finally offers an explanation of what he was doing to a hushed audience. He begins by stating, 'From what I can see, no matter what system of government we have, there will always be leaders and always be followers.' This statement alone seems to adhere to a hierarchical order of government. He goes on to say from the witness box:

> It's like the road out in front of my house. It's on a steep hill. Every day I watch the cars climbing up. Some go lickety-split up that hill on high, some have to shift into second – and some sputter and shake and slip back to the bottom again. Same cars – same gasoline – yet some make it and some don't. And I say

the fellows who can make the hill on high should stop once in a while and help those who can't. That's all I'm trying to do with this money. Help the fellows who can't make the hill on high.[92]

Longfellow's symbolic use of the car, that symbol of the assembly line, coupled with the biblical hill on high, emphasises the continuity of American values and American manufacturing. He goes on to make it clear that this is not a handout when he finishes by saying, 'I was going to give each family 10 acres – a horse, a cow and some seed. And if they work the farm for three years, it's theirs'. The film cuts to an image of farmers in the audience nodding their support. Longfellow's vision within the film was not a form of permanent socialism but rather a hand-up in the existing system, modelled to an extent on the New Deal. An ethic of hard work for profit would still remain in place within the film. Longfellow as a hero himself is simply offering his services to those in need, in this case American farmers suffering from the depression rather than the explicit effects of World War I.

Historical epics also offered ways for films to promote the figure of the soldier without tying him to the contemporary world of war. Philip Dodd notes that history as a subject became compulsory in schools in 1900, thereby granting the teaching of Englishness throughout the ages the comfort and authority of an academic discipline.[93] Britain's history thus became an important and sanctioned way of negotiating definitions of Englishness. Historical dramas became a vital tool in this process with the advent of film, as Harper's study on costume drama illustrates.[94] Yet American films were also absorbed with British history in this period and beyond.[95] Popular films like *Mutiny on the Bounty*, *Lives of a Bengal Lancer*, and *Captain Blood* were all produced by American companies and often starred American actors, yet addressed British history.[96] *Mutiny on the Bounty* was the second most popular film of 1935 while *Lives of a Bengal Lancer* was the top film in 1936. Audience confusion understandably resulted from these American productions of British history, with one respondent to an audience survey by Mass Observation assuming that the two films were British and indeed holding them up as an example of what British films were capable of: 'British films could attend with better results to exactness of detail. Such films as *Mutiny of Bounty* [sic] and *Last of the Bengal Lancers* [sic] would I believe improve the public's following.'[97] Regardless, these films were popular with film-going audiences of the 1920s and 1930s. Other historical epics included *Captain Blood* (1935), which was itself a bestseller.[98] All these narratives showed a hero who fought bravely for British ideals even in the face of death.

Mutiny on the Bounty (1935) was the film account of the real-life mutiny on a British ship in 1789, based on the 1932 novel by the British-born Charles Nordhoff and James Norman Hall, an American who had served in the British army during World War I until his nationality was discovered. The film was incredibly popular with British audiences when it made it to their screens in 1936. Harper notes that it was a runaway hit in Portsmouth, drawing 26,136 people into stuffy theatres during a heat wave in August 1936, and Sedgwick identifies it as the second most popular film of 1936 after Chaplin's *Modern Times*.[99] Although the film begins in 1787 and covers the two-year voyage of the *Bounty*, the types of characters would have resonated with audiences of the interwar period. The story was told from the perspective of Roger Byam, a young upper-class man naively eager to join the British navy as a midshipman and who plans to compose a dictionary of the Tahitian language. On the *Bounty* Byam meets the handsome, charismatic, and friendly Lieutenant Fletcher Christian, played by Clark Gable. Christian is the protagonist of the story, although it begins and ends with Byam's entrance into the story and his eventual trial and pardon for treason. Both Byam and Christian embody a particular type of British soldier that we are now familiar with. Byam is naively excited at the prospect of an adventure that exemplifies Englishness. As the family friend, Sir Joseph Banks, tells Byam's mother, 'This is England's new venture in science, in trade, in discovery. Who else but Sir Austin Byam's son should go?'[100] Byam is reminded again of his duty and his Englishness by Sir Joseph after he introduces him to the tyrannical Captain Bligh, 'This won't be all cakes and ale, Roger...but your family's followed the sea for seven generations. Not one ever failed in his duty. In a tight place, that's all you'll need to remember.' Byam's British and soldier credentials are sketched out in these simple exchanges and he stays true to them throughout the *Bounty*'s journey as he shows a fascination with documenting the Tahitian language and refuses to mutiny against Captain Bligh.

Lieutenant Fletcher Christian also shows himself devoted to Britain, just not the captain who runs the ship. Christian demonstrates his pride for Britain through affection for the men under his command, an affection that Captain Bligh clearly does not share. Christian first confronts Bligh when he notes that the supplies for the ship are inadequate, saying, 'This ship has less food than a prison hull', and 'Can't get much from a hungry man. I have to work these men we feed.' Finally Christian says angrily and defensively of the men, 'They may come from jails and taverns, but they're English and they'll sail anywhere.' For Christian, the British background of the men signals a certain quality of endurance. He says to Bligh after Bligh has been particularly hard on them,

'These men aren't king-and-country volunteers. They've been brought aboard by press gangs. In a week, I'll get some spirit without flogging.' Christian remains optimistic about the Englishness ingrained in the men, which will make them capable and loyal seamen. Indeed, his relative kindness does foster loyalty to him instead of to Captain Bligh. The tension between Christian as protector of the men and Bligh as captain comes to a head after one man dies during Bligh's flogging of him and when it comes to light that Bligh has diverted some of the ship's supplies to his own house before the voyage. The ship is portrayed as increasingly claustrophobic, emphasised through relatively tight camera angles. Yet mutiny is avoided when Tahiti is seen in the distance. The vastness of the vista shown in the film positions Tahiti's freedom as a potent counterbalance to the limited life on the ship. After the mission to Tahiti is completed, tensions again rise as Bligh continues to abuse the men through a shortage of water and food, unjust punishment, and generally cruel orders. Although Christian has rebuked some of the sailors for talking negatively of the captain and whispering of mutiny, he finally revolts:

> I've had enough of this blood ship! He's not master of life and death on a quarter-deck above the angels ... I'm sick of blood! Bloody backs! Bloody faces! Bligh, you've given your last command! We'll be men again if we hang for it![101]

For Christian, Bligh's great crime is undermining the manhood of the sailors under him and that alone is worth hanging for. When Bligh is being set adrift on a tiny boat with minimal provisions he cries, 'But you're taking my ship! My ship!' Christian responds, 'Your ship? The king's ship, you mean, and you're not fit to command it.' Thus Christian's loyalty to king and nation are not questioned; rather he expresses his loyalty to the crown by rejecting the harsh governance of an unfit captain. In many ways, this position is one and the same with the heroes of the aforementioned novels, where ex-soldiers remain loyal to institutions of Englishness yet question the futility of war and those who control both the politics and the economy of Britain.

A similar figure exists in *Lives of a Bengal Lancer* in the character of Lieutenant McGregor, who is serving in India with the 41st Regiment of the Bengal Lancers. McGregor is a 'Scotch-Canadian' devoted to service to the Empire and moved by poetry about Britain, as we shall see.[102] The film revolves around the arrival of two men into the Lancers, a Lieutenant Forsythe and Lieutenant Donald Stone, son of the regiment's Colonel and conveniently raised in America to account for the actor's accent. The younger fresh-faced Stone provides a challenge to Colonel Stone, referred to repeatedly by McGregor as 'old ramrod', who is loath to show favour to his offspring.

The younger Stone becomes embittered with this lack of affection, causing him to engage in some doubtful behaviour that ends up leading to his being kidnapped by the evil Mohammed Khan. Forsythe and McGregor mount a rescue of the son and end up contributing to Khan's downfall in the process.

Central to the story is the pitting of two types of soldiering against each other: an older type of military behaviour symbolised by the portly and buttoned-up Colonel Stone and a more emotional yet active type of soldiering symbolised by the lanky, often sloppily dressed McGregor. Forsythe and McGregor debate the merits of the Colonel's type of governance throughout, with McGregor calling him an 'old fool' and a 'terror for drilling' while Forsythe takes a more tempered view of the Colonel's style. When discussing the increasing bitterness of Stone Jr. and the Colonel's approach, McGregor says, 'The old man doesn't know what to do about his kid and wants us to help him but just couldn't get it out. I never thought he cared that much. I never thought he was that human ... Boy's pretty bitter and ugly. Largely the old man's fault of course.' Forsythe responds, 'Partly the old man's, partly our system's. But mostly the boy's.' This discussion of the 'system' of soldiering is again taken up after Mohammed Khan kidnaps Stone Jr. and the Colonel refuses to send the regiment to retrieve him. McGregor objects strongly and is cited for insubordination and put under house arrest in the care of Forsythe. McGregor is railing against the Colonel when the Colonel's comrade and friend, Major Hamilton comes into the tent:

> MCGREGOR: And I suppose if it were your son, you'd sit here too, like a dummy.
> MAJOR HAMILTON: No, I probably should have ordered the regiment out but that's because I'm not the man the Colonel is. Or the soldier.
> MCGREGOR: Well if that's what you call being a man or a soldier, I don't want any part of it. Not me. That kid needs him. It's his own blood.[103]

Here McGregor clearly articulates warring masculinities entrenched in ideas of soldiering. McGregor's approach is one that believes no man shall be left behind, while it is made clear through Major Hamilton that the Colonel takes a larger view of the situation. The Major finally loses his temper with McGregor, saying angrily

> Man you are blind! Have you ever thought how for generation after generation here, a handful of men have ordered the lives of 300 million people? It's because he's here and a few more like him. Men of his breed have made British India. Men who put their jobs above everything. He wouldn't let death move him from it and he won't let love move him from it. When his breed of men dies out, that's the end. And it's a better breed of men than any of us will ever make.[104]

This is a demonstration of the white man's burden articulated by Kipling, and the Colonel is thus entrusted with the representation of Englishness and the care of the people under Britain's command. Such a position is ultimately endorsed in the film when Forsythe responds after this outburst and after the colonel's man leaves, 'I didn't think the old boy had it in him but he's right'. Yet the film also makes room for tacit approval of McGregor's position when he decides to go after Stone Jr. himself with Forsythe's aid.

McGregor and Forsythe are quickly captured by Mohammed Khan, aided no doubt by their poor attempts to imitate Indian men by painting their faces brown. Once captured they and Stone Jr. are tortured for information on the Colonel's location. McGregor and Forsythe undergo the torture without breaking, yet Stone Jr. breaks after watching their ordeal. The three men are then placed in a small cell together where the ramifications of Stone Jr.'s actions are debated. Stone Jr. is sullen and feeling guilty for giving in, finally saying hysterically of the torturing, 'Why should I stand all that? For what? For him? For a service that makes [my father] like he's been to me? … He wouldn't come after me. Not him, [imitating Stone] Regiment, service, duty! Why should I stand what you did for them? Why should I? Why should any of us?' McGregor slaps him and then in a self-conscious but sloppy imitation of the Major's speech says, 'Why? Well … there are some things they don't teach you in military college. Can't I guess. India's big, you know. There are 300 million people, and run by, uh, just a handful of men. The-the-the job comes first. Like old ramrod, you can't let death move you, nor love. And it's like … well how can I tell you what it's all about when I don't know myself?' There is then silence until Forsythe comes up with the answer to why that silences them all. In the quiet earthen cell he cites poetry, 'Ever the faith endures / England, my England. / Take and break us, we are yours./ England, my own. / Life is good, joy runs high. / Between English earth and sky. / Death is death and we shall die to the song on your bugles blown, England. / To the stars on your bugles blown!'[105] This poem, 'Pro Rege Nostro', written at the end of the nineteenth century by W. E. Henley, became a sentimental favourite during World War I and captured an older type of masculinity that articulated soldiers as one with the nation. The film endorses this connection between soldiering and the nation. As McGregor and Stone Jr. listen quietly to the poem it is clear that this is their answer, commitment to the nation at bodily cost; immediately after McGregor formulates a daring plan for them to escape and demolish the weapon supply of Khan. Heroics follow with McGregor sacrificing his own life to save Stone and Forsythe and also to protect the regiment. Stone

Jr. finally redeems himself by single-handedly attacking and killing Khan in a spectacular final scene that emphasises the prowess and quick thinking of the three soldiers. All three, McGregor *in memoriam*, are cited with medals for bravery from the Colonel, their devotion to the nation acknowledged by the military institution, which embodies Englishness in India.

The soldier hero and the prospect of World War II

The interwar rebuilding of the soldier as a hero faced a particular challenge in the heady years just prior to World War II, when Britain in particular strove to achieve a peace with Germany at any cost. In July 1937, the same summer that most of Europe, including Germany, Soviet Russia, and Britain peacefully participated in the Paris Exhibition, Oppenheim's novel, *Envoy Extraordinary* (1937) was published; Britain's self-appointed 'Prince of Storytellers', making his contribution to a temporary calming of the waters in Europe.[106] In *Envoy Extraordinary*, Oppenheim's hero, a British diplomat, solves the tensions in Europe by restoring to Germany the colonies it had lost with the signing of the Versailles Treaty. In the process Oppenheim casts a charismatic German Hitler-like figure in the novel as simply misunderstood. The novel anticipated by eight months the actual meeting on 3 March 1938 of Neville Henderson, British Ambassador to Berlin, with Hitler on the very subject of German claims to colonies in Africa. At this meeting, Britain raised the possibility of a central Africa controlled by a European Union of sorts, which Hitler rejected less than two weeks before the Anschluss with Austria.[107] Oppenheim's solution to the crisis met more success on the page than it did in real life, yet key to his novel's conclusion was the work of the British diplomat Mattresser. In this characterisation we see an example of the shift towards the diplomat as hero rather than the soldier in some of the action novels and thrillers before World War II.

There is an uneasy embrace of peacemaking for the hero, if not a complete abandonment of his soldier status, evident in some of the popular works from the period. Soldiering still certainly functions as a vital means of defining heroic qualities in the period, yet it is often tempered by diplomatic activity. Oppenheim's *The Spymaster* from 1938 introduced two of its main characters as members of the army and navy who also are involved in intelligence gathering in the interests of peace. One general remarks to the other, 'There are millions of English people who do not know that I am the head of the real Secret Service so far as the Army is concerned, and that you occupy exactly the same position with regard to the Navy.'[108] The roles of both army and navy commanders were vital to the story and, most importantly, to peace. A number of these novels did strongly advocate rearmament and engagement in warfare and they are, after all, thriller or action adventures so there is inevitably a scene where someone is tied up, guns are brandished, and someone is probably knocked unconscious; but in the case of novels from roughly 1937 to the autumn of 1939 this violence is inevitably in the service of peace. It is not to rescue a woman or restore lost jewels, but rather to avoid World War II.

The violence that the heroic characters engage in is against those invested in war making. The majority of the heroes in these works are explicitly and openly committed to peace, and indeed, long speeches are given to that effect. Heroes are not always using soldiering as shorthand for heroism, but rather we have heroes who are publishers of the *European Review* in the case of Oppenheim's *Exit a Dictator*; adventurers like the Saint who works to protect naive young socialists in France in *A Prelude for War*; diplomats; financiers; or heroes who are themselves profiteers. In the case of Oppenheim's *The Spymaster* of January 1939, the story's key figure to be protected was a banker, who although he played international polo, was 'head of the most famous banking firm in the world'.[109] The Italian Ambassador to Britain says, towards the novel's end, of the banker, 'It was a terrible blow to our Minister of Finance when he practically destroyed every hope we had of a foreign loan.'[110] The Admiral and General who meet at the outset of the novel have somehow prevented Italy's rearmament by protecting this banker and his immense financial power. This act goes unrecognised by the wider international community, but as the Admiral says to an old love-interest, 'the men who work on the lines which I have done and for the purpose which I have had in mind think nothing or know nothing of honours. We live in the shadows. I go back to my old job, except that they have given me a new ship and six months' leave.'[111] The crisis is averted without a shot fired. Films were much more tightly controlled prior to the war in how much they could show of tensions in Europe.[112] Yet the odd filmmaker made allusions to the tensions through methods meant to evade censorship. Hitchcock's *The Lady Vanishes* (1938) set a dramatic espionage thriller in an eastern European town that looked somewhat like Czechoslovakia. In this narrative a young couple take up the cause of a seemingly frail woman kidnapped by soldiers wearing Nazi-like uniforms. This results in an eventual shoot-out as they desperately try to enlist the help of the doubting British bystanders. Violence is undertaken, but as a last resort as the hero and heroine work to protect the older lady, who turns out to be a British spy aiding the cause of peace.[113] This is a different landscape to that which had characterised the 1920s and first half of the 1930s, when Bulldog Drummond was also Captain Drummond. In a period when the possibility of war was confronted head-on, low and middlebrow works embraced, with some obvious reservations, a type of hero who works for peace. The soldier, when faced with war in Britain, ultimately chooses peace in these narratives.

This, to some extent, challenges Michael Paris's characterisation of British mass culture as being military minded from 1850 onwards. In many ways, the 1920s and early 1930s use the soldier identity as shorthand for a certain type of British heroism, yet there is this important pause or hesitation in that narrative in the late 1930s when the authors of these novels were faced with the very real prospect of a war. Paris himself acknowledges the public's desire for peace, but maintains that popular culture nevertheless contributes to the 'pleasure culture of war' throughout the period. While I do not disagree with this, I think it is important to make note of a brief but important period where heroes seem to be invested in avoiding participation in war and identification as soldiers. We must be careful to apply a monolithic culture of war-making throughout the entire interwar period, and make note of moments where war-making served specific causes at certain times. These works show us what immanent war can do to popular culture and concepts of the hero, for we see a concerted effort within mass culture to foster new heroes: diplomats, journal editors, financiers, bankers fostering economic stability, and the occasional arms producer. When faced with war, British action writers demonstrated a notable reluctance to rush the British, even steely-eyed, stern-jawed heroes, into the maelstrom.

Conclusion

The novels and films that were most popular with British audiences in the interwar period featured a hero who had been returned to the centre of the nation and the economy within the narrative. These were men who had been fighting against not just the odds but also the society surrounding them, and were often devalued by those in power and struggling to maintain their masculine independence. Thus British audiences saw some acknowledgement of the disillusionment that many felt after the war, but also ultimately witnessed a conservative solution that revisited the traditional relationship between masculinity, work, and nation. These works are striking in their repetition of male anxieties about the economy, the nation, and the deception that surrounded the soldier. They highlighted the injustice of unemployment and unrecognised service to the nation. Although the majority of the characters discussed achieved a happy ending, prior to this triumph these men were positioned within British society in remarkably tenuous ways. The presence of characters like the Baron in *Grand Hotel* who did not rise above the war and hard economic times also acted as important and dramatic reminders of the long-term impact of the war upon men. The comfortable and assumed role that the soldier had with the nation and the economy was no longer a given, but rather a cause to be actively pursued within arenas such as bestselling novels and popular films. The hero's return from exile, we will see, was also predicated increasingly upon the actions of characters that surrounded him such as the villain and the love-interest. These characters were instrumental in the defensive process of buttressing the role of the hero and the breadwinner within the nation and the economy. The centrality of the hero's role also received help from outside of the narrative itself through the actions of censors at the Home Office and the British Board of Film Censors, all indicating that the maintenance of the soldiering and breadwinning ideal was one that demanded constant upkeep and negotiation in the 1920s and 1930s. This was not an easy continuation of pre-war patterns of masculinity but rather the signs of a struggle to make sense of changing patterns of masculinity, work, and nation.

Notes

1 'I found my manhood', *Daily Express* (30 May 1919).
2 See Kent, *Making Peace*.
3 'Ex-soldiers and police', *Daily Express* (27 May 1919).
4 Stevenson, *British Society 1914–45*.
5 Melman, *Women and the Popular Imagination in the Twenties*.
6 R. Graves, *Good-Bye to All That: An Autobiography* (London: Jonathan Cape, 1929); E. M. Remarque, *All Quiet on the Western Front*, trans. A. W. Wheen (Toronto: McClelland and Stewart, 1929); S. Sassoon, *Memoirs of an Infantry Officer* (London: Faber & Faber, 1930).
7 Fussell, *The Great War and Modern Memory* (Oxford: Oxford University Press, 1975, 2000); Watson, *Fighting Different Wars*.
8 G. Dawson, 'The Blond Bedouin: Lawrence of Arabia, Imperial Adventure and the Imagining of English-British Masculinity', in Michael Roper and John Tosh (eds), *Manful Assertions: Masculinities in Britain since 1800* (London: Routledge, 1991), pp. 113–44.
9 P. Dodd, 'Englishness and the National Culture', in Robert Colls and Philip Dodd (eds), *Englishness: Politics and Culture 1880–1920* (London: Croom Helm, 1986), pp. 1–22.
10 Adorno, 'Culture Industry Reconsidered', p. 17.
11 'Fierce riot in London', *Daily Express* (2 March 1920).
12 McKibbin, *Classes and Cultures*; Stevenson, *British Society 1914–45*.

13 See McKibbin, *Classes and Cultures*; S. Pederson, *Family, Dependence and the Welfare State: Great Britain and France, 1914–45* (Cambridge: Cambridge University Press, 1994); Stevenson, *British Society 1914–45*.

14 'The appalling cost of everything', *Daily Express* (10 June 1919).

15 McKibbin, *The Ideologies of Class*, pp. 259–293; K. O. Morgan, *Consensus and Disunity: The Lloyd George Coalition Government 1918–1922* (Oxford: Clarendon Press, 1979).

16 'The British government', *New Statesman* (4 September 1920).

17 Dodd, 'Englishness and the National Culture'.

18 M. Paris, *Warrior Nation: Images of War in British Popular Culture, 1850–2000* (London: Reaktion, 2000).

19 Light, *Forever England*.

20 G. L. Mosse, *Nationalism and Sexuality: Respectability and Abnormal Sexuality in Modern Europe* (New York: Howard Fertig, 1985).

21 K. Boyd, *Manliness and the Boys' Story Paper in Britain: A Cultural History, 1855–1940* (Basingstoke: Palgrave Macmillan, 2003); A. Caesar, *Taking It Like a Man: Suffering, Sexuality and the War Poets Brooke, Sassoon, Owen, Graves* (Manchester: Manchester University Press, 1993); M. Green, *The Adventurous Male: Chapters in the History of the White Male Mind* (University Park, PA: Pennsylvania State University Press, 1993); J. Tosh, *A Man's Place: Masculinity and the Middle-Class Home in Victorian England* (New Haven: Yale University Press, 1999).

22 H. R. Haggard, *King Solomon's Mines* (New York: Longmans, Green, 1916 [1885]); J. M. MacKenzie (ed.), *Popular Imperialism and the Military 1850–1950* (Manchester: Manchester University Press, 1992).

23 G. R. Wilkinson, *Depictions and Images of War in Edwardian Newspapers, 1899–1914* (New York: Palgrave Macmillan, 2003).

24 Boyd, *Manliness and the Boys' Story Paper in Britain*.

25 Bloom (ed.), *Literature and Culture in Modern Britain: Volume I*, p. 12.

26 N. F. Gullace, *'The Blood of Our Sons': Men, Women, and the Renegotiation of British Citizenship during the Great War* (New York: Palgrave Macmillan, 2002).

27 P. Gibbs, *Now It Can Be Told* (London: Harper, 1920), p. 29.

28 S. Hynes, *A War Imagined: The First World War and English Culture* (London: Pimlico, 1992).

29 Waites, 'Effect of the First World War'.

30 For a discussion of the uneven experience of unemployment, see Stevenson, 'Myth and Reality: Britain in the 1930s', in *Crisis and Controversy*.

31 A. Clark, *The Struggle for the Breeches: Gender and the Making of the British Working Class* (Berkeley, CA: University of California Press, 1997); E. P. Thompson, *The Making of the English Working Class* (London: Penguin, 1963).

32 'Pay without work', *Daily Express* (28 April 1919).

33 'Labour's unemployment proposals', *New Statesman* (29 January 1921).

34 R. C. Davison, *The Unemployed: Old Policies and New* (London: Longmans, Green, 1929), pp. 170–1.

35 G. D. H. Cole, *Out of Work: An Introduction to the Study of Unemployment* (New York: Alfred A. Knopf, 1923), p. 61.

36 Gibbs, *Now It Can Be Told*, 517–18.

37 David Lloyd George, 'Fontainebleau Memorandum' (1919) quoted in M. MacMillan, *Paris 1919: Six Months that Changed the World* (New York: Random House, 2003), p. 197.

38 Morgan, *Consensus and Disunity*, pp. 133–8.

39 'Criminal Bolshevist regime. Mr Churchill on Russia and Ireland', *The Times* (19 November 1920).

40 Morgan, *Consensus and Disunity*, pp. 134–6.

41 Leslie Charteris, *Prelude for War* (London: Hodder & Stoughton, 1938), p. 11.

42 *Roman Scandals*, VHS, dir. Frank Tuttle (1933; New York, NY: HBO Video, 1995); Sedgwick, *Popular Filmgoing in 1930s Britain*.

43 Sedgwick, *Popular Filmgoing in 1930s Britain*, p. 312; *Mr Deeds Goes to Town*, dir. F. Capra, 1936.

44 P. Gibbs, *Young Anarchy* (New York: G. H. Doran, 1926).

45 Charteris, *Prelude for War*, pp. 45–6.

46 Pilgrim Trust, *Men without Work: A Report Made to the Pilgrim Trust* (Cambridge: Cambridge University Press, 1938), p. 5.

47 McKibbin, *Ideologies of Class*, pp. 228–58.

48 See Clark, *Struggle for the Breeches*; L. Davidoff and C. Hall, *Family Fortunes: Men and Women of the English Middle Class 1780–1850* (London: Routledge, 1997).

49 A. S. M. Hutchinson, *If Winter Comes* (Toronto: McClelland & Stewart, 1921), p. 61.

50 Gibbs, *Young Anarchy*, p. 27.

51 Harper, 'Lower Middle-Class Taste-Community in the 1930s', 581.

52 *Cavalcade*, VHS, dir. F. Lloyd (1933; Beverly Hills, CA: Fox Video, 1993).

53 P. Gibbs, *The Middle of the Road* (New York: G. H. Doran, 1923), pp. 30–1.

54 *Ibid.*, 31.

55 Deeping, *Sorrell and Son*, p. 3.

56 *Ibid.*, 4.

57 *Ibid.*, 12.

58 Hutchinson, *If Winter Comes*, p. 53.

59 *Ibid.*, 309.

60 *Ibid.*, 295.

61 McNeile, *Bulldog Drummond*, p. 86.

62 The film was ranked the 22nd most popular film in 1936 by Sedgwick and brought in 16,158 people to the Portsmouth cinema according to Harper ('Lower-Middle-Class Taste-Community in the 1930s', 584); Sedgwick, *Popular Filmgoing in 1930s Britain*, p. 258.

63 *Captain Blood*, DVD, dir. M. Curtiz (1935; Burbank, CA: Warner Home Video, 2005).

64 *Ibid.*

65 *Grand Hotel*, DVD, dir. E. Goulding (1932; Burbank, CA; Warner Home Video, 2005).

66 E. Ambler, *Cause for Alarm* (London: Penguin, 2009 [1938]), p. 7.

67 *Ibid.*, pp. 7–8.

68 *Ibid.*, p. 267.
69 Gibbs, *Middle of the Road*, p. 87.
70 *Ibid.*
71 *Ibid.*, p. 77.
72 *Ibid.*, p. 118.
73 *Ibid.*, p. 115.
74 Hutchinson, *If Winter Comes*, p. 59.
75 *Ibid.*, p. 51.
76 *Ibid.*, p. 295.
77 Deeping, *Sorrell and Son*, p. 3.
78 'Sorrell and Son', *Bioscope* 74:1110, 52.
79 Most notably Sorrell capitalises on the presence of two famous film actors whose elopement brought them to Roland's hotel. He asks them to do an interview with a local paper at the end of their stay as a form of promotion.
80 Mayer, *Sociology of Film*, pp. 190–1.
81 H. C. McNeile, *Bull-Dog Drummond* (London: Hodder & Stoughton, 1935 [1920]), pp. 173–4.
82 *Ibid.*, p. 19.
83 *Ibid.*, p. 125.
84 *Ibid.*, pp. 104–5.
85 *Ibid.*, p. 314.
86 Harper, 'Lower Middle-Class Taste-Community in the 1930s', 579.
87 *Mass-Observation at the Movies*, p. 51.
88 R. Berkeley, 'Cavalcade Comes to the Screen', *Picturegoer Weekly* 2: 75 (1932), 8.
89 Sedgwick, *Popular Filmgoing in 1930s Britain*, 313; Harper, 'Lower Middle-Class Taste-Community in the 1930s'.
90 *Arrowsmith*, DVD, dir. J. Ford (1931; Los Angeles, CA: MGM, 2005).
91 *Mr Deeds Goes to Town.*
92 *Ibid.*
93 Dodd, 'Englishness and the National Culture', 4. See also Chris Waters's article for a discussion of Englishness and history throughout the 1930s and 1940s ('"Dark Strangers" in Our Midst: Discourses of Race and Nation in Britain, 1947–1963', *Journal of British Studies* 36 (1997), 207–38).
94 S. Harper, *Picturing the Past: The Rise and Fall of the British Costume Film* (London: BFI, 1994).
95 Glancy, *When Hollywood Loved Britain*; P. Swann, *The Hollywood Feature Film in Postwar Britain* (London: Croom Helm, 1987).
96 The films were produced by Paramount, MGM, and Cosmopolitan Productions respectively.
97 *Mass-Observation at the Movies*, p. 50.
98 Bloom, *Bestsellers*, p. 140.
99 Harper, 'Lower Middle-Class Taste-Community in the 1930s', 536; Sedgwick, *Popular Filmgoing in 1930s Britain*, p. 313.
100 *Mutiny on the Bounty*, VHS, dir. F. Lloyd (1935; Burbank, CA: Warner Home Video, 2001).

101 *Ibid.*

102 *Lives of a Bengal Lancer*, DVD, dir. H. Hathaway (1935; Universal City, CA: Universal Studios Home Entertainment, 2005).

103 *Ibid.*

104 *Ibid.*

105 *Ibid.*

106 E. P. Oppenheim, *Envoy Extraordinary* (Boston: Little, Brown, 1937); R. Standish, *The Prince of Storytellers: The Life of E. Phillips Oppenheim* (London: P. Davies, 1957).

107 A. J. Crozier, *Appeasement and Germany's Last Bid for Colonies* (London: Macmillan, 1988).

108 E. P. Oppenheim, *The Spymaster* (Boston, Little, Brown, 1938), p. 11.

109 *Ibid.*, p. 4.

110 *Ibid.*, p. 292.

111 *Ibid.*, p. 297.

112 J. Richards, 'The British Board of Film Censors and Content Control in the 1930s: Images of Britain', *Historical Journal of Film, Radio and Television* 1:2 (1981), 95–116; J. C. Robertson, 'British Film Censorship Goes to War', *Historical Journal of Film, Radio, and Television* 2:1 (1982), 49–64.

113 *The Lady Vanishes* (1938), dir. Alfred Hitchcock (Gainsborough Pictures, Gaumont-British).

2

The shape of villainy: profiteering and money-men

He bore a certain resemblance to a stunted whale. He was chiefly abdominal. His legs appeared to begin, without thighs, at his knees, and his face, without neck, at his chest. His face was large, both wide and long, and covered to its lower part with a tough scrub of grey beard. The line of his mouth showed through the scrub and turned extravagantly downwards at the corners. He had a commanding, heavily knobbed brow, and small grey eyes of intense severity. His voice was cold, and his manner, though intensely polished and suave, singularly stern and decisive. He had an expression of 'I have decided' and Sabre said that he kept this expression on ice. It had an icy sound and certainly had the rigidity and imperviousness of an iceberg. Hearing it, one might believe that it could have a cruel sound.

A. S. M. Hutchinson, *If Winter Comes* (1921)

Avarice is as old as human nature. From the earliest times the greed of gain has tempted men to exploit to their own advantage the public need ... History is full of records of the attempts that have been made by communities to defend themselves against the activities of these evil doers.

1919 Profiteering Act

These passages from A. S. M. Hutchinson's 1921 bestseller *If Winter Comes* and from the introduction to the 1919 Profiteering Act might seem to occupy separate spheres. Yet both address the persistent conflation of wealth and evil that defined villainy in interwar popular culture. The colourful description of Mark Sabre's boss Mr Fortune and his iceberg-like management style helps the reader to identify Fortune as one of the main villains in the text. Fortune's girth is highlighted as exceptional, and the stark differences between Fortune and Sabre become apparent: while Fortune is heavy and stern, Sabre is of average size and affable; while Fortune does not serve in the war, Sabre does so eagerly and is dismissed by Fortune because of it. Fortune's actions against Sabre throughout the story illustrate his lack of sympathy for his workers, yet his real crime lies in his disregard of the returning soldier and his single-minded pursuit of profit. The Profiteering Act, introduced by the coalition government as a weak effort to address the post-war scandal of businessmen profiting from the war, acknowledged that this was indeed *the* interwar crime, making connections between villainy and a pursuit of wealth that jeopardised the soldiers at the heart of the nation. The 'evil-doers', the 'avarice', and the 'greed of gain' invoked by the Act drew upon a rather effective language of villainy to portray those who profiteered, even while the Act itself was largely denounced before it had even been passed. As Neil Rollings points out, public concern with profiteering simmered throughout the interwar years and the onset of World War II led to an outcry in the press against a potential repeat of the practice, and the hasty and ineffectual passage of a second profiteering act in Parliament.[1] The public memory of profiteering and its evils was easily provoked.

That anger at the outset of World War II towards profiteering was exacerbated by the continued presence of the profiteering villain in popular culture throughout the 1920s and 1930s. The characterisation of villainy found in both *If Winter Comes* and the Profiteering Act was repeated across the bestselling novels and popular films examined here right up until the outbreak of war in 1939. Profiteers rivalled fascist dictators in the frequency of their appearances. Audiences continued to see and read of wealthy men who exploited penniless soldiers and, in the more fantastic instances, hatched evil plans about destroying Britain and gaining world domination. I argue that the social and economic conditions of Britain following World War I fostered a characterisation of both businessmen and government officials as villains within popular film and fiction. This marked a shift away from a type of villainy that had previously resided largely within the aristocracy, to multiple new types of villainy that existed in seemingly respectable middle-class personages. Almost anyone and everyone in the 1920s and 1930s could be a villain in disguise. These multiplying types of villainy and their reoccurrence across popular narratives are the focus of this chapter.

In order to examine developments in the characterisation of villains in interwar popular culture, there is a need to historicise the role of the antagonist. Although villains have long existed as a way for authors to comment upon and interpret the realities of the contemporary world, the components of the villainous character has not been timeless. The dastardly deeds and behaviours of villains in the 1920s and 1930s took forms that emphasise not just greed, but a betrayal of Britain, while the just behaviour of the hero includes selfless love of nation and a belief in a type of moral economy. Philip Gibbs's wealthy 'Oxford dons', whom he chastises in the non-fictional *Now It Can Be Told*

(1920) for being so 'proud of their prowess with the pitchfork – behold their patriotism! – while the boys were being blown to bits on the Yser Canal', are fictionalised in Gibbs's subsequent novels as interwar villains.[2] Newspaper commentary that emphasised war profiteering or ran cartoons lancing the wealthy, non-mobilised man played an important part in affirming and promoting the villainy depicted in both fiction and film. Warwick Deeping's *Sorrell and Son* describes 'the women going to the rich fellows who had stayed at home, the bewilderment, the sense of a bitter wrong, of blood poured out to be sucked up by the lips of money-mad materialism', and reproduces these 'rich fellows' as villains in his work.[3] Deeping was not alone, for across an entire body of bestsellers, films, and newspaper articles, discourses surrounding post-World War I villainy were represented and multiplied.

The traits of villainy within the mass culture of the interwar period marked moral boundaries that reflected intensely contemporary concerns. The actions, speeches, beliefs, and appearances of villains constructed a definition of what was wrong with society for the reader and viewer and drew upon headlines of the day to do so. The villain, as a result, is very much entrenched in the period in which he or she was formed. This connection is something that tends to be overlooked by both historians and scholars of media studies in favour of an emphasis on the affirmative values embodied by the hero. As we have seen, popular film and fiction made noticeable efforts in the post-World War I period to connect post-World War I heroic ideals with pre-war ideals. The character of the villain, on the other hand, did not need to emphasise such continuity. Villains could be a symbol of modern evils. Adorno and Horkheimer tend to emphasise the role of the hero as central to the formula of the culture industry, yet it is the changeable and contemporary aspects of the villain that are key to the enduring qualities of the hero at the formula's centre.[4] For the historian of popular culture, the intensely contemporary villain is a particularly fruitful window into the period itself. The transgressions of the villain underscored the just actions of interwar heroes who were the only characters capable of revealing and disciplining the villain's wrongdoings. The extreme behaviour of the villain, be it aggressive profiteering or the fanatical beliefs of a Bolshevik or fascist, became an important vehicle for the hero's articulation of a moderate middle road that tended to reinforce the status quo, rather than advocate radical reform.

In the popular fiction and film of the 1920s and 1930s, two dominant types of male villains can be identified: the older, wealthy, and large man already discussed, and the younger, wealthy man. The imposing figure of Mr Fortune and his physical embodiment of villainy found cinematic equivalents, if not in the lost 1923 film version of the novel, then in countless other films of the interwar period. The large, scheming wealthy man was so common in bestsellers and films on both sides of the Atlantic as to be almost a stock caricature by the end of the 1930s. In comparison, the pairing of a handsome and sometimes even ordinary young man with villainy seems to further signal real concerns by the reading and viewing audience with the interwar economy, ideas of 'Englishness' and performance. The relationship between performance and wealth and its expression within popular culture is consequently central to this chapter.

This chapter starts with an examination of the changing role of the villain in the modern era before moving on to examine villainous characters consumed by British audiences within the social and economic context of interwar Britain. Wartime anxieties about both a capitalist economy and the role of government led to a uniquely interwar embodiment of villainy – one that foregrounded an older traditional type of 'knowable' villain alongside a newly mysterious 'unknowable villain'. Villains in the narratives discussed here were engaged in overt or covert performances of respectability. The hero either recognised the villain for what he or she was, but no one else did, or the villains were not even recognised as such by the hero until later in the narrative. The latter's disguise was convincing and the dramatic tension in popular novels and films was based on the hero seeing through and ultimately knowing the villain for what he or she is. The performance of the villain was a central part of his or her shifty and evil characteristics. The hero, in contrast, embodied 'good' because he did not engage in performance. His heart was true, and that 'truth' was very much related to his supposed disinterest in wealth or power, a disinterest communicated even more potently in the case of the unemployed ex-soldier. This disinterest, not coincidentally, made him a natural leader and allowed him to see easily through the performances of others. Thus performance for all of the characters becomes the expression of unease about wealth and power in the interwar period. The porous divide between the knowable and unknowable villain spoke to numerous anxieties about shifting epistemologies of good and evil in the aftermath of World War I. On the eve of World War II, we will see that further confusion abounded in mass culture's construction of knowable and unknowable villains. Prior to the introduction of an enduring template for modern villainy in the form of the evil Nazis, I examine the wide array of villains housed in popular fiction, demonstrating the extent to which villains can be a vital entrance into interwar Britain.

The changing villain

For the most part villainy as a subject has been relatively unexplored by cultural historians of the modern period. In part this may be that while rogues and scoundrels have abounded in fiction and theatre for centuries and have traditionally driven the plots of novels and plays, the villain in the modern era, as Juliet John writes, seems somewhat outdated. John argues that the changes of the eighteenth century caused the villain of the nineteenth century to 'seem old-fashioned and incredible as a real-life concept and consequently simplistic or primitive in fiction'.[5] Villainy became doubly unfashionable in the twentieth century for its naive conceptions of evil in the era of psychology and psychoanalysis, and for its persistent presence within devalued popular forms of culture. Virginia Woolf and T. S. Eliot, for instance, did not deal in such black-and-white categories. The Cold War era offered up new types of villains within the likes of the James Bond films and spy novels, but the interwar villain in particular has remained woefully obscure.

The lack of scholarly attention to interwar villainy is, in part, a casualty of the developing schism between high and low culture. For the cultural elite such as Q. D. and F. R. Leavis and others the presence of villainous charac-ters, along with the sentimental happy endings discussed in the next chapter, marked out the middle or lowbrow novel. These works were subject to a disdain that lingers in the historical record. In highbrow works, villainy could at best only be inferred and it was almost always justified by circumstances.[6] Villains were moulded by their environment, not by natural instincts towards evil. The characterisation of bestselling authors, on the other hand, inevitably lacked the subtlety of serious modernist literature. Hence, while Philip Gibbs and E. Philips Oppenheim likely did not consider themselves to be writing in the same genre (Gibbs, after all, still warranted a review in the *Times Literary Supplement*), the sometimes clumsy presence of villains in their novels distin-guished them both from highbrow authors.

Middle and lowbrow associations with villainy were inevitably aided by the presence of highly theatrical villains in films eagerly attended by the working and middle classes. In popular films villainy functioned, at times, in very obvious ways that drew upon a tradition of melodrama and theatre. Film made extensive and sometimes exaggerated use of the villain through physical appearance, broad winks, and exaggerated actions of actors playing the villains. Silent films, in particular, had to depend upon such visual clues to aid the narratives, while the 'talkies', introduced in the late 1920s to Britain, increas-ingly experimented with less obvious forms of villainy. *Film Weekly* summed it up best in 1935 when it remarked, 'in the old days villains were villains indeed. They hissed and leered and twirled their moustaches triumphantly; there was no mistaking them. Nowadays, they are more of a puzzle.'[7] The 1930s and the talking film saw the production of new types of villainy that embraced a type of nuance and indeed deception in the construction of the film villain.

The hissing and leering villains of the 'old days' stemmed from the working-class culture of the eighteenth and nineteenth centuries. Melodrama never tired of its villains and was an important form of entertainment throughout this period.[8] Villains within popular melodramatic plays and early films were often black-hearted, licentious, aristocratic types. Vilifying the aristocracy as well as the monarchy became an important means to articulate one's own role in a class society. The villain's role had to be clearly defined in order for an opposing view to be taken. Colin Watson, like his predecessor in *Film Weekly*, argues that the villain in the late eighteenth and nineteenth centuries was marked by his visibility:

> The villain of the old melodrama was identifiable at his very first appearance. He wore the face of wickedness and spoke in the approved accents of his kind. He was the Devil of the miracle plays with tail and horns concealed by frock coat and top hat. The costume was significant. In the eyes of Victorian labourers and artisans it was the uniform of the man they believed they had most cause to hate – the man who, by reason of advantages of birth, education or wealth, was able to cheat them. He was generally a lawyer or a landlord … And the cause of conflict had to be immediate and personal – a seduction, a piece of legal sharp practice, a fraud or injustice of some kind. Such matters were either within the experience of the audience or easily appreciable at second hand.[9]

The evildoer's role as a member of the upper class became recognisable not only through his costume but through his crime. It was the gentry that were able to perpetrate fraud, legal injustice, and the seduction of poor working or middle-class girls in the plays because they wielded that power in reality.[10]

By the late nineteenth century, the shape of villainy was beginning to change. The working and middle classes could no longer set themselves against the considerable power of the aristocracy. By the time Dickens and Arthur Conan Doyle were writing their novels and short stories, the aristocracy was considered to be in decline within the economic and political landscapes of the day. Popular representations of the aristocratic villain, such as in Bram Stoker's *Dracula* (1897), now only emphasised a degenerate and declining class that was unreasonably attached to outdated symbols of wealth.[11] In order to carry emotional weight within a narrative, villainy had to be redefined. Villainy began to be associated with the financial world of the city, although in highly ambivalent ways. The successful banker or financier could occupy both the role of a benevolent patriarchal figure and also a greedy and devious villain.[12] Ranald Michie argues that this characterisation of the developing world of finance was linked to the health of the British economy. Certainly the obvious villains of the eighteenth and nineteenth centuries were difficult to replicate as economic and political power shifted to the growing middle classes who were alternately lauded and condemned in popular culture.

The proliferation of detective stories in the late 1880s and the early twentieth century speaks to that class confusion. Detective stories, when not blessed with an arch-villain such as Sherlock's Moriarty, displaced the role of a trans-parent villain. The audience did not immediately know the perpetrator in the modern crime novel. The bad man did not appear on the narrative stage twirling a sinister moustache. Rather, villainous attributes were conferred upon the transgressor retroactively, after the detective had identified their role. This mystery and the danger involved were further heightened by the revelation of the proximity of the villain throughout the story. Within film, this effect could be especially powerful as the audience witnessed the villain appearing and behaving in ways indiscernible from the surrounding innocents. In this regard, the boundary between innocence and guilt were blurred as the villain walked among the middle-class societies envisioned by the likes of Agatha Christie and Dorothy Sayers. As Alison Light writes of Christie's works, the detective novel was a profoundly paranoid genre that constantly invoked a middle class that was threatened from without, as well as within; yet central to this threat was the economic instability implied.[13] Stacy Gillis argues that the detective novel reflected middle-class concerns about individual property and capital.[14] Jerry Palmer maintains in his study of thrillers that protection of individual property by the twentieth century had become tantamount to the 'natural order' of things in popular fiction; a violation of this property was in turn a violation of natural order and all the more heinous.[15] The skill of the detective was his ability to both restore this natural order and expose evil when it was no longer clearly recognisable as such.

This dichotomy between the all-seeing hero who protects the right order of things and the villain who threatens to skew this order and therefore must be discovered was repeated to varying degrees across detective novels and other developing genres of bestsellers, such as the thriller and the social melodrama. Thrillers tended to mimic some aspects of the detective formula, while hastening exposure of the villain and punctuating their plots with considerably more action and violence; the villain still had to be discovered, but this tended to happen early on compared to Christie's works. Dramas and the slightly more serious narratives of A. S. M. Hutchinson and Warwick Deeping also mimicked the close proximity of the hero and villain, making the exposure of the villain to the community within the narrative and the triumph of the hero somewhat less suspenseful and definitive but nevertheless key to the narrative arc. The villains in these stories also had to be revealed but in less outrageous ways than in the thrillers.

Yet, while the discovery of the 'unknowable' villain became more central in these works, in many popular films and novels of the interwar period the more recognisable type of villain that had been so popular in nineteenth-century melodrama was still readily apparent. The 1920s and 1930s act as an important and overlooked bridge between nineteenth-century and post-war representations of villainy.[16] The James Bond villains in the late 1950s and early 1960s are highly visible examples of the knowable villain.[17] Whatever can be said about the Bond villains, Dr No and Goldfinger were not particularly subtle characters. Yet this type of villainy was rooted in the interwar period. James Chapman, citing authors Sydney Horler and H. C. McNeile, argues that the post-World War II Bond villains were built upon the sensational thrillers of the 1920s and 1930s, which presented criminals who were 'caricatures rather than characters, often of bizarre physical appearance, invariably bent on the acquisition of wealth and power, and with a tendency to devise ingenious death scenarios for the hero'.[18] As an example, one need only think of the illustrious career of the actor Peter Lorre who played first a foreign and rotund villain with an impressive facial scar in Hitchcock's *The Man Who Knew Too Much* (1934) and then reprised the role of villain in other notable films including *The Maltese Falcon* (1941) and a TV version of James Bond's novel *Casino Royale* (1954).

What is remarkable about popular culture in interwar Britain is that this older type of knowable villain continued to exist alongside the newer type of villain – the seemingly ordinary middle-class and unidentifiable villains of Christie, Deeping, and Hitchcock. The 1920s and 1930s was a significant moment when the older villains of melodrama shared the stage with an emerging not-so-obvious 'uknowable' villain. Wallace Beery, the popular film villain (who played the murderous Preysing in *Grand Hotel*), in his interview with *Film Weekly* in 1935, spoke of the new type of villains, saying 'Of course, there are villains and villains, and not all of them are what you might call the fighting kind. There's the smooth, calculating type, and there's the unscrupulous business-man type, and then there's the villain you don't recognize at all until the end of the last reel.'[19] Interwar bestsellers and popular film offered up this particularly peculiar amalgamation of an older and newer type of villainy.

Concerns about the British economy and the strength of the nation following World War I grounded this fractured type of villainy. The cold, calculating businessmen that Beery describes, as well as the ham-fisted violent thug, found a receptive audience. The *Daily Mail* wrote somewhat mournfully of the demise of Bulldog Drummond's own calculating arch-enemy, Carl Peterson, in the novel *The Final Count* (1925): 'We are sorry to think that his long duel with Carl Peterson is at an end. And yet there seems to be a promise of something to follow.'[20] A British society that had been destabilised by a devastating war, changing meanings of work, and a profound blurring of gender roles, had to look to new types of villains to reflect these shifts. What resulted was a number of villainous types who could take on multiple forms, some of which were seemingly benign. Many of the scoundrels that audiences increasingly saw were ordinary men who were, nevertheless, capable of extraordinarily wrongful pursuits. This disjunction between what appeared to be and what was, was central to the new construction of villainy, for this revelation revolved around the axis of wealth.

Wartime wealth

The predominance of the wealthy villain in the popular culture of the interwar period reflected the very negative meaning ascribed to wealth following the war. The existence and representation of wealth on the pages and the screen as well as in reality was simply irreconcilable with the loss of human life on the fighting front in World War I and the domestic trials of those on the home front. The experience of soldiers within the war was certainly not the experience of luxury, even when the disparity between staff officers and infantry is taken into account. While soldiers in the trenches felt the lack of pre-war wealth and amenities most keenly, the home front was not the land of plenty that many soldiers believed it to be.

Scarcity of foodstuffs and rising inflation were particular characteristics of the latter half of the war and the first years of peacetime in Britain. While hardly reaching starvation or the levels of shortage experienced by the Germans, food scarcity did become a pressing issue and one that seemed to find Parliament scrambling to respond. The Ministry of Food itself was not established until early 1917 and rationing was not introduced until January 1918. The rationing that did come into existence did not apply to all food; rather, items like sugar and meat were rationed in the face of an anticipated shortage and sometimes as the result of an already existing shortage.[21] Rationing continued until as late as 1921, with milk being rationed after the war.[22] As the *Economic Journal* noted in 1920, 'all the conditions which have made food so dear could have been better handled if in the earlier stages of the War the Government had regarded supplies of food for the civilian population as a matter only second in importance to the supplies of munitions for the armies and the navy'.[23] Rationing was something Parliament was slow to embrace as part of the domestic wartime economy.

Food scarcity highlighted the government's inability to control prices, resulting in drastic inflation on all goods during and after the war and leading to a widespread denunciation of profiteering in the press. Columns comparing pre-war prices of goods to post-war prices were run regularly in the press, from the *Daily Express* and *Daily Mail* to the relatively conservative *The Times*. Inflation commonly stood at 200 per cent for some goods. Arthur Conan Doyle, the creator of Sherlock Holmes, was compelled to write two passionate letters to the editor of *The Times* on just such a topic, stating that 'unless something is done quickly, and done thoroughly, to check rising prices in the necessaries of life, there will be violence in this country. Man must live, and these wicked prices are making it a hard matter.'[24] *The Times*, usually not supportive of government intervention in the market, called attention to the problem of the price of food, scolding grocers for price gouging.

The more sensational press such as the *Daily Express* and the *Daily Mail* not only dwelt upon profiteering among food merchants, but also among businessmen at large. The contention of the *Daily Express* was that all profit from the war should be taken for the state either through taxation or a number of other, sometimes bizarre, schemes. Although happy with proposed legislation to deal with those selling goods at inflated prices, the paper proclaimed, 'It is absurd, while doing this, to leave intact those great increases in actual wealth which were the consequence of a way which has impoverished those who did the fighting. Clearly no one should be allowed to make and keep fortunes at the expense of human life and national bankruptcy.'[25] Following the war, a capital levy was widely considered as a means of securing wealth for a debt-ridden economy. A capital levy would have taxed existing capital, capital that was supposedly maintained and amassed during the war. The appeal of this programme following the war was fairly widespread among left-leaning newspapers as well as economists such as Sydney Webb. The *Daily Express* declared dramatically in October 1919, 'The agitation in favour of a tax on war profits is a vital and living movement which will have to be met fairly and squarely by Ministers. It has gathered an immense force of public opinion behind it, as the letter bag of the *Daily Express* continues to testify, and has reached a point where to ignore the proposal is no longer possible.'[26] Indeed the capital levy was a plank in Labour's manifesto as late as 1923; yet by the mid-1920s the prospect of a levy had been effectively contained through the efforts of the conservatives.[27]

Although the idea of a capital levy had been rejected, the coalition government under David Lloyd George did attempt to at least give the appearance of addressing public concerns with wartime wealth by passing the Profiteering Act in 1919. The Act made efforts to address price gouging at the daily level, by policing the price of food, clothing, and building materials. Charles A. McCurdy, the Liberal MP and Minister of Food Control from 1920 to 1921, who authored the Profiteering Act, likened profiteers to rats in the pages of *The Times* in 1919, arguing that 'while some of the minor horrors infest the trenches, the profiteer preys on the civilian population at home'.[28] McCurdy had initially envisioned and spoken of its grand powers of prosecution, saying, 'The Act deals with two kinds of profiteers – the big and the little ones. First the big profiteers who may be found among the trusts and combines and the wholesale trades – then the smaller offenders.' However, the Act was considered ineffectual from the outset. McCurdy's foreword to the Act admitted that its provisions 'can hardly be said to deal with profiteering at all, in the popular sense of the word, but are intended to create new machinery for the purpose of acting as a bureau of information and statistics'.[29] The Act was envisioned in this statement as a means of gathering information, rather than an instrument for prosecution.

The main purpose of the Act, a number of historians have noted, was to allow Parliament to appear as though it was actively interested in maintaining a sense of economic fairness.[30] One of the primary tenets was to protect trade while satisfying some of the most pressing complaints of the public. In 1920, McCurdy was still attempting to implement the Act, in the process outlining in the chairman's report the tricky position between business and consumer, and also indicating the flaw at the heart of it: 'I hope and believe that [the report] will be found to contain a practical solution to the problem of how the consumer may be protected and the profiteer eliminated without any injurious or harassing consequences to the trades concerned. The solutions consists [*sic*] in enlisting the voluntary co-operation of the traders themselves.' The Act's foreword engaged in a lively discussion of the practices enacted against

forestalling, engrossing, and regrating in the old market economy, only to end
with another rather ambivalent statement:

> Throughout the whole world drastic measures are being taken to counter a
> universal evil which appears to be one of the normal concomitants of war. If this
> be so, perhaps the final remedy rests not with any legislative enactment (though
> legislation may do much to mitigate the mischief), but with the course of time,
> and the natural re-adjustment of economic and moral forces.

Here, again, the strong language of evil and avarice is ultimately mitigated by
the ambivalent attitude of Parliament towards its role as prosecutor of businessmen.

The government's ambivalence towards the profiteering businessman was
further highlighted in 1922 by the 'honours scandal', which plagued Lloyd
George. As Kenneth Morgan has noted, Lloyd George engaged in a practice that
had been quite common in preceding governments: the sale of honours for party
contributions. Lloyd George's coalition government pursued this course rather
more enthusiastically than past governments, an enthusiasm which eventually
resulted in a general inquiry. An inquiry was seen as especially necessary after
the controversial South African diamond mine magnate Sir Joseph Robinson
was granted a peerage. Robinson had been successfully prosecuted after the
war for numerous illegal business transactions in regard to his diamond mines
in South Africa, resulting in the payment of almost half a million pounds.[31]
The outcry over his peerage resulted in its withdrawal. Morgan argues that the
controversy over the affair was motivated by the usual efforts by the conservatives to oust Lloyd George and by general concerns about the lengths Lloyd
George would go to hold on to power.[32] Yet the extent of public objection is
more easily explained when one takes into account the villainous presence of
the profiteer in film, fiction, and the press. The honours scandal presented a
real-life example of the cosy relationship between government and profiteer.
Little came of the scandal, yet it was an important contributing factor to the
public's negative view of the Lloyd George coalition.

The government's uneasiness regarding the prosecution of profiteering
businessmen ironically reflected not the cosy relationship that the honours
scandal would seem to indicate but a much tenser relationship, for the outbreak
of war had severely tested an industrial economy dependent upon the laissez-
faire approach of its government. Both business and Parliament had been slow
to realise the implications of a war economy upon their respective spheres:
business in regard to the uninterrupted regular movement of goods and profits,
and the government in its contrasting role as a wartime regulator of goods and

prices. That businessmen would be expected to abandon international trade and would potentially lose profit in areas of trade because of an international conflict was only discovered as the war wore on. The government from the outset had advocated a 'business as usual' approach for industry, one that did not see it interfering any more than the industrial market economy had previously witnessed; yet this was next to impossible to maintain as much of Britain's market was based on supplying goods to Germany and enemy countries.[33] National rhetoric and popular opinion simply could not tolerate open trading with the enemy. Instead, the government was forced to intervene in business to an unprecedented extent in order to feed and supply both the fighting front and the home front. While popular with the people, the government was relatively quick to abandon this role following the war. The idea that the economy should be left to re-stabilise itself through 'business as usual' and a laissez-faire economy appeared to be paramount in the government's actions, and indeed seemed to manifest itself in the ineffectualness of the Profiteering Act and the conservative-led dismissal of the capital levy.[34] The capital that was threatened by the one-time tax levy was ultimately seen as necessary to stimulate an economy dependent upon the free exercise of that money, for undoubtedly some business sectors, such as munitions, had realised a profit during the war.

The high price of food items, the widespread unemployment of returning soldiers, and the continued presence of profiteering were widely seen as failures of both the government and business in the press and popular film and fiction. In the context of World War I and a capitalist economy that had not previously been subject to such a disaster, the resulting economic instability and the actions of profiteers were scandalous. All sectors had simply been unprepared for the collapse of a wartime economy and indeed, the interwar years were marked by Parliament's reluctance to address the prospect of a second world war and further profiteering, a prospect that was all but inevitable in 1920. The amount of coverage granted to profiteering by the general press is surprising to the cynical modern eye – an eye that is all too familiar with the notion of wars bringing economic benefits to a chosen few – yet following World War I, profiteering was seen by some as a shocking grab for money, something that did not naturally fit with ideas of a capitalist economy or of a modern British government.

Consequently, a profound disillusionment existed not only with the experience of war, but with both government and business. In 1930, a series of articles examining 'What is right with Britain?' in the *Daily Express* invited a number of notable figures to contemplate the topic. Labour MP Ellen

Wilkinson argued that what was right with Britain was 'Our splendid workers – and their wives', noting that the British worker will never go Bolshevist and that 'while great fortunes have been made over their heads, British working men and women have borne with philosophic cheerfulness the fact that they have to bear the main burden of paying for the war they won – a cheerfulness that is a salutary contrast to certain doleful millionaires'.[35] Here Wilkinson attempts to emphasise the passive stability of the working man and women while acknowledging the continued presence of profiteers and 'doleful million-aires', a position that was radicalised by 1936 when she participated in the hunger march of men from the severely depressed town of Jarrow.

In 1930, following the American stock market crash of 1929, many had difficulty avoiding the topic of the government's ineffective role in the realm of business. Collinson Owen, a conservative journalist, in his contribution to the series entitled 'English – And Still Proud of It', tried to positively portray politicians while mounting a defence of soldiers whose noble image had been somewhat undermined according to him by the publication of *All Quiet on the Western Front*. What instead resulted were rather backhanded comments about the government. According to Owen, following the war 'the country realised that the politicians meant well, even if they were doing badly', however, 'this quiet acceptance by a nation of its own impoverishment for the benefit of others certainly cannot be matched in all history'.[36] Other more searing studies of the phenomena of wartime corruption of politicians and businessmen continued to circulate in both America and Britain. Indictments of profiteering like *Merchants of Death: A Study of the International Armament Industry* by American authors Engelbrecht and Hanighen, published in Britain by Routledge in 1934, did little to make the topic go away, even in the face of a growing fascist threat in Europe.[37] Leslie Charteris's hero, Simon Templar or 'the Saint', in 1938's *Prelude for War* identifies one Mr Luker as 'king-pin of what somebody once called the Merchants of Death' and notes his close affiliation with Members of Parliament and businessmen in Britain who stood to profit from another war. Profiteering was a spectre that continued to be paired with the prospect of another world war, as the latter increasingly became a reality.

Antagonism towards politicians and businessmen thus ran close to the surface in the 1920s and 1930s, further reflected in popular film and fiction that depicted men of wealth as villains. In the novels and films consumed by British audiences villains acted reprehensibly in ways that would have been strikingly familiar to interwar readers and viewers. This cynicism on the part of authors, filmmakers, and audiences in both the depiction and consumption of wealthy and powerful villains, is, in many ways, the most enduring legacy of World War I and contributes even further to our understanding of 1945 and an election of a government for the people by the people.

The knowable villain

The knowable villain, with his noticeable and gratuitous displays of wealth, spoke in obvious ways to the cynicism of interwar audiences. The obese profiteer in his dress clothes came to replace the thin, leering, aristocratic villain. He took on the face and body of new wealth, which was acquired through trade and business, not through inheritance. The recent acquisition of wealth was often portrayed as part of a performance that hid the real aims of the coarse profit-hungry businessman. One could now purchase the accoutrements of wealth and perform an upper-class status rather than inheriting it through bloodlines and kinship. As such, wealth was negatively associated with class performance. Likewise, one could easily pretend to care about the nation through employment in certain positions within government or other institutions that represented and upheld normative Englishness. Concerns about the authenticity of one's class position and one's devotion to the nation subsequently dominated the interwar portrayal of the knowable villain.

Reverend Fortune in *If Winter Comes* embodied many of the typical traits of the knowable villain: distinctive physical characteristics and a thinly disguised performance that attempted to hide both his greed and his false devotion to Britain. Hutchinson's depiction of Fortune's girth drew upon a longstanding association between the accumulation of wealth and consumption. Fortune's weight also makes him a physically unappealing figure. Yet in Fortune's case this bulk implies a rather inactive role as manager rather than worker. Fortune is inactive in two areas: the workplace that he controls and the battlefield that he avoids.

Recall that Fortune is head partner of Fortune, East, and Sabre, a company that furnishes both schools and churches. It is not coincidental that the areas of business Fortune, East, and Sabre are involved with are the moral battleground for British minds and hearts. The close proximity of Fortune and Sabre to these institutions upon which Britain rests is significant for both characters. The Sabre in the title of the company is not our own Mark Sabre, but rather his grandfather, who was bought out by the Reverend Fortune when he was a keen young man. The account of the takeover implies a degree of ruthlessness on the part of Fortune:

In his thirty-four years of association, indeed in the first twenty, he had, by fortuitous circumstances, and by force of his decisive personality, achieved what amounted to sole and single control. Coming in as a young man of force and character, he had added to these qualities, by marriage, a useful sum of money (to which was attached a widow) and proceeded to deal decisively with the East and Sabre (Mark, Sabre's grandfather) of that day. Both were old men.[38]

Fortune thus took advantage of his inheritance and went on to enlarge and maintain his share of the business. Yet, although Fortune had acted to acquire riches, which was in keeping with the productive accumulation of wealth encouraged by a capitalist economy, it is made clear within the text that Fortune's ability to manage his affluence is questionable. That the firm represents the foundations of Britain implies that Fortune is mismanaging not simply the company, but the nation as well.

The first clue for the reader regarding Fortune's poor business skills is his mismanagement of the office and his treatment of Sabre, who is clearly a good worker. The office space is organised in a rather haphazard way:

This arrangement was highly inconvenient to the performers of the various duties thus carried on, but was essential to the more rapid execution of Mr. Fortune's habit of 'keeping an eye' on everything. This habit of the Reverend Sebastian Fortune was roundly detested by all on whom his eye fell. He was called Jonah by his employees; and he was called Jonah partly because his visits to the places of their industry invariably presaged disaster.[39]

This passage and Fortune's incompetence were satirised in 1922 by a stinging parody called *If Winter Don't* by 'Barry Pain'. Fortune, renamed Sharper is introduced to the reader: 'He had achieved this position by unscrupulousness and low cunning. For of real ability he had not a trace. In fact, the staff mostly called him Cain, because he was not able.'[40] Fortune continues to display poor business skill when he passes over Sabre for a promotion to partnership. This incident, as noted earlier, is terribly demoralising for Sabre, due in no small part to Fortune twice assuring him that he would become a partner. Part of Sabre's desire for partnership is expressed in the novel not as a desire for money but as an honest desire to do better: 'He desired it largely for what he knew he would make it bring in the form of greater freedom from Mr. Fortune's surveillance, but more for the solid personal satisfaction its winning would give him. It would be a tribute to his work … and he was keenly interested in and proud of his work.'[41] As noted in Chapter 1, Sabre's devotion to his work also implies his devotion to the nation.

Instead of the promised promotion Sabre experiences Fortune's dishonesty. Sabre discovers second-hand that the partnership is going to a fellow named

Twyning. When Sabre confronts Fortune about this subterfuge, Fortune refutes his claim and his presumption to hold him as the employer account- able to his employees, saying, 'I recollect no *promise*. Either twice or any other number of times, greater or fewer. I *do* recollect mentioning to you the *possi- bility* of my making you such a proposal in my good time [original emphasis].' Fortune goes on to accuse Sabre of forcing or prematurely 'bouncing' him into the partnership. Fortune rails against Sabre, 'I most emphatically am not to be *bounced*, Sabre. I never have been *bounced* and you may quite safely take it from me that I never propose or intend to be *bounced*.'[42] Fortune's refusal of partnership to Sabre is indicative of his unease with what he views as Sabre's presumptuous claim to power. Fortune asserts that nothing except his own decision produced in his own good time will bring about a partnership, and Sabre is left without acknowledgement of his labour and having discovered the truth behind Fortune's false promises.

Finally, the last and most devastating event within Sabre's career with Fortune, East, and Sabre is his protracted dismissal from the firm while he is serving in the war. Although earlier within the novel Fortune had declared to all of the soldiers that their places would be kept for their return, it is made clear to Sabre that he is no longer wanted in the firm. This decision is disguised as good business by Fortune. In the novel, this is the epitome of poor govern- ance for it does not adequately recognise Sabre's work for his country both in his manufacture of textbooks for schools and his physical defence of the nation. Sabre, however, is relatively circumspect in his reaction.[43] Mr Fortune again deceives Sabre, yet this deception is not entirely shocking to either Sabre or the reader as it is in keeping with Fortune's villainous character. Fortune's subterfuge is exposed early on in the story and then simply repeated, thus quickly defining him as a villain within the narrative. He is, for all intents and purposes, constructed as a knowable villain, obvious from the novel's outset.

Warwick Deeping's subsequent bestseller *Old Pybus* (1928), released after the popular *Sorrell and Son*, presents a character similar to Mr Fortune. In *Old Pybus*, the protagonist, Old John Pybus, resembles Stephen Sorrell, right down to occupation. Pybus is a porter at a hotel and the story revolves around the relationship between Pybus and his young grandson, Lance. Like Sorrell's son Kit, Pybus's grandson Lance grows to appreciate his grandfather's hard work and honest work ethic, even while Lance's father (Probyn) and uncle (Conrad) scorn Pybus's methods and have long since lost touch with their father.

The crime of both sons, Conrad and Probyn, in *Old Pybus* is that they did not serve in the war, although they were able in body. To Old John Pybus this was unacceptable, 'for John Pybus was old English. When there was war there was war, and if his country was involved in it, then it was his – John Pybus's war, and his sons' war. He was an old-fashioned patriot.'[44] John Pybus is profoundly devoted to his country, and, as a result, actually travels the countryside speaking at recruiting meetings.[45] Yet, as the war entered its second year, the absence of Pybus's sons within the enlistment lines was notable and increasingly embarrassing to one of the country's top recruiters. Pybus undertakes their recruitment as a mission and visits them in their respective homes.

The visit does not go well, for influenced by a weak, socially aspiring mother who tended to offer them sweets instead of discipline, the boys have decided to cash in on the war. For Conrad especially, the war presented a financial opportunity that, for Old Pybus, was tantamount to stealing. When Pybus visits the sons, Probyn, 'a little sheepish', reveals that his father-in-law had produced some money in order to make him 'indispensable' in the eyes of the government because of his interest in the wool industry. However, Conrad was not so excused: 'Conrad, unearthed somewhere near Fenchurch Street, was less explanatory than his brother. He was busy, arrogantly and perspiringly busy. Ships – you old fool – ships and more ships! He did not call this meddling old fire-eater a fool, but implied it. Besides he was a careful fellow; he was out to make money.' In response to this Pybus 'had called them shirkers, gunshies, opportunists. Such burs stick even to sleek jackets.'[46] Here Deeping mobilised some of the rhetoric surrounding profiteers, profiting from the death and disablement of Britain's finest. Pybus, in reaction to Probyn's wartime profiteering and Conrad's shirking of duty, dismisses them from his life and does not lay eyes upon them for many years.

Conrad Pybus's chance meeting with his father Old Pybus opens the novel and in the first scene many of the stock characteristics of the interwar villain are deployed. Conrad is clearly the anti-hero in the story, as his brother Probyn's crime is somewhat lesser. We first see Conrad through the eyes of an upper-class socialite, Ursula Calmady, to whom Conrad wishes to propose and with whom Conrad is lunching at the very hotel at which his father is employed as porter. Ursula is not at all enamoured of Conrad and through her cool appraisal of him the reader becomes witness to Conrad's true character. He, like Fortune, is a large man, 'solid and obvious, all black and white, a heavy man who could not sit comfortably'. He also 'possessed one of those heavy white skins which resemble greasy vellum'.[47] Conrad perspires throughout lunch and Ursula wonders to herself why she accompanied him on the outing.

We see, through Ursula, first the performance of Conrad as he acts the wealthy, overbearing man, and then the stripping away of this act. His façade of culture crumbles after the shock of seeing his father: 'That he as a man should sit calmly down to lunch after cutting his own father was beyond Mr. Conrad Pybus's capacity. Obviously he was not himself, or rather – he was too much himself.'[48] Ursula sees the veneer of wealth quickly stripped away and as she thinks of his country home, Chlois Court, she realises the artifice involved in its decoration: 'She thought of Chlois Court, and his pictures, and his library with its multitudinous classics all bound in red leather. Culture – culture spelt with a very big K, Teutonic, a little pathetic. And yet, in spite of his carefulness and his contrivings, the trotter protruded in proximity to the trough.'[49] Conrad responds to this slip in authority by bullying the servants and waiters, but even they recognise that he was 'the kind of new gentleman who raised his voice and made a fuss when things were not going well'.[50] The narrative makes Conrad's performance of wealth and power unsupportable and the unpleasant man beneath is revealed: 'It seemed to her that she was watching a materialisation of the real Conrad Pybus, of the man who sat in his office chair in his shirt-sleeves and smoked rank cigars, and bullied people. His voice appeared to slip back into his throat and to become thick and aggressive. She was vividly aware of his crudities, of the inherent vulgarities of the man.'[51] Thus the reality was as unappealing as the performance.

Conrad's performance as a member of the cultured classes and the subsequent dismantling of the performance to reveal the lower-class man behind it was drawn in even broader strokes across some of the thrillers and adventures stories of the period. One of the first villains that we meet in E. Phillips Oppenheim's bestseller *Murder at Monte Carlo* (1931) is a man named Viotti. When we first encounter him, he is drunk and chasing after a young and beautiful girl. In the course of this chase the girl latches onto the story's protagonist, Roger Sloane, and his friend Reginald Phillip Erskine (Pips), begging them for help. Sloane, upon seeing Viotti, needs little encouragement: 'From the higher part of the orchard descended the disturbing object and as soon as Sloane had seen him he scented trouble. Here was a man in a passion, a black-browed, heavy built man, cutting the air with a switch as he moved, an ugly protruding jaw reminiscent somehow of the dragon in a child's story.'[52] Sloane rescues the girl – Jeannine – with whom he, of course, falls in love, and we are duly informed about Viotti's role within the village by Sloane's housekeeper: '"He is a bad man, Pierre Viotti", she declared, "but he is the mayor and he owns all the land, the *épicerie* and the café. He does what he pleases with the girls and all the people about the place".'[53] Although Viotti would at first glance seem to be an uncouth peasant, he is, instead, a person of importance in the village who in fact holds a monopoly on the land, its businesses, and by proxy its women. Like Conrad, he possesses wealth, yet no upper-class breeding.

Viotti's prominent role in the village and beyond is conveyed later in the novel when Sloane and Jeannine see him again as they are exiting a salon:

> A large automobile turned off the main road and came to a standstill in front of the café – a powerful Voisin, but hideously painted in a violent shade of lilac. A fat little man descended from it, a man who wore tight, glossy clothes, over-elaborate linen and a beflowered tie. He wore gloves, he was smoking a cigar and he carried a cane. His thick lips pursed themselves into a whistle as he recognised Jeannine.[54]

Viotti is clearly playing the role of a wealthy gentleman, yet with a certain ineptness. Everything is a bit off: the tight clothes, the linen, and the overabundance of accessories. The lilac car and the beflowered tie also hint at an effeminate side, one that would seem to contrast with his swarthy Neanderthal shape. Yet this is just another aspect of an awkwardly arranged costume, for the reader has already been presented with Viotti in his natural setting and with his emotions unchecked. Whereas with Conrad we watched the unravelling of a performance, with Viotti we are first presented with his true nature and then the subsequent performance that disguises it. In both cases, this performance is contrasted against the relatively prestigious roles of Conrad as a businessman and Viotti as a businessman and mayor.

In Viotti's case the brute reality of his nature is also racialised as his character is marked out as decidedly un-British. The *Murder at Monte Carlo* justifies Clive Bloom's assertion that Oppenheim's villains anticipated those of the later era.[55] Oppenheim did indeed furnish his stories with 'foreign, evil-genius villains', and although Viotti does not count as a genius, his French origin undoubtedly made him sufficiently foreign in the eyes of British readers. French characters also continued to take the brunt of negative characterisations, even competing with Nazi Germany in the case of Charteris's 1938 *Prelude for War*. Throughout the bestsellers and popular films of the interwar period, foreigners were presented as villainy literally embodied and, consequently, very thinly disguised. Jews were also particular targets across these narratives, from John Buchan's Richard Hannay novels to Dorothy Sayers's stories featuring Lord Peter Wimsey, and their appearances as moneylenders in the novels of Edgar Wallace.[56]

Foreigners were actively linked with villainy, and the European continent often produced notable villains. Germans were a particularly easy target after

World War I. Peter Lorre in Hitchcock's first version of *The Man Who Knew Too Much* has a heavy German accent, along with a deep scar across his face and eye and a white patch in his black hair that comes down over the scar.[57] He is part of a group engaged in an assassination attempt on a diplomat, activities sure to undermine European stability. The film was first proposed to the British Board of Film Censors under the title 'The Hidden Hand' as a Bulldog Drummond story featuring Peterson as the villain.[58] While Bulldog Drummond's cultural and economic cache was lost for the film, Hitchcock was able to modify his villain, in both physical and geographic ways that seemed to resonate with audiences. *Picturegoer* marked Lorre's role as 'the best performance' in the film.[59] I noted in Chapter 1 that the popular actor Wallace Beery, who made a career of playing villainous men such as *Grand Hotel's* Preysing, was the only character to speak with a German accent even as the rest of the cast had German names. In the film Preysing is both a coarse and dishonest German businessman, and eventually a murderer. Preysing also preys upon the typist he hired by making passes at her and then hiring her to accompany him on business. The film's audience was invited to contemplate the lecherous aspects of such an arrangement in scenes where he engaged in exercises in his hotel room, his ample and not very attractive body cloaked only by a towel around his waist. Beery's immense girth was front and central every time he emerged on-screen.

In the British silent film, *The Rat* (1926), which acted as a showcase for the actor Ivor Novello and produced two sequels, the antagonist within the Parisian world dominated by the dashing conman, the aforementioned 'Rat', was also a portly but wealthy German named Hermann Stetz. In the film, Stetz, played by Robert Scholtz, is a violent and powerful man of considerable girth and immense wealth. He is described to a female patron at the bar, The White Coffin, through the film's inter-titles as 'a powerful brute, Madame; even more powerful than Inspector Caillard himself'. Stetz throws his weight around both financially and physically as he attempts to rape the love-interest of the Rat. Stetz's nationality is never commented on but his identification as a German is enough to indicate his role from the very outset. Germans were certainly easy villains in interwar popular culture, but as we shall see they also competed with numerous other European and colonial groups for this role.

The role of Empire within popular culture in the early twentieth century has produced its own growing historiography, but it is worth noting here the significant presence of colonial villains within low and middlebrow works throughout the 1920s and 1930s.[60] Sax Rohmer's Dr Fu Manchu, first penned prior to World War I and with multiple sequels after the war, provided perhaps an even more memorable villain as he unleashed the 'yellow peril' on Britain and the rest of the world.[61] Fu Manchu's considerable wealth and prestige in the Orient, along with his dastardly acts and snake-like green eyes complete with a second transparent lid, allowed readers to make links between villainy, wealth, and race. *Shanghai Express* (1932), Britain's third most popular film in 1932, which brought in 22,811 people to the Portsmouth Regent cinema, also exemplified the terror of the Orient by featuring a half-white and half-Chinese villain, Mr Chang.[62] Mr Chang appears to be sympathetic to the British, escorting a number of British and American men and women through tumultuous China on the *Shanghai Express*, but then is revealed as 'Commander-in-Chief of the revolution' and hijacks the train.[63] Chang is thus vilified through not only his race but his sympathies with communism as well. He threatens to kill the British protagonist, a captain and a doctor in HMS, until the female love-interest convinces him to exchange his life for her services. Chang is eventually killed by a Chinese woman, played by the well-known Chinese actress Anna May Wong. Chang's deception as pro-capitalist and sympathetic to the British is thus undone.

Spectacular villains from the colonies were central to the popular 'empire' films of the 1930s. Empire films tended to emphasise the duplicity of the colonial subject, making each appearance of an Indian or African man on-screen particularly fraught with tension. The assumption in these narratives was that this was a villain, and it was up to the film to establish loyal colonial subjects. Colonial villains were also wealthy for the most part. The villains in the so-called empire trilogy by the Korda brothers were politically powerful and well armed. The fortresses and guns held by the villains establish them as both wealthy and resistant to British rule.[64] Wealth in the hands of villains from the colonies was thus constructed as particularly problematic. This was true of other empire films such as the American-directed *Lives of a Bengal Lancer* (1935) that introduced the wealthy and Oxford-educated Mohammed Khan. Khan's double identity as a man educated in England but dominating the North Western frontier in his effort to lead an uprising against the British was signalled as deviant on a number of levels. The heroes in these empire films ironically engage in their own type of performance, as soldiers often don coloured face make-up to successfully infiltrate the camps of the rebels. *Lives of a Bengal Lancer* demonstrated this, although Zoltan Korda's *Four Feathers* deployed this most extravagantly as the hero, attempting to demonstrate his bravery to the regiment he abandoned, successfully disguises himself as a mute native in order to rescue his friends and protect British interests in Egypt.

Few groups within the British Empire escaped the stigma of bred-in-the-bone villainy, yet one of the most interesting examples of the relationship between the mutual construction of race and villainy is the reversal of the two in the character of Sheik Ahmed in E. M. Hull's novel *The Sheik* and the film of the same title. Set in tumultuous Arabia, Sheik Ahmed acts in villainous ways by kidnapping the British woman Diana Mayo at the outset of the film, closeting her in the desert and having his way with her, all the time making use of Rudolph Valentino's infamous bulging eyes in a menacing way. By the end of the novel and film, his parentage has been revealed as half-British and half-Spanish, rather than Arab, and he is consequently deemed to be not a villain but rather a passionate and worthy man. His European background, in this instance, exempts him from villainy and makes him an appropriate object of heterosexual love for a British woman.

While racialised villains were popular with audiences, low and middlebrow films and novels of the interwar period did not spare the home-grown villain either, who was negatively portrayed as possessing considerable wealth within Britain, or in the case of American films, America itself. American films popular with British audiences, such as *Roman Scandals* and *You Can't Take It with You* (1938) made ample use of the trope of the rich fat-cat villain. The 1930s saw this character come to life in popular American films that found a receptive audience in Britain. The economic downfall of the United States in 1929 had aligned the American depression with the sustained depression experience by Britain, making for a common pillorying of wealthy businessmen in the transatlantic film industry. American films showed wealthy businessmen profiteering in a way that exploited American land, and displaced the farmer. Both *Roman Scandals* and *You Can't Take It with You* showcased powerful American businessmen securing land deals that benefited their businesses and displaced ordinary working and middle-class townsfolk.[65] The antagonist in *Roman Scandals*, Warren F. Cooper, is intent on buying land on which to build a prison, and bribes the town's police officers to throw off the people inhabiting the land. The powerful and portly Mr Kirby in Frank Capra's *You Can't Take It with You* is head of a bank intent on gaining a monopoly on munitions manufacturing. Capra's *Mr Deeds Goes to Town* also sees Mr Deeds's scheme to offer land to poor farmers thwarted by a group of lawyers and businessmen intent on gaining his fortune for themselves. Villains in these roles are inevitably portrayed as obese, unattractive, and overdressed. They bark orders at the subservients, by whom they are constantly surrounded. As opposed to the heroes surrounding by family or love-interests, the villain on film is an isolated, bloated individual. All of these films, although American in origin, problematised wealth in a period of economic duress and seemingly struck a chord with British audiences who watched the films and saw features on 'film villains' such as Wallace Beery in *Picturegoer*.

The British had also long been producing their own version of the large money-hungry villain of 1930s American films. Jean Louis Roberts points out that the profiteer had a visual life in cartoons produced in the British, French, and German press during World War I.[66] Yet this fascination with the profiteer and his crimes persisted in the landscape of fiction well beyond 1918. The 1920s, in particular, saw a host of British novels dealing with the intricacies of profiteering in the food industries, but on a vast scale which leapfrogged the inflated prices of the local grocer. In Oppenheim's *The Profiteers* (1921), John Wingate, the protagonist, undertakes an investigation into and the eventual punishment of British and Imperial Granaries (BIG) for inflating the price of grain, describing the profiteers as men of 'diabolical cleverness', commanding 'immense capital' with agents working in secrecy. These were businessmen working 'inside the law', whose immense fortune and shady activities were directly leading to a high cost of bread.[67] In the novel, Wingate embarks on his own form of vigilante justice causing the accidental death by heart attack of one of the profiteers, something the novel condones in its last pages as a newsboy shouts out a headline regarding a lowered cost of bread. The price of bread further had also preoccupied Edgar Wallace in 1919 when he published his novel, *Green Rust*, whose hero was, of all things, a 'Wheat Inspector' working to ensure the safety of America's wheat fields and against a diabolical plan by Bolsheviks and Germans to sabotage Great Britain's access to grain.[68] The monopoly of wartime wealth and access to basics such as food was fodder for writers who nevertheless imagined these plots in highly imaginative and outlandish ways and did not hesitate to target British businessmen as the villains of the day.

The British author Sydney Horler's novel *Tiger Standish* (1932) offered a vision of a British villain literally throwing his weight around. The heroic Standish's encounter with one-quarter of a typical criminal ring bent upon such a scheme follows lines made familiar in McNeile or Wallace's works. Standish meets 'Hamme' first in the street, roughing up an attractive girl. Standish rescues the girl and removes her to his own home, at which point a more genial Hamme comes knocking. We see that Standish is immediately able to see through the subterfuge of civility: 'The speaker was a brute of a man, weighing at least sixteen stone, Tiger judged, and belonging to the type which England turns out occasionally. He was a mixture of well bred gentleman and country oaf. He was pink of face, seemingly stupid of eye, and, although his tailor was obviously expensive, gave the idea of feeling uneasy in his clothes.'[69] Hamme, like Viotti, possesses some power but is British and has the type of money that buys a certain class status; yet the violent episode prior to this meeting with Standish undermines Hamme's performance and exposes him as brutish and unrefined, undercutting his claims to anything beyond the class of nouveau riche. The deceptions committed by Hamme and Viotti are undone early on in the story, revealing them almost immediately as villains. Their villainy is presented to us primarily as a class deception for they are clearly the nouveau riche filling an ill-fitting part.

Tensions around class deception as well as access to rations were also apparent in one of the interwar period's most popular films, *Mutiny on the Bounty* (1935). The captain of the ship, William Bligh, stands in high contrast to the charismatic Fletcher Christian, whom I discussed in Chapter 1 and who cuts a figure much like Hamme's in Horler's novel. In comparison to the handsome Christian played by the dashing Clark Gable, Bligh is pudgy, with impressively bushy eyebrows, a facial mole, a permanent scowl, and a slightly effeminate voice; the actor Charles Laughton making Bligh a figure that could justify the mutiny of his shipmen. Tightly wound, curt, and dictatorial Bligh is immediately an unsympathetic character. After the audience is introduced to Bligh's lack of physical appeal, his further lack of personal appeal soon follows as he orders that the lashings of a midshipman who struck him in anger be continued even after the man is declared dead. Bligh is not above inflicting cruel and even unusual punishment upon the king's men in order to assert his power.

In an exchange between Christian and Bligh after this scene it becomes clear that the motivations for Bligh's behaviour stem, in part, from his own uneasiness with his class status. Christian is called down into the Captain's quarters to discuss the upcoming voyage as they prepare to set sail. Their respective backgrounds are revealed as Bligh informs Christian: 'I requested you. I like having a gentleman as my subordinate, being a self-made man.' Christian pauses and then responds evenly, 'I admire you for that sir', to which Bligh snaps 'and for very little else'. This is followed by a tense moment as Bligh glowers at Christian. It is clear that Bligh is self-conscious of his self-made status and is very aware of social and economic hierarchies. He sits behind his desk in the scene as Fletcher stands reporting to him, leisurely assessing him. Blight takes pleasure from his superior rank on the ship even if his class status does not afford him that outside of it. In this way, his command on the ship allows him to perform as a superior. As the scene continues, it is foreshadowed, however, that Bligh's economic superiority is maintained at the expense of the crew who are eating inferior rations. Bligh seems unconcerned with their rations and belittles the crew: 'Men? Rascals and pirates. Did you see them growl at the flogging. I'll teach them what flogging is like.' Christian is disturbed by Bligh's attitude but agrees to enforce his orders.

Food supplies become a more pressing issue as the voyage wears on, with the sailors complaining about the quality and quantity of food allotted to them. The bedraggled appearance of the crew stands in stark contrast to the well-fed and sleek Bligh in his captain's dress. This inequality among the rations is on top of the regular and extreme floggings to which the Captain submits the crew. The issue of food comes to a head during an inventory of supplies. A crewman notes that two 50-lb cheeses are missing from the casks and informs Bligh, himself embodying the excess of that cheese in his round frame, as Christian passes by. Bligh's response is immediate and angry: 'Thieves and jailbirds! A hundred pounds of cheese gone. They'd steal the canvas off a corpse.' Christian is puzzled, saying, 'That's strange, I checked the stores myself', to which Bligh snaps, 'Cheeses can't fly you fool. They've been stolen of course.' Regardless of the poor condition of the crew, Bligh orders that the cheese allowance for the crew be stopped until the culprits are found. However, an elderly crewman of low rank pipes in, 'Begging your pardon sir but back in Portsmouth that cask was opened by your orders and Mr Maggs [another crewman] had them cheeses carried ashore.' Bligh shouts at him, 'Silence!' yet the man carries on innocently, 'Perhaps you'll recollect sir. Maggs had me take them to your house.' Incensed, Bligh yells 'You insolent scoundrel!' even as the sailor prattles on, inadvertently illustrating Bligh's rather cruel pattern of behaviour, 'But I remember very well sir because I didn't get to see my wife that day.' The camera cuts to Christian as the sailor says this, and Christian's mouth thins as this explicit description of behaviour fits with what they all know of Bligh. Bligh, however, chooses to punish the man and orders the 'liar' to be tied spreadeagle to the rigging until sundown. Christian and the rest of the officers in the close confines of the officers' dinner refuse to take part in the Captain's cheese. (See Figure 2.1.) The scene, shot in the claustrophobic setting of the captain's quarters, shows Bligh spectacularly losing his temper and banning the officers from eating with him.

Later in the film, the issue of food is again raised as Bligh orders Christian to add his signature to the ship's inventory book. Christian refuses, saying

The officers' dinner and heightening tensions about rations in *Mutiny on the*   **2.1**
Bounty (1935). Captain Bligh sits centre with Fletcher seated at his left.

'I can't sign this book. No such amounts have been issued to the men.' Bligh responds, 'Now look you here, You've signed daybooks with a few extra kegs that the ship never carried … And why not? We all do it. We'd be fools if we didn't on a lieutenant's pay. I want to stow away enough to keep me out of the gutter when I'm too old for service.' Christian acknowledges that this happens on ships and says, 'I understand, a captain's prerogative. Ordinarily, I wouldn't mind … the captains I've served with didn't starve their men. They didn't save money by buying up the stinking meat that you put aboard. They didn't buy yams that would sicken a pig.' Bligh's awful behaviour to the crew, not only in restricting and diverting portions but in knowingly choosing inferior food, is now openly acknowledged by them both. Bligh brings Christian on deck before the remainder of the crew and accuses him of mutiny unless he signs the book, which Christian does. Moments later Tahiti is seen in the distance as a land of plenty in direct counterbalance to the tight, hungry confines of the ship's deck. The issue fades to the background until the ship is about to set sail again and Christian leads a mutiny.

Bligh undoubtedly fits the part of the profiteer as he profits from his power and rank on the ship in order to secure supplies for himself. Such a negative portrayal of a captain of the navy benefiting himself at the expense of the ship's soldiers may not have easily existed during World War I or even prior to it, yet in the context of post-World War I discussions of profiteering and a Parliament that did not seem to govern properly, this narrative was immensely popular. Bligh's villainous behaviour only lessens when Christian casts him and his loyal crew members off to sea in a boat with very few supplies and no land to be seen. They are all quite literally in the same boat in terms of food and water, and Bligh, in an impressive show of seamanship that seems to rehabilitate his role as a soldier, manages to bring them to land after months on the sea seemingly without sufficient supplies. Still, Bligh's initial bad behaviour becomes the lesson of the film as the opening screen writing indicates: 'neither ship nor breadfruit reached the West Indies. Mutiny prevented it – mutiny against the abuse of harsh eighteenth century sea law. But this mutiny, famous in history and legend, helped bring about a new discipline, based upon mutual respect between officers and men.' The lesson of the film was that profiteering only leads to rebellion and potentially violent reform.

An interesting perspective on the villains already outlined is presented by Arnold Bennett's acclaimed bestseller *Lord Raingo* (1926). *Lord Raingo* was, in some respects, a response to Virginia Woolf, who criticised Bennett's straightforward writing style, a style made popular in bestselling novels and his weekly column on reading for the *Evening Standard*.[70] With a narrative arc whose absence Bennett noted in Woolf's work, it deals with a relatively short span in Sam Raingo's life. It opens in 1918 with Raingo being called from his country home to the Prime Minister's office in Whitehall. Raingo is a childhood adversary of the Prime Minister and they are on familiar, if somewhat antagonistic, terms. However, this shifts when the Prime Minister informs Raingo that he wants him to take over as the Minister of Records. Raingo accepts after some clever negotiation, out of which he is able to procure himself a place within the House of Lords and a peerage, something that would have resonated with readers familiar with the honours scandal. The narrative is entirely produced from Raingo's perspective, and it becomes increasingly fragmentary and confused as he lies at his home waiting to die at the end of the novel.

The importance of *Lord Raingo* to this discussion is that Bennett constructs Raingo, to all intents and purposes, as the wealthy, large, performative, and knowable villain who highlights numerous anxieties regarding performance, wealth, and nation. Yet Bennett provides this villain with a conscience and a first-person narrative that allows the reader to view his internal dialogue. The first lines of the book describe Raingo: 'Fifty-five. Tallish – but stoutish. Dressed like the country gentleman which he was not and never would be.'[71]

Although Raingo does not fit in well with country life, it is made immediately apparent that he is wealthy – a millionaire in fact. Raingo is the epitome of the self-made nouveau riche businessman, who has earned multiple millions during his lifetime. Yet he was not a wartime opportunist, at least not in the typical way; instead he 'behaved nobly in the matter of subscriptions to British war loans … He turned down all Swetnam's clever proposals for making an honest penny out of the necessities of war. He could, for example, have amassed millions by manipulating shipping interests – and did not.'[72] Still, Raingo does capitalise upon the war by becoming Minister of Records and joining what he eventually terms the 'circus' menagerie of Whitehall. Raingo gains power, prestige, and a title due to the desperation of his country, yet repeatedly throughout the novel he is reminded of his own futility in the face of the war by the presence of his son, a prisoner of war just returned home.

What distinguishes Raingo from the typical villain is both his unrealised devotion to his country and his crippling insecurities. Raingo's wish to partici-pate in the war is introduced early on in the novel, as his faulty heart is checked out by the town doctor who himself has just returned from the war: 'Raingo, in his secret humiliation, admired the fellow, and had a wild, absurd desire to justify his own inactivity to the simpleton.'[73] When Raingo takes on the job as the Minister of Records he feels that he has emerged from a coma, one induced by the war among other things. He had lost his penchant for business, an exercise that defined him. He had 'lost the touch, the flair, for big buyings, big sellings, mergers, monopolies, spectacular flotations'. But now his appoint-ment at the Ministry had 'quickened him suddenly into eager life, and he had found out that his mental facilities, though they had been dormant, were as good as ever, better than ever … He could put the whole of himself into the Ministry of Records, whether as a peer or only as commoner. He would work for the country at war as nobody had worked.'[74] Raingo, through this work for his country, finds salvation and redemption from the foolish old man that he felt he was becoming. However, as his political star rises and falls, Raingo's confidence is undermined both by the presence of his soldier son who symbol-ises the 'reality' of war to him, and the women in his life. These figures undo Raingo's performance of power and wealth.

Raingo's son Geoffrey is a soldier who has been imprisoned as a prisoner of war in Germany for a number of months. Geoffrey does not enter the novel until halfway through and, when he does, it is at a tragic moment: the funeral of his own mother. Raingo is shocked at Geoffrey's appearance: 'Tall, emaci-ated, with prominent eyes that had a permanent childlike stare of wonder at the world, and unruly hair that stuck out under his cap. His uniform, with the stars of a captain, did not fit him.'[75] Geoffrey is in a bad way, undone by the war in many respects. He has a facial twitch, is unable to sleep indoors, tends to cry, and above all is very cynical about the government. This to Raingo is the war literally brought home and he is alarmed by it, thinking to himself of his recent successes: 'Politics! Titles! Propaganda! What odious, contemptible tinsel and mockery. Here was the war itself, tragedy, utterly distracted fatherhood.'[76] Geoffrey's presence forces Raingo to face his own performance and the futility of a government position that he feels is uncomfortably close to profiteering.

Raingo is constantly engaged in a performance, one that he sees as necessary to maintain his hold in the economic and political arena. This performance of ease and grace is what he partially attributes his success to:

> In a hundred financial deals, in some of which millions of money and triumph and ruin had hung in the balance for days of protracted and intricate negotiations, Sam had learnt how to wear a mask falsifying all his wishes and emotions. He prepared it and wore it now. The Prime Minister, unsurpassed for force, enterprise, originality of resource, courage and chicane, was not Sam's equal in the manipulation of masks.[77]

This ability, honed through business, serves him in his grasp for political power. In many ways, the loss of this mask is the subject of the novel. Raingo's internal dialogue reveals that he feels giddy and 'girlish' with excitement at the thought of being called Lord Raingo. His entrance into the Ministry of Records on the first day is a calculated and successful performance, he misleads his advisers and the Prime Minister in an effort to maintain power, and he is naked and exposed and depressed before the figure of Delphine, his mistress, who holds the key to his inner reality. When Raingo begins to suspect that Delphine may be cheating on him, he is overcome with grief: 'A formidable, revolting thought, that in the next room, on the other side of the door there, a man – a young man – was awaiting, in bravado or terror, the upshot of her adroit acting. And he, Sam, was the old man, deceived, exploited – and humiliated.'[78] The virile young hero more suitable to an Edgar Wallace novel, in this case, undoes Raingo, his performance is revealed and his role as lover is likewise revealed as a farce. By the end of the novel Raingo is increasingly worrying about his weight, 'ashamed of his girth, which made him too old and unworthy'.[79] By the end of his life his position with the family has also been usurped. Geoffrey has recovered from his war experiences, and ironically, in the absence of the war, he becomes even more soldierly. He commands the household that is nursing Raingo, a role that seems natural to him. Physically he had vastly improved: 'He had apparently grown not only in girth but also in height. His khaki was tight on him. He had an air of great strength' while Raingo withers away into death.[80] Geoffrey has regained a sense of stability and a sense of purpose, while Raingo's trappings of wealth fall away from him.

Thus we see that performances that disguise actions against the nation and in favour of wealth often went hand in hand. This was a shift from nineteenth-century fiction, which emphasised the knowable aristocratic villain in his black frock coat. Instead, interwar audiences saw largely middle-class villains who were knowable not through their obvious aristocratic dress, but rather through their strained efforts to appear upper class. This performance of wealth accompanied their efforts to gain wealth and power at the expense of the nation and the nation's economy. Knowable villains were immediately apparent to the hero and the audience, who was invited to view them from the hero's perspective. Knowable villains were constantly held up to the scrutiny of the audience and negative meaning was produced in the narratives surrounding wealth, performance, and villainy.

The unknowable villain

While the above examples outline what I term the knowable villains of interwar film and fiction, the villain who was not immediately apparent to the reader – the unknowable villain – was perhaps the more interesting. His role as villain is not obvious to the community or the hero initially, and consequently he often has a closer relationship to the hero than the ham-fisted, obviously evil villain. This villain is similar to the double agent within the Bond novels and films and John le Carré's later spy novels. Yet within interwar popular culture the construction of the unknowable villains is still closely related to anxieties about wealth and performance. He, like the knowable villain, is also exposed as being primarily interested in wealth. This character, however, threatens the hero not only in areas of economy and nation, but sometimes on the field of love as well.

Some unknowable villains in fiction did not survive the transfer to screen and were converted to the physically sensational knowable villain. The best example of this is the conspicuous absence of Carl Peterson from most of the film versions of the Bulldog Drummond series. Drummond's Carl Peterson, as mentioned, had his role reimagined in *The Man Who Knew Too Much*, but also in the numerous and relatively low-budget Bulldog Drummond films of the 1930s. *Bulldog Drummond's Peril* (1938), which dealt with an absent-minded professor who manufactures diamonds in his laboratory, erased Peterson's role in favour of a rival scientist who had a small role in the novel.[81] Likewise, Peterson's role was similarly excised in the adaptation of the novel *The Final Count* (1926), which featured his death, to the screen version of *Arrest Bulldog Drummond* (1939). In the film deadly poison is transformed into a 'death ray' and Peterson is replaced by a German named Rolf Alferson. The reasons for this removal are unclear but perhaps those involved in the franchise felt that they could support only the continuity of Bulldog Drummond's name and not the villain's.[82] When Peterson did appear in the widely popular 1929 version of *Bulldog Drummond*, which starred Ronald Colman, he appeared as a large, portly and somewhat older man played by Montagu Love.[83] This was in contrast to Peterson's often-changing description in the novel as he was billed as a master of disguises from the first book onwards, very much an unknowable villain. The film chose to privilege visual representations of the 'knowable' villain rather than the unknowable villain.

Yet the unknowable villain did gain in popularity in film over the course of the interwar period, and his average and sometimes above-average countenance stood in contrast to the large, stocky, uncouth man with which we are already familiar. The unknowable villain was often non-descript, much like the hero himself, or devastatingly handsome. The audience and reader were nevertheless often given clues that allowed them to 'know' the unknowable villain. These clues generated meanings that were similar to the knowable villain by attributing substantial wealth, power, and/or foreign traits to the unknowable villain.

In Philip Gibbs's *The Middle of the Road* (1923) the handsome villain is Kenneth Murless, much hated by Bertram Pollard: 'Murless whom he detested most of all [Joyce's] friends because he was too beautiful to live – one of those tall, curly-headed, Greek God sort of fellows – and elaborately brilliant in conversational insincerities'.[84] In *If Winter Comes*, Lord Tybar, the husband of Sabre's childhood love Nona, 'was thirty-two, was debonair and attractive of countenance to a degree. His eyes, which were grey, were extraordinarily mirthful, mischievous. A supremely airy and careless and bold spirit looked through those eyes and shone through their flashes and glints and sparkles of diamond light.'[85] The face of Medina, the villain in John Buchan's *The Three Hostages* (1924), is described in the novel by the protagonist Richard Hannay as 'beautifully cut, every feature regular, and yet there was a touch of ruggedness that saved it from conventionality'.[86] One of the multiple villains in *The Murder of Monte Cristo* by E. Phillips Oppenheim, Terence Brown, seems to be well known to the protagonist, calling out to him upon his arrival,

'Roger Sloane, by all that's amazing!' Then 'the young man came up to them smiling pleasantly'.[87] Carl Peterson, when we first meet him as the arch-villain in *Bulldog Drummond*, is tall with a firm jaw and gives off the impression of immense power. At the beginning of one of its sequels, *The Third Round* (1924), Peterson's companion Irma contemplates 'the clear blue eyes under the deep forehead, the aquiline nose, the firm mouth and chin … the thick brown hair … the great depth of chest, and the strong powerful hands'.[88] These were the deceptively attractive features of the unknowable villain.

Other unknowable villains may not have been handsome, but held positions within the larger community that allowed them to appear to act in the interests of the nation. The unknowable villain was usually the brains and not the brawn behind the operation, and it was his brains that fostered proximity to the mechanisms of the nation's economic and political power. These villains could possess positions of authority in politics or business or simply be part of an upper middle-class profession that lay at the foundation of Britain's public institutions. The medical profession occupied a rather ambivalent role within this popular fiction, with evil doctors hatching far-fetched plans for chemicals as weapons or the like. Yet almost as often, hapless absent-minded doctors were victims to be protected by the soldier hero. In *The Murder of Monte Carlo* the most surprising villain is the aforementioned Brown's associate Major Thornton, who is introduced as a liaison between the Foreign Office and Scotland Yard. Thornton is described as fairly ordinary, even heroic: 'Thornton was lean and grey, slow of speech, with steely blue eyes and a strangely shaped mouth, owing to his long upper lip. His voice was soft and pleasant. He had the air of an absent-minded man – which he certainly was not.'[89] In retrospect his strangely shaped mouth and his association with the Foreign Office were meaningful clues to his deviancy.

The villain in Edgar Wallace's *The Joker* (1926), Stratford Harlow, was another villain marked out by 'unusually small ears' and pale eyes, who nevertheless seemed to be an upstanding citizen within England. As head of 'Rata Syndicate' he is in charge of immense amounts of money and has the rubber market cornered. The novel notes that 'There was nothing furtive or underhand about the Rata Syndicate. It was registered as a public company, and had its offices in Westshire House, Old Broad Street, in the City of London, and its New York office on Wall Street.' Yet the novel goes on to document that the firm had hired a thug from New York who arrived the night before Rata's main competitor's factory burned to the ground. Harlow's plot to introduce insecurity into the world markets by having a man disguised as the Foreign

Secretary declare a coming war with France is foiled by the heroic inspector Carleton, but the novel notes at its end that Harlow continued to be unknowable to the bulk of the British public:

> If he gave, he gave cold-bloodedly, and yet without ostentation. True, he had offered to build, on the highest point of the Chiltern Hills, an exact replica of the Parthenon as a national war memorial, but the offer had been rejected because of the inaccessibility of the chosen spot. There was a certain freakishness in his projects; and Jim suspected that they were not wholly disinterested. The man baffled him: he could get no thread that would lead him to the soul and the mind behind those cold blue eyes.[90]

In Wallace's novel and other narratives that dominated the interwar period, the villains imagined were disturbing in their proximity to the systems of governance, and as such their undoing became all the more urgent. It was the hero alone who recognised the evil at work and it was him, not government, that enforced the villain's removal.

Alfred Hitchcock, in particular, favoured the unknowable villain as a narrative tool and featured this character in a number of films. Even in a romance such as 1928's *Champagne*, Hitchcock made use of an ambiguous character to hint at the potential evil residing within. The audience discovers at the end of the film that the father of the female protagonist, a spoiled heiress, has hired someone credited in the film as 'The Man', to watch over his daughter Betty. Yet, up until that moment, the Man, played by an older actor with a thin black moustache, black oiled hair, and a knowing stare, seems to occupy a villainous role. His show of wealth as he dines with the heiress seems to fit with the stereotypes of the consuming villain. This is apparent to the audience and Betty, who vividly imagines him sexually assaulting her in one scene. Even when he is discovered to be much more benign than this, the heiress, played by popular British actor Betty Balfour, looks at him and shudders as he drinks from a champagne glass and leers at the screen.[91] Hitchcock reversed the reveal of the villain, but questioned the extent of this reversal within an otherwise romantic narrative.

Professor Jordan in Hitchcock's film adaptation of John Buchan's novel *The Thirty-Nine Steps* (1935) remains the most striking demonstration of Hitchcock's use of the unknowable villain. Jordan is a respectable-looking professor living in a stately gated home in the countryside. When Hannay, played by Robert Donat, first meets him, he is hosting a gathering for his recently engaged daughter and we discover he is a friend of the local sheriff in attendance. As the professor himself says to Hannay, 'You see, I live here as a respectable citizen'. He is a person of some repute among the community, so much so that the sheriff is outraged and disbelieving when Hannay tells him of the professor's real identity, declaring angrily, 'Why he's my best friend in the district!'. Yet at the outset of *The Thirty-Nine Steps*, we know from the female agent who attempts to describe the spy villain before she dies that 'He has a dozen names and he can look like a hundred people'.[92] Only the missing top of his little finger gives him away as a foreign agent taking air defence secrets out of the country. The professor freely admits his identity to Hannay when exposed, holding up his maimed finger and complaining, 'You must realize my whole existence would be jeopardized if it became known that I'm not, what shall we say, not what I seem … I can't lock you up in a room or anything like that. You see, there's my wife and daughter to think of.' Instead he tries to shoot Hannay and plans to plead self-defence. His performance as a respectable and wealthy citizen is the perfect foil for him to commit crimes against Hannay and the nation.

In the case of *If Winter Comes*, Nona's husband Lord Tybar is constructed as not only handsome and wealthy but also likeable and apparently devoted to his country, hardly an unlikable rival for the novel's protagonist. When Sabre first runs into them for the first time in two years, Lord and Lady are out on their horses and Lord Tybar is surveying his landholdings. Through Tybar's joking exchange with his wife, it is indicated to the reader that this is no typical wealthy and pompous lord; rather he is a young sympathetic man who self-deprecatingly refers to himself as a 'bloated aristocrat' and a 'bloodsucker'.[93] Throughout the novel, he is presented as likeable and well known in the community. True to form, Tybar is friendly and jovial with Sabre and invites him to come up to visit him and Nona, although he is well aware of their past relationship. Thus Tybar seems to betray the formula of most bestsellers, which equated wealth with villainy. Tybar, like Sabre, also joins the war. He immediately enlists upon the outbreak and serves valiantly throughout. In fact Tybar is killed in action at Vimy, 'shot down leading his men'.[94] Tybar's actions parallel the hero's in almost every way, yet this valiant death is ultimately undone in the novel by actions prior to his death, which betray the real Lord Tybar.

Readers ultimately discover that Lord Tybar is not what he seems. The novel hints at this in the very first meeting. The passage that has Sabre contemplating his sparkling eyes also ends on this rather sombre note: 'There were people – women – who said he had a cruel mouth. They said this, not with censure or regret, but with a deliciously fearful rapture as though the cruel mouth (if it were cruel) were not the least part of his attraction.'[95] As the narrative progresses and Sabre rekindles his friendship and then love with Nona, audiences learn that the cruel mouth indicates a darkness at the core of Lord Tybar. After Sabre and Nona run into Tybar with a buxom and overly friendly female companion, Sabre starts to suspect that all is not well in their marriage and that Tybar's comic tone contains more than a hint of mockery. Nona eventually haltingly confesses to Sabre the countless affairs that Lord Tybar has engaged in and his cruel treatment of her as he details painful and graphic aspects of the trysts. Nona describes the treatment: 'There have been women all the time we've been married and he simply amuses himself with them until he's tired of them, and until the next one takes his fancy, and he does it quite openly before me, in my house, and tells me what I can't see before my own eyes just for the love of seeing the suffering it gives me.'[96] On Tybar's deathbed, to which Nona had rushed, he deliberately gives her a written message meant for another woman – his last act of cruelty.

Tybar by the end of the novel has been stripped away of any claims to heroic attributes. Instead he has been revealed as an inherently cruel villain, incapable of love. Although his physical appearance had confused this, his wealth and power consequently seem much more in keeping with the villains outlined above, the implication being that wealth must always be corrupting. His acts of cruelty as he lay dying also seem to undermine his actions in the war. These were, in some respects, constructed in the novel as simply another performance, an attempt to gain prestige and admiration rather than authentic efforts to defend his country.

Medina in *The Three Hostages* is also an upstanding citizen at the outset of John Buchan's novel, who is then revealed to be something quite different. Hannay's friend Macgillivray describes Medina to him as such:

> He's not in the least the ordinary matinee idol. He is the only fellow I ever heard who was adored by women and also liked by men. He's a first-class sportsman and said to be the best shot in England after His Majesty. He's a coming man in politics, too, and a most finished speaker. I once heard him, and though I take very little stock in oratory, he almost had me on my feet. He's knocked a bit about the world, and he is also a very pretty poet, though that wouldn't interest you.[97]

Medina, in almost all respects, seems to be the quintessential British man. Sports, politics, and poetry complete the scene of immense likeability and all the qualities of the public schoolboy. Hannay reads of his achievements in the local papers and is himself swayed by Medina's charm when he meets him. They talk about rifles and politics; Medina is interested in reviving the conservative party, that party of the public,[98] and harnessing the conservative voting power of women. Hannay, impressed 'that the man's reputation was justified', decides to take him into his confidence in the hopes of rescuing a young man, a girl, and an older man taken hostage by an evil villain who writes cryptic clues within lines of poetry.[99]

Of course, Medina is the arch-villain and the reader is clued into this through hints such as the poetry, as well as less subtle hints that indicate Medina's racialised tendency to villainy. When Hannay contemplates his face at the outset he notes, 'It was very English, and yet not quite English; the colouring was a little warmer than sun or weather would give'. This colouring is explained primarily through his Irish background. At the outset, his Irishness is identified neutrally, yet later it becomes a morbid explanation for Hannay's friend Sandy's increasing suspicions of him: 'To begin with, there's a far-away streak of the Latin in him, but he is mainly Irish, and that never makes a good cross … There's plenty of decent plain folk in Ireland, but his kind of *déraciné* is a ghastly throw-back to something you find in the dawn of history, holy and cruel like the fantastic gods of their own myths.' This atavistic tendency towards myth making on the part of the Irish is used to explain Medina's entrancement with an Indian 'guru' named Kharáma who is a master of mind control. To further complete Medina's increasingly bizarre set of features, he also possesses an extraordinarily round head, which Buchan comes back to again and again throughout the novel. The roundness, it is implied, indicates 'madness – at any rate degeneracy'.[100]

The ultimate goal of this particular degenerate is to bring people under his hypnotic control and thus exercise absolute power. The text is somewhat vague about how this power would be put to use but it is implied that Medina's influence in the political sphere is related to this goal. Medina states explicitly that he wishes not to control just the minds of women and children, but of men as well. Although the goal is clearly evil in subverting the will of freeborn English men, as a crime it is rather intangible, which becomes problematic in the novel's narrative when his exposure is brought about, yet he cannot be charged with anything. Rather than taking him to the police, Hannay and his friends bargain to release the hostages in exchange for not exposing him. This would be a relatively anticlimactic ending, which is remedied by a final chase across the craggy hills of Scotland where Medina meets his end in a fall off a cliff. The crime that Buchan constructs in the novel cannot be prosecuted; Medina's use of hypnotism to undermine the independent free will of British subjects. Medina wishes to destabilise the foundations of a normal British life, as personified by Hannay. Speaking of Medina, Hannay describes this process: 'He seemed to take pains to rout out the codes and standards, the points of honour and points of conduct, which somebody like me was likely to revere, and to break them down with his cynicism ... He broke down, too, my modest ambitions. A country life, a wife, and family – he showed me that they were too trivial for more than a passing thought.'[101] Medina, instead, possessed considerable ambition to be the most powerful man in the world. His crime was subsequently this hubris but also his rejection of the 'country life, a wife, and family' as ideals central to the English, but certainly not the Irish or the Indian.

Medina's ambitions for power and prestige are not unlike Carl Peterson's, although Peterson's were perhaps more crassly monetary, a comment Drummond himself makes in the first novel. At the outset of *Bulldog Drummond*, Peterson makes it clear that he wishes to destroy Britain's economy by working with Bolshevist union agitators, and much of his criminal activity seems bent on undermining Britain's security. Behind the undermining of the nation lay the ultimate goal of acquiring money. This aim caused him to involve himself in the theft of a secret regarding the manufacture of diamonds and a poison that could wipe out hundreds of people at a time. Peterson hoped to bribe the government and its business partners with his possession of these weapons (with the diamonds, to undermine the world's diamond industry, and the poison had more obvious effects). To this end, Peterson uses ten different disguises across the four books in which he appeared before perishing in *The Final Count* (1926). The bulk of disguises involved him masquerading as respectable citizens such as a scientist with an academic interest in diamonds and a wealthy Australian businessman who owned a fleet of Zeppelins and was the toast of British society.

While the scale of wrongdoing could vary, villains usually had the same goal in mind across popular narratives, even while the execution of these goals became increasingly fantastic. Some had grand plans of dominating the world and its finances, corrupting markets to favour their product be it grain or diamonds, while others, like Major Thornton and Terence Brown in *The Murder at Monte Carlo*, Warren F. Cooper in *Roman Scandals*, or Longfellow Deeds's distant relative in *Mr Deeds Goes to Town*, simply wish to swindle people out of their money for their personal gain. Yet what is striking about both the unknowable villain and the knowable villain is that the way they executed their crimes tend to be out of all proportion to what their real goal was. Terence Brown and Major Thornton kill a man and plan multiple meetings across Europe and America in order to achieve a goal that could have easily been accomplished by fixing a deck of cards. Carl Peterson's exploits are breathtaking in their complexity, as he commandeers country home after country home to house his flesh-eating acids, murderous gorillas, and tarantulas. The villain of Wallace's *Green Rust* engineers a green dust that can wipe out crops in North America, Peter Lorre's gang hold elaborate church ceremonies to cover their activities in *The Man Who Knew Too Much*, Longfellow Deeds is declared insane and put on trial in *Mr Deeds Goes to Town*, while even Lord Tybar's dramatic note-giving to his wife Nona on his deathbed seems entirely unnecessary in the face of already acknowledged adultery and impending death.

This scale of wrongdoing, however, obviously seemed to strike a chord and if anything makes the connection to the 1919 Profiteering Act somewhat telling, if only for highlighting the great gap between how the Board of Trade envisioned profiteering and how it was envisioned by producers of popular culture. The Act, while using the language of villainy, was unable to speak to people's real concerns about profiteering, partly because it targeted the small-scale grocer and merchant. These were not the large-scale companies such as 'British Imperial Grains' in Oppenheim's *The Profiteers*, or 'The Green Rust Syndicate' of Wallace's novel of the same name. It is worth revisiting the complaints mentioned earlier of the *Daily Express*: 'By their Profiteering Act the Government are making war on those who sell goods at unjustifiably inflated prices. Thus it is hoped to reduce the cost of living and to check illicit prices. It is absurd, while doing this, to leave intact those great increases in actual wealth which were the consequence of a way which has impoverished those who did the fighting.'[102] Some local districts also registered frustration with this when they reported to the Board of Trade on why they had suspended their local tribunal sessions. One district, Wood Green, reported of its activities: 'Suspended till question of profiteering is dealt with in a manner less irritating to small tradesmen and directed more to profiteering on a large scale. Will reconsider Amending Act', while Lambeth local tribunal noted that it 'Serves no useful purpose'. Southport also reported that it shut down 'In view of limited powers given in Act. May reconsider in view of Amendment Act.'[103] The amendments to the Act actually have further reduced the limited powers of the Act. Two amendments in the spring of 1920 indicated that the Board of Trade would pursue fair price 'agreements' with trade with the understanding that the trade 'should not be liable to any proceedings under the Profiteering Act' and that names under investigation should remain private.[104] The naming and shaming aspect of the Act was effectively undermined and the vague and unenforceable agreements with trade were set as the way forward. The Act clearly did not address popular views of profiteering yet profiteers continued to have an active life in the realm of mass culture.

It was the spectre of profiteering that raised its head again as mass culture began to grapple with the ever growing reality of another world war in the late 1930s. Leslie Charteris's *Prelude for War*, along with the relatively new author Eric Ambler in his *Cause for Alarm*, also of 1938, pointed to profiteers as people who would directly benefit from another great war. The language in these novels shifted from a preoccupation with the term 'profiteering' to a more specific indictment of the 'arms manufacturer' or 'dealer'. Charteris's villain, Mr Luker, the aforementioned 'Merchant of Death' was also 'one of the biggest shareholders in the Stelling Steel Works in Germany, and the Siebel Arms Factory in France, and the Wolverhampton Ordnance Company in England'. After this introduction, the Saint goes on to note cynically of Luker:

> At home, of course, he's a staunch patriot. He's one of the most generous subscribers to the Imperial Defence Society, which spends its time proclaiming that Britain must have bigger and better armaments to protect herself against all the European enemies of peace. In fact, the IDS takes a lot of credit for the latest fifteen-hundred-million-pound rearmament program which our taxes are now paying for. And naturally it's just an unavoidable coincidence that the Wolverhampton Ordnance Company is now working night and day to carry out its Government contracts.[105]

The novel spends much of its time tracing the connection between this arms dealer and the rise of the fascist group the Sons of France, and notes their willingness to murder the poor socialist student who discovers their plan in the process. In *Prelude for War*, Europe's problems are directly related to the growing industry of arms manufacturing, something that Eric Ambler would also address in 1938's *Cause for Alarm* as a critique of British arms manufacturing in Italy. Its hero finds himself entangled in a plot that exposes the terrible aims of Italy's war-making and Britain's blind willingness to look the other way. Another popular writer, Hammond Innes, follows a similar condemnation of the arms dealer in his book *Sabotage Broadcast* when his heroes show some compassion for the background of one Professor Pasman, the son of a profiteer from World War I. The main character notes sympathetically that

> He had a specific reason for hating war more savagely than other men. His father had made a packet out of selling death in metal containers and that money had been inherited by him. A man's mind might easily revolt from that. Some people – certainly a man of fine feeling – would consider it as bad if not worse than inheriting money from the owner of a chain of brothels or from a man who had made his pile out of murdering ignorant natives with vile whiskey.[106]

Profiteering is thus put on the same plain as prostitution or morally corrupting the ignorant, and the racially inferior according to this novel. Frank Capra's film *You Can't Take It with You* also weighed in on the dubious role of the resurgent profiteer in the late 1930s. Capra's antagonist, Mr Kirby, as mentioned was intent on securing a monopoly on arms manufacturing through his powerful Wall Street bank. Kirby says gleefully to his son at the film's outset, 'Do you realise that there wouldn't be a bullet, gun or cannon made in this country without us?' – a stance the film does not celebrate.[107] Yet the difference in the late 1930s is that profiteering occupies an increasingly ambivalent place within popular culture. Innes's novel ultimately loses sympathy for Pasman when it turns out that Pasman is broadcasting plans for rearmament in order to make the weapons meaningless and avoid another war. The hero says of Pasman, 'The man was so eminently sane, yet so terribly misguided' after saying to Pasman himself 'I have no choice but to do all in my power to defeat your object, which, when all is said and done, is nothing more than to undermine the morale of the country.'[108] Pasman ultimately throws himself off a cliff and Britain is able to go on to safely rearm, although against who is left deliberately vague in the novel. Even Mr Kirby, while criticised for ruthless business habits and not allowing for hobbies in his life, is never really targeted for his role in arms producing.

The willingness in the novels to condemn profiteers but not necessarily rearmament seems to be perfectly in tune with popular sentiment in the period. The 1935 Peace Ballot conducted by the League of Nations Union showed when respondents were asked 'Should the manufacture and sale of Armaments for private profit be prohibited by International Agreement?', 90.1 per cent of the respondents, almost 38 per cent of the population, responded 'Yes'. Yet thoughts on rearmament were less straightforward as 58 per cent responded yes to the statement, 'if a Nation insists on attacking another the other Nations should combine to compel it to stop, by, if necessary, military measures?'.[109] The public was not conflicted about the evils of making profit from wartime industry and seemed strongly against it, but was somewhat ambivalent about the act of rearming itself and did not necessarily connect the two. Oppenheim, who wrote 1919's fictional condemnation of the profiteer, himself exonerated arms dealing with 1937's 'An Opportunist in Arms' where his protagonist, an arms dealer named Mr Bresson redirects arms in Abyssinia towards the natives and against Italy. The story's protagonist describes Bresson's activities to him, saying he knows that 'you are able when it pleases you to finance governments, that in many of the smaller wars you have supplied both sides with all the arms and munitions they required, and that you have built up a gigantic fortune chiefly by being in the position to supply armaments and sometimes even an odd battleship just at the moment it was required'.[110] Bresson, in this case, however, is interested in financing the right side and Colin Rooke, the protagonist goes through harsh travails in Africa to make sure that the weapons land in the hands of the King of Abyssinia, who hails Bresson as a hero. The arms dealer does nothing but good in this story. Oppenheim's endorsement of arms dealing is certainly a change from 1919 and reflects confusion about the relationship between arms manufacturing and profiteering in a period of considerable international tension. New threats existed and profiteering was unfortunately just one of many that were troubling Britain.

The ambivalence towards the profiteer at the end of the 1930s was reflective of a striking period in mass culture. Villainy, particularly in the popular fiction of the late 1930s, which avoided many of the constraints of film censorship, was rather more unknowable than it had ever been. The complex political landscape had, by 1937, produced a vast array of bizarre plots within low and middlebrow fiction. *Prelude for War* places the blame for Europe's troubles squarely on the shoulders of British armament producers for selling to both Nazi Germany and fascist Italy, and then sponsoring the fictional French fascist group the 'Sons of France'. The efforts of the arms producers, aided by a former MP from the conservative Party, to sweep France into fascism and Europe into further uncertainty, is foiled by the hero and jack-of-all-trades Simon Templar. Two months later, *Sabotage Broadcast* (1938) by Innes was published, which features the aforementioned misguided peace activist (and professor) and the son of a profiteer trying to prevent rearmament by widely broadcasting on the BBC secret British weapon designs, thus moving Europe towards a détente.[111] Two journalists ultimately find out about the sabotage, and stop the plan for the sake of the 'morale' of the country. In January 1939 Oppenheim published another tome, *The Spymaster*, which shows an Italian dictator and his German allies who retreat from brinkmanship with Britain and realise that they cannot win, once they see Britain's plans for rearmament and their 'genius' military strategy.[112] Finally, in August of 1939, in a terrible stroke of timing, *Exit a Dictator* by Oppenheim is published, in which the fictional Stalinesque dictator of Soviet Russia peacefully abdicates once he is allowed to read the works of the then fictional British journal, *European Review*. The journal shows the Russian dictator the true state of his people and illustrates the failure of communism.[113] Seldom has an academic journal had such impact. The baffling complexities of the period are certainly captured in the plots outlined here, which point the finger at armaments dealers, pacifists, fascists, France, and Russia as just some of the villains at work in Europe.

Popular fiction was hard pressed to keep pace with international events, as evidenced by mixed assessments of the practice in the press. Oppenheim's 'An Opportunist in Arms' was deemed by the *Observer* in October 1937 'an epic on the arming of Abyssinia [by the British] against aggression' that 'comes a little after the fair'.[114] Yet the *Observer* condemned the villain in Inness's *Sabotage Broadcast* as 'an *ubermensch* who torpedoes the newest destroyers and interrupts the BBC all in the cause of peace – the kind of peace that passeth all understanding' while applauding the book and its ending as 'a high-class thriller in word as well as deed'.[115] Authors of low and middlebrow works still continued to explicitly tie their hero and villain to events of the period, drawing upon the latest headlines to inform their narratives.

When looking at depictions of the villain within these works on the eve of the war, it is clear that popular conceptions of villainy were heavily influenced by the government's pursuit of appeasement and the aforementioned lingering resentments about the profiteering scandal. Perhaps the most striking theme to the contemporary reader is the noticeable reluctance in these novels to explicitly identify Germany as the primary villain in Europe's unrest. Oppenheim's *Extraordinary Envoy* from 1937 takes pains to present Germany as misunderstood, going as far as to draw a sympathetic portraiture of a charismatic Hitler-like character named Hellstern, the self-titled 'President' of his country who abdicates when he realises he has created a 'Frankenstein' in the form of a German army, and that his goal has been achieved when his 'friend Great Britain' restores to Germany its colonies. This process is hastened by the diplomat hero, Mattresser, who visits central Africa and determines that the natives there would welcome back German rule, allowing Mattresser to state philosophically at the novel's end: 'Germany has been granted her greatest desire. Her colonies have been restored to her. It is Great Britain who has to pay the price, but when you sit down to consider this matter seriously I believe that everyone in the Empire will agree that no price could be too great to pay which guarantees peace.'[116] President Hellstern abdicates in favour of a return to a limited monarchy saying, 'A dubious war is a thing with which I will have nothing else to do. I have struck my blow for Germany.'[117] The leader of Germany is thus portrayed as rational, logical, and above all placated through appeasement. This villain is not actually a villain at all – something only the British hero can truly know and understand.

The journalist characters in Innes's *Sabotage Broadcast* likewise have a discussion at the beginning of the book that clearly absolves Germany from blame in the European tensions, as its hero complains of the press's tactics, saying, 'Trying to pin the blame on to Germany', observed Barry. 'Rather clumsy, wasn't it?' is the response to which Barry says, 'Very'. The heroes further complain of the press's efforts to demonise Germany, declaring, 'I'm sick of their sensationalism for sensation's sake. They never seem to think of the effect of some of their perniciously inaccurate stories on the reading public.'[118] In *Exit a Dictator* (1939) Germany, through the figure of Baron Adolf von Hertzfeldt, is portrayed as an uneasy, but ultimately willing friend of the British editor of the *European Review* and endorses the hero's plan to bring Soviet Russia out of communism. The British editor states first to the German politician, 'I am a friend of your country', then acknowledges in a stilted discussion that communism is a greater evil than even fascism. Von Hertzfeldt then expresses hope that Russia will move to fascism. The British editor says only that, 'the fundamentals of every modern political faith have been, during the last twenty years, torn to ribbons … therefore I shall not accept the terms of any one of them as a definition of our new faith. The existing system has reduced its citizens to bondage. It will be the scheme of the part I represent to set them free.'[119] Fascism is not endorsed but communism is strongly condemned. And indeed the *European Review* does free Russia, with German help. Even in novels like *Prelude for War*, which explicitly identified German Nazis as enemies of Britain and 'Jew-baiters', a lone voice in identifying anti-Semitism in Germany among these novels, Germany never acts alone but rather in conjunction with Italy, Russia, or even France.[120] Europe as a whole is thus cast as problematic before World War II, rather than Germany as the primary villain.

The influence of Chamberlain's policy of appeasement is evident in this reluctance to cast Germany as the primary antagonist. Germany is alternately portrayed as misunderstood, a friend of Britain, or as just one of many aggressors within Europe. Germany is denied the role of dominant villain that it would shortly take on and confusion about its aims persisted within mass culture until the very start of the war, as demonstrated in *Exit a Dictator* in the summer of 1939. It should be noted that all of these novelists and filmmakers shift radically and easily into the demonisation of Germany once the war starts. The next instalment of Charteris's Saint series was *The Saint in Miami* and revolves around hunting down a Nazi spy-ring in Florida, and Capra went on to produce the successful *Why We Fight* film series which offered scathing indictments of Germany and Japan on-screen. Yet, in the late 1930s, villains were surprisingly unknowable and lacked uniformity in the mass culture of the period. Germany was just one of many contenders in the field while older fears about political corruption and big business persisted before the war's start. This was cast as just as dangerous, if not more so to the producers of popular film and fiction, than Germany's fascist leanings.

Conclusion

While World War II would change the face of the popular villain in the twentieth century, villainy had a much more dynamic and contemporary life throughout the 1920s and 1930s. In popular film and fiction audiences responded to the villains they had known and villains they thought they knew in the faces of politicians, businessmen, and respected figures. The sheer array of villains and the banal and ordinary unknowability of villains in government and business fostered a climate of paranoia in popular novels and on the screen. This, if anything, spoke to the widespread diffusion of cynicism about profiteering following World War I and a reworking of the 1919 Profiteering Act into the Goods and Services (Price Control) Act when war broke out. Under this new Act, local committees again reported to a central committee but were encouraged and empowered to fix prices on goods and food. The Act was passed through Parliament relatively easily, ushering in large-scale rationing. *The Times* trumpeted its passage with the subheading 'New powers against profiteering'.[121] Tensions related to profiteering were obviously easily evoked at the outset of a new world war, indicating the extent to which it remained an issue throughout the 1920s and 1930s. When the 1919 Profiteering Act deployed the language of villainy, it likely did not anticipate the role it would play within politics or mass culture. Yet mass culture preached, through the figure of the knowable and unknowable villain, constant vigilance against wealthy businessmen and the politicians who failed to keep them at bay. Villainy, after all, could lurk in the most comforting of faces.

Notes

1 'Whitehall and the Control of Prices and Profits in a Major War, 1919–1939', *Historical Journal* 44:2 (2001), 517–40.
2 Gibbs, *Now It Can Be Told*, p. 534.
3 Deeping, *Sorrell and Son*, p. 5.
4 Horkheimer and Adorno, *Dialectic of Enlightenment*.
5 J. John, *Dickens's Villains: Melodrama, Character, Popular Culture* (Oxford: Oxford University Press, 2001), p. 10.
6 Jane Austen's rogue male characters were often well-meaning men brought down the wrong path through a weakness of character and a quest for money. It is often

implied in her works that a love of a good woman could reform him and indeed these characters teeter in that predicament and fall one way or the other.

7 A. Vesselo, 'Villains of To-Day', *Film Weekly* (5 July 1935).

8 P. Bailey, *Popular Culture and Performance in the Victorian City* (Cambridge: Cambridge University Press, 1998); Clark, *Struggle for the Breeches*; Gledhill, *Reframing British Cinema 1918–1928*; T. W. Laqueur, 'The Queen Caroline Affair: Politics as Art in the Reign of George IV', *Journal of Modern History* 54 (September 1982), 417–66; N. Rogers, *Crowds, Culture, and Politics in Georgian England* (Oxford University Press, 1998); Thompson, *Customs in Common*.

9 C. Watson, *Snobbery with Violence: Crime Stories and Their Audience* (London: Eyre & Spottiswoode, 1971).

10 This vilification took place not only in melodramatic plays but songs and scandalous cartoons as well; Davidoff and Hall, *Family Fortunes*; Laqueur, 'Queen Caroline Affair'; I. McCalman, *Radical Underworld: Prophets, Revolutionaries, and Pornographers in London, 1795–1840* (Cambridge: Cambridge University Press, 1988); Rogers, *Crowds, Culture, and Politics*.

11 D. Pick, *Faces of Degeneration: A European Disorder, c.1848–1918* (Cambridge: Cambridge University Press, 1993).

12 M. C. Finn, *The Character of Credit: Personal Debt in English Culture, 1740–1914* (Cambridge: Cambridge University Press, 2003); J. McVeagh, *Tradefull Merchants: The Portrayal of the Capitalist in Literature* (London: Routledge, 1981); R. C. Michie, *Guilty Money: The City of London in Victorian and Edwardian Culture, 1815–1914* (London: Pickering & Chatto, 2009); M. Poovey, *Genres of the Credit Economy: Mediating Value in Eighteenth- and Nineteenth-Century Britain* (Chicago: University of Chicago Press, 2008); R. Stern, *Home Economics: Domestic Fraud in Victorian England* (Columbus: Ohio State University Press, 2008); J. Taylor, *Creating Capitalism: Joint Stock Enterprise in British Politics and Culture, 1800–1870* (London: Royal Historical Society, 2006).

13 Light, *Forever England*.

14 S. Gillis and P. Gates (eds), *The Devil Himself: Villainy in Detective Fiction and Film* (London: Greenwood, 2002).

15 J. Palmer, *Thrillers: Genesis and Structure of a Popular Genre* (New York: St Martin's Press, 1979).

16 M. Woolf, 'Ian Fleming's Enigmas and Variations', in Clive Bloom (ed.), *Spy Thrillers: From Buchan to le Carré* (New York: St Martin's Press, 1990).

17 See Bloom (ed.) *Spy Thrillers*; Deborah Banner, 'Why Don't They Just Shoot Him?: The Bond Villains and Cold War Heroism', in Stacy Gillis and Philippa Gates (eds), *The Devil Himself: Villainy in Detective Fiction and Film* (London: Greenwood, 2002).

18 Chapman, *Licence to Thrill*.

19 Vesselo, 'Villains of To-Day'.

20 *Daily Mail*, 20 January 1926.

21 Tea, butter, and margarine were also rationed.

22 Stevenson, *British Society 1914–45*, pp. 72–4.

23 J. R. Clynes, 'Food Control in War and Peace', *Economic Journal* 30:118 (1920), 147–55.

24 'Profiteering. Where the guilt lies. The middlemen's gains', *The Times* (9 July 1919).

25 'War profits', *Daily Express* (11 October 1919).

26 Lord Beaverbrook, 'Tax war profits. A just method to meet our desperate needs. More than £1,000,000,000', *Daily Express* (21 October 1919).

27 M. J. Daunton, 'How to Pay for the War: State, Society and Taxation in Britain, 1917–24', *English Historical Review* 111:443 (1996), 882–919.

28 'Fighting the trusts. The Profiteering Act. Mr McCurdy's warning', *The Times* (16 September 1919).

29 *The Profiteering Act, 1919, Fully Annotated* (London: Stevens & Sons, 1919), p. vii.

30 Daunton, 'How to Pay for the War'; Rollings, 'Whitehall and the Control of Prices and Profits in a Major War'; P. MacLachlan and F. Trentmann, 'Civilizing Markets: Traditions of Consumer Politics in Twentieth-Century Britain, Japan and the United States', in M. Bevir and F. Trentmann (eds), *Markets in Historical Contexts: Ideas and Politics in the Modern World* (Cambridge: Cambridge University Press, 2004).

31 D. M. Cregier, 'Robinson, Sir Joseph Bejamin, first baronet (1840–1929)', *Oxford Dictionary of National Biography* (Oxford University Press-Online Edition, May 2006).

32 Morgan, *Consensus and Disunity*, pp. 339–42.

33 S. Broadberry and P. Howlett, 'The United Kingdom during World War I: Business as Usual?', in S. Broadberry (ed.) *The Economics of World War I* (Cambridge: Cambridge University Press, 2005), pp. 206–35; J. McDermott, '"A Needless Sacrifice": British Businessmen and Business as Usual in the First World War', *Albion* 21:2 (1989), 263–82; MacLachlan and Trentmann, 'Civilizing Markets'.

34 Clynes, 'Food Control in War and Peace'; Daunton, 'How to Pay for the War'.

35 E. Wilkinson, 'What is right with Britain. Our splendid workers – and their wives', *Daily Express* (6 January 1930).

36 C. Owen, 'English – and still proud of it', *Daily Express* (10 January 1930).

37 H. C. Engelbrecht and F. C. Hanighen, *Merchants of Death: A Study of the International Armament Industry* (London: Routledge, 1934).

38 *Ibid.*, p. 54.

39 *Ibid.*, p. 53.

40 B. Pain, *If Winter Don't* (New York: Frederick A. Stokes, 1922), p. 11.

41 Hutchinson, *If Winter Comes*, p. 56.

42 *Ibid.*, p. 103.

43 *Ibid.*, p. 309.

44 W. Deeping, *Old Pybus* (New York: Grosset & Dunlap, 1928), p. 17.

45 *Ibid.*

46 *Ibid.*

47 *Ibid.*, pp. 4–5.

48 *Ibid.*, p. 8.

49 *Ibid.*, p. 10.

50 *Ibid.*, p. 9.

51 *Ibid.*

52 E. P. Oppenheim, *Murder at Monte Carlo* (Boston: Little, Brown, 1933), p. 17.

53 *Ibid.*, p. 21.

54 *Ibid.*, p. 77.

55 Bloom, *Bestsellers*.

56 Almost all of J. Buchan's novels exhibit negative references to Jews, while Dorothy Sayers's first Lord Wimsey novel, *Whose Body* (1923), mounts a rather bizarre defence of Jews through Wimsey's mother, the Duchess, that is undone through-out the novel. In Edgar Wallace's work they are identified as of 'Hebraic origin' but always shifty and always playing the moneylender, as in *The Man Who Was Nobody* (1927). See T. Kushner, *The Persistence of Prejudice: Antisemitism in British Society during the Second World War* (Manchester: Manchester University Press, 1989) and *We Europeans? Mass Observation, 'Race' and British Identity in the Twentieth Century* (London: Ashgate, 2004).

57 *The Man Who Knew Too Much*, DVD, dir. A. Hitchcock (1935; Los Angeles, CA: Laserlight DVD, 1999).

58 'The Hidden Hand', in *British Board of Film Censors: Scenario Report* (1934), 'The Man Who Knew Too Much', in British Board of Film Censors: Scenario Reports (1934).

59 L. Collier, 'On the Screens Now', *Picturegoer Weekly* (2 February 1935).

60 J. M. MacKenzie (ed.), *Imperialism and Popular Culture* (Manchester: Manchester University Press, 1986); L. Grieveson and C. MacCabe (eds), *Empire and Film* (London: BFI, 2011); L. Grieveson and C. MacCabe (eds), *Film and the End of Empire* (London: BFI, 2011).

61 S. Auerbach, *Race, Law, and 'The Chinese Puzzle' in Imperial Britain* (New York: Palgrave Macmillan, 2009).

62 Sedgwick, *Popular Filmgoing in 1930s Britain*, p. 311; S. Harper, 'Lower Middle-Class Taste-Community in the 1930s', 580.

63 *Shanghai Express*. Videodisc, dir. Josef Von Sternberg (1932; Los Angeles, CA: Paramount [year unknown]).

64 See *The Drum*, dir. Z. Korda (1938; London, UK: Alexander Korda Films); *Sanders of the River*, dir. Z. Korda (1935; London Film Productions); *The Four Feathers*, dir. Z. Korda (1939: London Film Productions).

65 *You Can't Take It with You* (1938) was the fifth most popular film in 1939 at the Regent cinema in Portsmouth and *Roman Scandals* was the third most popular film in Britain according to Sedgwick in 1934 when it was released. See Harper, 'Lower Middle-Class Taste-Community in the 1930s', 587; Sedgwick, *Popular Filmgoing in 1930s Britain*, p. 311.

66 J. Robert, 'The Image of the Profiteer', in J. Winter and J. Robert (eds), *Capital Cities at War: Paris, London, Berlin, 1914–1919*, vol. I (Cambridge: Cambridge University Press, 1997), pp. 104–32.

67 E. P. Oppenheim, *The Profiteers* (Boston: Little, Brown, 1921), pp. 76–7.

68 E. Wallace, *The Green Rust* (1919). Project Gutenberg Australia. http://gutenberg. net.au/ebooks06/0600131h.html (accessed 12 July 2010).

69 S. Horler, *Tiger Standish* (New York: Crime Club, 1933), p. 25.

70 See R. Squillace, *Modernism, Modernity, and Arnold Bennett* (Lewisburg: Bucknell University Press, 1997); V. Woolf, *A Moment's Liberty: The Shorter Diary*, ed. Anne Olivier Bell (San Diego: Harcourt Brace Jovanovich, 1990).

71 A. Bennett, *Lord Raingo* (New York: G. H. Doran, 1926), p. 11.

72 *Ibid.*, p. 47.

73 *Ibid.*, p. 12.

74 *Ibid.*, p. 47.

75 *Ibid.*, p. 176.

76 *Ibid.*, p. 184.

77 *Ibid.*, p. 41.

78 *Ibid.*, p. 25.

79 *Ibid.*, p. 227.

80 *Ibid.*, p. 282.

81 *Bulldog Drummond's Peril*, DVD, dir. J. Hogan (1938; Narberth, PA: Alpha Video, 2003).

82 Two different actors played Bulldog in the 1920s, and then Ronald Colman, the popular and quintessentially British star, played Bulldog in 1929's *Bulldog Drummond* and *Bulldog Drummond Strikes Back* (1934). John Howard went on to play the part in seven increasingly low-budget Bulldog productions in the late 1930s.

83 *Bulldog Drummond*, 35 mm, dir. F. R. Jones (Hollywood, CA; Samuel Goldwyn, 1929).

84 Gibbs, *The Middle of the Road*, p. 11.

85 Hutchinson, *If Winter Comes*, p. 85.

86 J. Buchan, 'The Three Hostages', in *The Complete Richard Hannay* (London: Penguin, 1992 [1924]), p. 702.

87 Oppenheim, *Murder at Monte Carlo*, p. 35.

88 H. C. McNeile, *The Third Round* (London: Hodder & Stoughton, 1925), p. 12.

89 *Ibid.*, p. 59.

90 Wallace, *The Joker* (1926) (Project Gutenberg Australia, http://gutenberg.net.au/ebooks07/0701181h.html, ch. 26) (accessed 10 October 2011).

91 *Champagne*, DVD, dir. A. Hitchcock (1928; Los Angeles, CA: Brentwood Home Video, 2005).

92 *The Thirty-Nine Steps* (1935), DVD, dir. A. Hitchcock (1935; Los Angeles, CA: Brentwood Home Video, 2005).

93 Hutchinson, *If Winter Comes*, p. 89.

94 *Ibid.*, p. 314.

95 *Ibid.*, p. 85.

96 *Ibid.*, p. 176.

97 Buchan, 'Three Hostages', p. 700.

98 McKibbin, 'Class and Conventional Wisdom in Interwar Britain', in *Ideologies of Class*.

99 Buchan, 'Three Hostages', p. 704.

100 *Ibid.*, pp. 701–2, 782, 757.

101 *Ibid.*, p. 745.

102 'War profits'.

103 BT, File 68/69 (1920).

104 'Profiteering Act to be retained: fair price agreement', *The Times* (23 April 1920); 'Profiteering Bill through Committee', *The Times* (13 May 1920).

105   L. Charteris, *Prelude for War* (London: Hodder & Stoughton, 1938), p. 39.

106   H. Innes, *Sabotage Broadcast* (London: Herbert Jenkins, 1938), p. 258.

107   *You Can't Take It with You* (1938), dir. F. Capra (Columbia Pictures).

108   Innes, *Sabotage Broadcast*, pp. 274–5.

109   H. McCarthy 'Democratizing British Foreign Policy: Rethinking the Peace Ballot, 1934–1935', *Journal of British Studies* 49:2 (April 2010), 358–87.

110   E. P. Oppenheim, 'An Opportunist in Arms', in *Curious Happenings to the Rooke Legatees: A Series of Stories* (London: Hodder & Stoughton, 1937), p. 231.

111   Innes, *Sabotage Broadcast*.

112   E. P. Oppenheim, *The Spymaster* (Boston: Little, Brown, 1938).

113   E. P. Oppenheim, *Exit a Dictator* (Boston: Little, Brown, 1939).

114   'Thorndyke and others', by 'Torquemada' *Observer* (10 October 1937), p. 7.

115   'Free for all', by M. Richardson, *Observer* (21 August 1938) p. 6.

116   Oppenheim, *Envoy Extraordinary*, p. 202.

117   *Ibid.*, p. 217.

118   Inness, *Sabotage Broadcast*, p. 45.

119   Oppenheim, *Exit a Dictator*, p. 115.

120   Charteris, *Prelude for War*, p. 157.

121   'Control of prices: new powers against profiteering; House of Commons', *The Times* (20 June 1941).

3

That magic moment: the female love-interest and the villainess

ARMAND: You mean you'd give up everything for me?
MARGUERITE: Everything in the world. Everything. Never be jealous again.
Never doubt that I love you more than the world – more than myself.
Camille (1936)

When actor Greta Garbo whispers the above words to Robert Taylor in *Camille*, Britain's eighth most popular film in 1937, she looks up into his face and he violently embraces her.[1] They kiss and he asks her to marry him. This moment stands out in the film as one of the most passionate of scenes between the characters Marguerite, otherwise known as Camille, and her beau Armand. It comes over halfway into the film, following a period of relative happiness for the couple once the initial barriers to their union had been overcome. As such it was constructed as an authentic moment of true love, upon which the rest of the narrative turned. This type of exchange dominated the popular films and novels of the interwar period as female lead after female lead pledged to give up everything for love.

Some bemoaned the popularity of this exchange as it, more often than not and in contrast to the ending of *Camille*, usually signalled a happy ending within the narrative. In 1920, the *Daily Express* ran an article entitled 'The death of the short story'. The article outlined a defining feature of the dominant lowbrow narrative: 'the written or unwritten rule is that it must have a happy ending … However original the beginnings may appear, the endings are tiresomely inevitable … No man or woman can write masterpieces with a perpetual climax of treacle.'[2] Ten years later, in the same paper the climax of treacle was still worthy of note in bestselling novels and popular films. Ruby M. Ayres, a popular writer of romances, responded to the ongoing derision of the syrupy exchange of love in an article entitled 'Well, let them despise Me!':

> Let me say that I am proud of being a lowbrow. Being a lowbrow means making so many friends through the medium of one's books that one is left humbly amazed; it means being thanked by hundreds of people who have never known much romance for bringing a little into their lives, even if it is only through the medium of a paper-covered novel or a serial story; it means trying to hold up the banner of happy endings above all the mire and sludge of the 'smart' modern world.

Ayres ended her defence by arguing that the masses would always side with the lowbrow happy ending: 'I admit that there is a great dividing line between us, but if that line came to be truly defined I wonder on which side of it would stand the greater crowd of people who really matter in the world? Somehow I do not think the lowbrow would feel very lonely.'[3]

Undoubtedly, the lowbrow author would not have felt lonely on his or her side of the great cultural divide between high and lowbrows. Ayres, who could write a sticky sweet masterpiece and did so quite regularly, seemed to have judged the masses accurately. These romantic exchanges and the happy endings that often attended them continued to be a defining trait of bestselling novels and popular films in 1920s and 1930s Britain. These novels encompassed not only romances by the likes of Ayres but also a variety of other genres. The popularity of this moment translated into multiple editions of novels and box-office sales for films. The appeal of it was widely acknowledged by authors, filmmakers, and producers who sincerely believed that this was what the mass public desired most. Charlie Chaplin, for example, rewrote the ending of his tremendously popular film *Modern Times* (1936) to satisfy this desire of audiences for a happy ending between boy and girl.[4] Originally *Modern Times* was to end with Charlie and his love separating as she comes down with an illness and grows tired of the roving life. Instead, at the urgings of early viewers, it ends with Charlie and the urchin girl walking hand in hand into the sunset. It was the happy ending that the public seemed to want and it was the happy ending that they repeatedly got.

In both films and novels the romantic exchange, or what filmmakers and songwriters alike have called the 'magic moment', tended to rely on particular narrative and visual devices. In popular novels, a declaration of love was usually followed by the first kiss or embrace, seldom described in detail. The absence of description granted it a finality that rejected words. In films, kisses and embraces were visually quite uniform, with the women's head usually positioned below the man's, her face upturned towards his, eyes usually closed, and then followed by a physical collapsing of the body into the kiss so that swooning and kissing were indistinguishable. This was filmed through a tight close-up that emphasised only the two figures and nothing of the world surrounding them. This movement of the camera angle was significant because film techniques at this time tended to remain static, with deep focus shots that encompassed all the actors in a frame. The close-up in this moment emphasised only the desire of the two characters and added an element of other-worldliness with the use of soft focus, which blurred the edges of the heroine and sometimes the hero as well. This declaration of love was consequently constructed as a crucial moment within the narrative as it ended a story happily or set up dramatic tension about whether the lovers would endure a tragic separation, as was the case in *Camille*.

This chapter examines changes within the female character's role as she subscribes to heterosexual love, and how this shift related to larger anxieties about women's place within the economy and the nation in interwar Britain. The 1920s and 1930s saw a marginal increase in the presence of women within the workplace as well as considerable gains within the political spheres of the nation. Women acquired footholds in light industry and clerical work, while winning limited female suffrage in 1918 and universal suffrage in 1928. Yet these gains – marginal and significant – were amplified within the press, creating a sense of significant female advancement, while men experienced declining status within the economy and nation.[5] This impression of changing roles was moderated by the popularity and repetition of heterosexual love within popular film and fiction. Indeed this magic moment was actively constructed as a moment removed from these economic and social anxieties even as it also responded to them. For instance, the exchange between Marguerite and Armand quoted above from *Camille* was instrumental in soothing Armand's fears about Camille's desire to acquire wealth. Her past work as a courtesan to wealthy upper-class men is renounced in this moment, as she pledges to give up 'everything in the world' as proof of her love and devotion to Armand. Thus even as true love was constructed as unworldly, it was informed by anxieties about women's access to wealth. Through an examination of similar moments and processes within bestsellers, popular films, and the press, I situate them within the 'mire and sludge of the 'smart modern world' and explore the changing depiction of the female love-interest who had to declare her interest in love and not in economic gain or status.

We have seen that the heroes of these stories often emerged as breadwinners and as politically and socially central to Britain. This was the end result of a narrative that showed an authentic male hero surrounded by people engaged in false performances. The hero's ability to survive lay in his skill at seeing through the performances of seemingly benevolent businessmen and politicians to the bleak reality behind them.[6] An examination of 'true love' in these narratives presents us with the female love-interest as a character whose own performance of love must be questioned and interrogated by the hero. The cathartic revelation of authentic love that lay at the heart of popular magic moments reflected the hero's insistent need to 'know' and to guard against false performance. Love within popular film and fiction of the 1920s and 1930s, I argue, was constructed as an authentic 'truth', while women's interests in economic gain and social prestige were negatively constructed as false performances. This was the 'truth' that the modern age demanded and the secret it must uncover, as Foucault argues.[7] For love-interests, wealth and status were depicted as unnatural trappings, often symbolised by material objects such as clothing, jewels, or disguises that impeded the character's own true self, or signal the woman's status as a villainess. True love was revealed as residing within a love-interest with no interest in wealth or power. The relationship between wealth and love consequently became an important yet unstable feature in the love-interest's performance of gender in this period. Within most low and middle-brow narratives a female character either gives it all up for love or chooses the loveless life of the villainess. Thus heterosexual love is constructed within popular interwar narratives as a bubble, strangely devoid of money, politics, or power, yet entirely framed by it. In contrast, the role of the villainess offered an example to readers and audiences of the pitfalls of choosing economic and social gain rather than love. This chapter consequently addresses the vital place of female characters in fostering criticisms of class performance within mass culture and promoting a realignment of the gender order, with the beloved male hero back at the centre of the economy and nation.

Although an argument could be made that the increased presence of working women within popular film and fiction was a partial acknowledgement of women's roles in the workplace and the nation, this presence was ultimately tempered by a negation of her breadwinning status that occurred during the revelation of her true love. Escapism is too simple an explanation for the complex process by which true love reflected, negotiated, soothed, and reproduced concerns about gender and work within the 1920s and 1930s. The popularity of this type of true love in many ways signalled a gender crisis not unlike the one that Anna Clark identified as a 'struggle for the breeches' in the 1820s.[8] A similar crisis of masculinity about work arose in interwar Britain. This manifested less as a crisis than as a constantly negotiated dance between

men, women, and work. As previously discussed, this shift in modern conceptions of masculinity was precipitated by the combination of a war that did
little to reaffirm old patterns of masculinity alongside new patterns of male
unemployment. The spectre of female employment added important dimensions to this movement, signalling it strongly as a crisis.[9] Mass culture, through
a newly improved printing press and the development of the cinema, was able
to provide a remedy that allowed men and women to concentrate not on the
real problems of work and politics, but on the newly reimagined game of love.
While Thompson may have characterised Methodism as the pap of the people
in the eighteenth century, the magic moment produced a new type of pap for
its age and became central to popular culture's promotion of the masculine
breadwinner.[10]

As outlined in my introduction, I have highlighted the persistence of heterosexual love and desire in the happy endings of male-authored novels and male-
directed films that were not portrayed by their contemporaries or by historians
as typically being concerned with love. Yet novels by writers such as E. Phillips
Oppenheim and Philip Gibbs as well as military movies such as *Mutiny on
the Bounty* (1935) frequently contained a love scene, however limited. The
heterosexual exchange of love was not only the domain of romances, nor was
it produced only by female writers or by female directors for female audiences.
This heterosexual moment of true love was also central to thrillers, adventure,
and detective stories made by and for men.

The appeal of the heterosexual love imagined in these narratives relates to a
point that has been argued throughout this book – that popular culture was an
important site for the articulation of concerns about the economy, politics, and
gender. The incongruity that Ruby Ayres noted between the lived experiences
and the fantasies of middle and working-class people who read the bestsellers
and watched the films speaks to a commitment by both the public and the
producers of film and fiction to an idea of love that was both increasingly available and particularly compelling in the interwar period. While acknowledging
that audiences, authors, and producers alike may have seen popular culture
and the type of love that it envisioned as escapist, the form that this escape
took, as it envisioned a relationship that held considerable appeal for both
sexes, says much about the intersection of economic and gender anxieties in
the period.

The mire and the sludge:
women within the economy and nation

In order to account for the popularity of the type of true love I have outlined, we first need to address the social and economic context of women's roles in the 1920s and 1930s. In doing so, it becomes clear that the idea of living on nothing but love had particular resonance for audiences who were experiencing high male unemployment, widespread disillusionment with the government, and new and controversial roles for women within the workforce and the nation at large. What had been a predominantly male workforce before World War I now endured the rise of industries dependent upon new methods of mass production. With this shift, male workers faced the entrance of newly enfranchised women into the labour force. Women were making steady gains in both working-class occupations, newly defined by lighter assembly-line technology, and middle-class occupations such as clerical work. Women's employment, while certainly not comparable to men's, was one of the few bright spots of growth in the interwar period. In comparison, those areas that constituted old industry, such as coal, steel, and iron, and that employed a large number of men were most affected by the depression. This movement undermined ideas of British masculinity built upon the breadwinner ideal.[11] British masculinity was challenged both by this shift in the economy and by the experience of war which had likewise shaken entrenched ideas of the heroic soldier working on behalf of the nation.

The restructuring of Britain's economy and its effect upon the male and female working class is well documented.[12] The new role of women within the workplace has often been attributed to World War I, but, as Miriam Glucksmann and Deborah Thom have pointed out, working-class women were present in Britain's workforce both before and after the war. Their presence had been minimised by the government which took pains to emphasise that women's roles within the workforce during the war was temporary and incongruous with the workplace itself.[13] After the war, women's work was only marginally more acceptable to the larger public, yet was increasingly vital to a struggling economy.

The primary reason behind women's newfound importance to Britain's economy was their employment in relatively new industries. Working-class women arguably benefited from the greater use of the assembly line in production, which ushered in a need for unskilled labour. A number of industries, such as electrical engineering, the automotive and aircraft industry, chemicals, synthetic fibres, food processing and canning, rubber, glass, and paper, 'took off' in the interwar period, and specifically in the 1930s. Employers in these industries were actively seeking out a new 'green' workforce of unskilled workers.[14] Women and young men were seen as potential employees as a result. Estimations of women's employment in 1931, based upon census records, indicate that women still experienced lower employment figures overall than men. Yet in certain industries both sexes were equally employed and in some areas women occupied the larger percentage of the workforce. Women regis-tered slightly higher levels of employment in food manufacturing and paper, significantly higher levels of employment in textiles and clothing and slightly lower levels than men in brick manufacturing and chemicals.[15]

The growth in female labour was not only among working-class women. Middle-class women, and specifically lower middle-class women, also experi-enced rising levels of employment. The census figures of 1931 tell us that women seemed to be enjoying relatively equal levels of employment with men in commerce, somewhat less equal positions in public administration, and substantially higher figures in professions and personal service. These last two fields encompassed women's movement into clerical work. Selina Todd notes in her study of patterns of female employment in the interwar period that by 1931 women made up 42 per cent of the clerical workforce.[16] The typist also became a highly eroticised figure within popular film and fiction as women began to displace men as personal secretaries, further eroding the positions of male clerks.[17] The visibility of the female typist in the office dovetailed with women's increasing visibility in the public sphere of department stores as they found work as shop girls and as 'mannequins' or clothing models.

Popular culture had to reconcile anxieties about women's roles within the workforce as well as within the social and political sphere of the nation. I have written that pre-war political suffrage and ideas of Englishness were identi-fied strongly with men. This encompassed their roles as voting citizens and involvement in institutions that embodied Englishness. With the advent of the war, women began to be incorporated into the idea of Britain, troubling the masculine conception of the nation. Women gained a powerful presence in the war as workers, nurses, and patriots, and also occupied positions as law enforcers on the domestic front.[18] Collectively these activities redefined notions of wartime citizenship, causing Gullace to state that 'war service, rather than male gender, became the basis of British citizenship'.[19] The duration of the war and its impact upon its soldiers forced the government to draw upon the very groups that had been most marginalised at the outset of the war – women and workers.[20] Women and workers were not only drawn upon but also increasingly conflated as one and the same, as women became workers in munitions factory and on the fields of war. This devotion to the nation and the economy was twice 'rewarded' in the interwar period when limited suffrage was granted to women over 30 years of age in 1918 and when universal suffrage was adopted in 1928. Women entered Parliament for the first time shortly after the war; in 1919 Lady Astor became the first female to sit in Parliament. This, along with women's presence within the workforce, universities, the streets, and the popular press, seemed to indicate that women were becoming more central within the British manufacturing economy and political conceptions of the nation.

This widening sphere of influence coincided with more expansive coverage of political roles for women within the popular press and a general courting of female readers, a point that Adrian Bingham has made about the interwar newspaper press.[21] Women in popular newspapers were now asked to imagine what Britain meant to them. The *Daily Express* series, mentioned in Chapter 3, entitled 'What is right with Britain', asked Ellen Wilkinson, as one of the country's few female MPs in 1930, to contribute. Her column's answer, 'Our splendid workers and their wives', was non-threatening enough in that it emphasised the male breadwinner and his role in the family.[22] Yet nevertheless, she was granted both the political and public forum to express this view. A similar series in the same year featured advice to give one's children about life's important lessons, and included such an array of titles as 'What I am teaching my children about God' and 'What I am teaching my children about war'.[23] Two women were asked to contribute, and Sylvia Thompson, billed as 'the brilliant young novelist', predictably was asked to discuss marriage, while Storm Jameson, perhaps strangely enough for a female novelist, was asked to contribute to one entitled 'What I am teaching my children about money'.[24] Women were invited and encouraged within certain pages of the press to express their views on how the nation should be run and to verbalise their own roles within that nation.

Although women were granted a greater voice within the press, this voice was nevertheless moderated by the highly ambivalent and masculinist view of women's activities. The examples already provided speak to that ambivalence as women were recorded on subjects usually related to the family. When it came to discussions of the young working girl, these papers, on the one hand, in a paternalist fashion expressed concern over her low wages, yet on the other hand, limited this concern to the young working girl that could not and would not ever easily accumulate wealth. Typists who were generally poverty-stricken were covered favourably and indeed the plight of the poor typist found some sympathy among even writers from the conservative *The Times*.[25] One article, 'Civil Service typists; girls "underpaid and under-nourished"', expressed concern that 'even the maximum for copying-typists and writing assistants – namely – 53s. 8d. – is inadequate to keep a girl in good health and respectably clothed if she has to live in lodgings'. It is unclear whether this was a cry for increased wages or an admonishment to women to not live in lodgings.

Marginal sympathy ended when it came to the displacement of male workers from the workforce. In periods of particularly high male unemployment, readers expressed their anger towards the presence of women workers, arguing that if women were kept at home, 'we should be spared the odious sight of heroes, many of them cripples, selling pencils, playing organs, and "queuing" to obtain a livelihood'. The writer of this particular letter goes on to note that 'any women doubtless took on "temporary" war work from patriotic motives but they cannot deny that their patriotism was well paid for'.[26] Indeed, although most writers in the *Daily Express*, the *Daily Mail*, and *The Times* offered up conflicting views of women's work, they all emphasised the novelty of it. This type of intensified coverage of what amounted to a fairly small section of the workforce, as indicated by Savage, tended to amplify the impact of that work within the economy. This, in turn, may account for the prominent role that wealthy and socially mobile woman took in interwar fiction and film, and the contrasts between the woman giving up work for love and the loveless villainess that seemed to define popular portrayals of female wealth.

Newspapers could be even more barbed in critiquing the general visibility of women in new roles. Some emphasised women's new and junior role within the nation by running articles that advised women how to behave in public. The *Daily Mail* argued that most women did not know how to conduct themselves on the telephone in a telling article entitled 'At the telephone. Women who waste time'.[27] The paper highlighted the activities of one woman who 'is less efficient, searches for money, where to put her bag, and then rambles on for 9 minutes while 7 people wait behind her'. Further down the column readers are asked to submit accounts of similar experiences under a further subheading 'Women who annoy'. Similar articles in the *Daily Express* lectured women in the early days of 1920 on the way they conducted themselves on the omnibuses and the Tube: 'She will stand waiting to alight, occupying the step on to which you were hoping to jump before the omnibus pulls up at its appointed stop. Similarly, in a tube she will stand and block the way, anxious only for her own chance of an early exit.'[28] The article advises that a 'woman, even emancipated woman, will find her way through life much the pleasanter for the little polite-nesses that man expects her to offer'. Women, in these pages, were actively constructed as needing training in order to perform the acts of a member of the public sphere. By emphasising the need of women to be trained and to learn this performance, the press simultaneously constructed women as being naturally not workers and naturally not part of the public sphere, let alone nation. Similar depictions pepper the narratives of popular fiction and film.

Although women seemed to be gaining more visibility in Britain's workforce and other social and political arenas in press accounts, it must be emphasised that this was only a partial representation of their experiences. While women were hired in somewhat larger numbers into the new industries, this was at a lower wage than their adult male counterparts and even the adolescent men with whom they were competing. The mass production used in the lighter manufacturing industries seldom made for an adequate living wage for either women or men. Likewise clerical work was also not an easy path to a living wage.[29] In many respects it further emphasised the role of marriage as a way out of such poorly paying work for women. Popular film and fiction further affirmed the economic benefits of love over work. The presence within popular film and fiction of wealthy women paired with men of a lower class and willing to abandon their own social and economic position to maintain that relation-ship can be viewed as a more dramatic, and indeed misogynist, reordering of the popular conception of increasingly skewed gender relations.

In reaction to the anxieties outlined above, audiences flocked to films that tended to present female love-interests in one of three ways: women who lacked wealth at the outset of the narrative; working women who possessed some means of earning wealth but abandoned it for love; and women who initially possessed and then gave up substantial wealth and social status for love. While these three types of women occupied different social and economic standings at the outset of the bestselling novel or the popular film, the experi-ence of heterosexual love tended to produce a similar effect for them – they were willing to abandon everything for love. This exchange acted as a levelling device against various forms of economic and social stratification. This chapter ends with a discussion of the villainess, a character whose role also buttressed a mutually exclusive relationship between wealth and female love by illustrating to audiences the negative results of making the wrong choice.

Poor girl! Women lacking wealth

Women who stood to gain wealth or social status at the outset of the narrative often had little to lose in terms of economic and social status and only love to gain. They were usually portrayed as lacking wealth based on circumstances around class, race or ethnicity, place, or age. These women were marginalised, like the hero, from the centres of economic and national prestige but in different ways, thus making them unthreatening, vulnerable, and singularly honest characters from the outset. These characters possessed some commonalities with heroines of nineteenth-century popular fiction and melodrama in that they were often presented as impoverished women elevated at the end of the story by love and money.[30]

For instance, the love-interest in E. Phillips Oppenheim's *Murder at Monte Carlo* (1933) is introduced early in the story to Roger Sloane as a young Italian savage, climbing trees and being persecuted by an evil and drunk man. The 15-year-old girl falls from the tree in which she is hiding into Sloane's arms. The helplessness and desirability of the girl and the subsequent 'truth' embodied in this moment is dependent upon the girl's age and her complete lack of performance in an extreme moment of fear:

> He was caught up in a blaze of incredible and incomprehensible sensation. This half-dressed, probably unwashed brat was clinging to him with all the abandon of her long supple limbs and pulsating body, her strange-coloured eyes aflame, her breath sweet as the flowers themselves falling hot upon his cheeks. She was nearly mad with terror. Her sobs told him that and the frantic rise and fall of her small bosoms.[31]

Jeannine, utterly exposed, is obviously in need of Sloane's protection on a variety of levels. Jeannine later acquires the trappings of delicate clothing and manners, yet makes it clear that she does so only in order to win Sloane's approval and love. By the age of 17 and in the proper dress she is a socially acceptable mate for Sloane and he is, of course, enamoured of her. The narrative allows for this acquisition of social performance after her true self and her true love has been established.

Lost Horizon (1933), the novel by the British writer James Hilton and later the most popular film with British audiences in 1937,[32] imagined its female love-interest in a place where her economic and social status could not possibly be threatening and where her disinterest in wealth was abundantly clear. In the film, its protagonist, Robert Conway, played again by Ronald Colman, is about to become Britain's new Foreign Secretary when his plane carrying exiled British citizens fleeing China crashes in the mountains of Tibet. Conway's love-interest Sondra resides in the film's fictional utopian land of Shangri-la.[33] Shangri-la is presented to the viewer through the turning pages of an old-fashioned storybook that the viewer is meant to read. The first page asks the viewer, 'In these days of wars and rumours of wars – haven't you ever dreamed of a place where there was peace and security, where living was not a struggle but a lasting delight?' The film presents Shangri-La as the answer, far removed from war as well as the mobile working woman. The novel emphasised the innocent and chaste pleasure offered up by Lo-Tsen, a woman exiled by both place and race (Shangri-la seems to be in Tibet); however, the film anglicised its female love-interest by having her portrayed by a white woman, Sondra, who is the daughter of the British man who founded Shangri-la, yet it still emphasised Sondra's inability to leave utopia. In the film, when another female character, Maria, tries to leave Shangri-la, Maria is struck down by accelerated ageing and perishes. In the novel, Lo-Tsen also ages rapidly outside of Shangri-la and subsequently dies. While the men can leave this land for British politics, women must reside in Shangri-la to achieve love, thereby demonstrating their disinterest in the political and economic sphere.

The film *Mutiny on the Bounty* also constructed female love-interests exiled by race and place.[34] The romantic interlude halfway through the film stands in marked contrast to the claustrophobic climate of the boat on which the bulk of the film takes place and where mutinous tensions are on the rise. Once the *Bounty* docks off Tahiti, Lieutenant Fletcher Christian and his friend Roger Byam cavort with two Tahitian women whose white cotton swim shorts somehow made it past the British Board of Film Censors. Fletcher as the dominant and more dashing figure allies himself with 'Maimiti, the grand-daughter of Hiti Hiti'. Hiti Hiti is the chief of the Tahitians that the Englishmen are trading with, indicating that Maimiti is not without status among her people. Yet the submission of her own status to Fletcher is key from their very first meeting when Byam translates her first words to Fletcher: 'She says, "You must be a king in your own country"', as Maimiti looks at Fletcher adoringly. When Christian leads the mutiny against Captain Bligh and then is forced to flee to a remote and inhospitable island to avoid trial for treason, Maimiti flees with him, giving up her happy homeland and her place within it. This goodbye does not elicit a comment in the film, as it occurs entirely off-screen. In contrast, Byam, who has also taken up with a Tahitian girl, Tehanni, goes back to Britain to face a trial and an eventual pardon. He says goodbye to Tehanni and they do not discuss her returning with him. She simply has no place, other than on the island, and her presence on-screen ends with his departure.

Similarly in *The Middle of the Road* by Philip Gibbs, Bertram the unemployed ex-soldier, is tortured by his love for his aristocratic wife Joyce, but finds comfort in the arms of a recently impoverished woman. Bertram journeys to Russia to document the plight of the poverty-stricken people there and takes up with a former Russian princess named Nadia. Nadia's title and aristocratic status carries a potential threat to Bertram's own status, but this princess is impoverished as a result of the war. Her parents are exiled from society and forced to live in a 'dilapidated building ... smelling of bad drains'. The princess herself is dressed in a 'shabby frock, in boots that would have been slung over a garden wall by any English tramp'. [35] She is also entirely devoted to Bertram and his socialist beliefs. When he tells her he wants to make his life with her, she responds, 'you are one of the great lovers of the world. How proud I am to be your handmaid! I will help you to do your work for poor humanity. Every word you write shall be a light to my love for you.' [36] Clearly, the princess offers only balms for any existing insecurities. Nadia offers up two 'truths' to Bertram: she is unencumbered by a performance of wealth or class, and due to this she is able to freely express her true love for Bertram and her support for his own working goals.

Margaret Kennedy's bestseller *The Constant Nymph* (1924) was remade as a film three times, once in 1928 with the popular British heartthrob Ivor Novello and then again in 1933 by the well-known director Basil Dean, and again in Hollywood in 1943. The novel featured a female protagonist made both desirable and marginalised through age, place, and class. Tessa Sanger is a pre-teen, penniless daughter who lives with her eccentric father, the great composer Sanger, and his other children from multiple marriages in a remote part of the Austrian Tyrol. The 1933 film emphasises the remoteness of their home to great effect while also highlighting the ruffian appearance of the unkempt children. [37] Tessa is in love with Sanger's young friend Lewis Dodd, who sees her as nothing but a child until he himself falls in love with Tessa's proper and upper-class older cousin Florence. After Florence reveals herself as preoccupied with his financial and social success as a composer, Dodd realises how precious are Tessa's innocence and her lack of desire for social or economic prestige. He objects to her learning the value of money or manners, and specifically the finishing school that Florence has forced Tessa into attending, saying, 'She was very nearly perfect before she went there'. Florence tells him she hates him. He responds, 'Women like you are fond of saying that. It means nothing. You have pretty ways. You go about the earth as if it belonged to you, but you'd eat dirt to get the man you want.' [38] Dodd and Tessa then run away together and in a decidedly unhappy ending Tessa dies from a weak heart shortly after they are reunited.

The book and both films were incredibly popular and Tessa's tragic devotion was a marketable aspect of it. Yet this marketability was not without discomfort, due to the character's young age. The exhibitors' book for the 1933 film advised theatres, 'In the ads it is wise to stress the youthful love angle with honest emotional copy, and to steer away from any temptation to make Tessa's great yearning for Lewis anything but a most natural, beautiful and enduring thing.'[39] One man responding to Mayer's survey in 1945 recounted his own identification with the 1933 remake:

> The remake of the *Constant Nymph*, tells you how a young girl in Pigtails falls for an older man than herself, who is a composer. The same thing has happened to me. It was last year when I went to a big job, in the Isle of Man, My Landlady had a beautiful Daughter, who was no more than sixteen, she was also in pigtails, and she fell head over heels in love with me. I tried to avoid her, but couldn't, until I came across to England again, she still writes to me, I am not a composer but a great lover of music, any kind of music, I sometimes make up little tunes in my head, I think it is a coincidence.[40]

The respondent, who identifies himself as a 26-year-old third-class cook and a Scotsman, seems as eager to identify as a musician as he does to claim a romance with a teenager. Such narrative and character associations were no doubt what cinema exhibitors hoped to avoid in early advertising of the film. The film's earnest equation between desire, true love, and innocence did not always sit easy with some, yet was undoubtedly appealing to others.

The cinema exhibitors' estimation of the audience's discomfort with adolescent love coupled with the perseverance of the theme across popular film and fiction raises a number of interesting points (worthy of their own study), but in particular it highlights the marginal place of the family within the popular formula.[41] The young innocent girls that increasingly populated the pages and screen were not easily associated with motherhood and indeed mothers seldom appeared in the narratives discussed. This absence was a departure from nineteenth-century narratives that often elevated the role of the mother. Working-class melodramas had entire plots centred on a woman's role as a mother as she sought to protect or retrieve her children from the wealthier villain.[42] Joyce Pollard in *The Middle of the Road* is one of the few characters introduced at the outset as a mother, yet her child dies immediately after childbirth and she seems stubbornly unaffected by this. Even Lady Tybar in *If Winter Comes*, who is described as having a face attractive to children, has no children herself.[43] The wife of Dr Martin Arrowsmith of *Arrowsmith* is a spunky nurse who suffers a miscarriage and is rendered sterile as a result, although this frees her to help her husband in his work of stopping the spread of tropical diseases. In part, this absence of motherhood was likely because these women were main characters subject to a star-crossed love and numerous tribulations that would have seemed especially scandalous to censors, if not audiences, if children were involved. The tragedy at the centre of the film *Anna Karenina* (1935), starring Garbo again, was undoubtedly Anna's inability to see her son after she chooses to live with the man she loves rather than the fact that her husband refused to grant her a divorce.

Further reasons for the absence of mothers can be traced to the controversy surrounding motherhood in the interwar period. Susan Pedersen and Stephen Brooke have illuminated the political, social, and economic meanings of motherhood in the interwar period. Women advocates, as Pedersen notes, struggled to tie the state's nascent welfare system to the role of the mother rather than to a male breadwinner wage; while Brooke has charted the conflict over women's access to abortion and birth control in a period when Marie Stopes's marriage guide *Married Love* was a bestseller that discussed sex for pleasure, not motherhood.[44] Motherhood was a political and economic issue in the interwar period and as such did not fit with the apolitical construction of romance that popular film and fiction promoted. Men and masculinity instead become the end result of the woman's desire. As Arrowsmith's wife Leila remarks to him tearfully after losing her baby, 'Now I can't have a baby. I'll have to bring you up. Make a great man that everyone will wonder at.' The masculinity of her husband and her heterosexual marriage becomes Leila's focus, rather than children.

Working for love, not money

One of the most interesting and common figures in film and fiction popular with British audiences was the working woman who gave up both her independent means of acquiring money and social prestige for love. Although narratives that brought wealth and love to female love-interests who had neither continued to exist, an important difference began to emerge in the interwar period in regard to the economic status of women at the outset of popular low and middlebrow works. Women on the screen and within novels often reflected the experience of women in the '"smart" modern world' by having economic and social status to lose. Working women were evident on-screen and on the pages. Yet women in popular novels and films still had to ultimately prove themselves willing to sacrifice all this for love. The threat of the working woman's social and economic mobility was effectively arrested in this movement and in some cases the trajectory took a turn downward. Although the epilogue often materially rewarded this sacrifice on the part of women, the moment of renunciation became increasingly significant in this period and replayed across films and novels. The relationship established between economic and social loss with the gaining of love in these narratives was effectively entrenched by the end of the 1930s.

One of the most well-known examples of a woman who gave up her work for love was the title character of the film *Camille*. The novel by Alexandre Dumas was remade as a film three times in the interwar period. The 1921 silent version starred Rudolph Valentino, but by far the most popular film was the 1936 version adapted by *Lost Horizon*'s writer James Hilton and starring Greta Garbo. Garbo was adept at playing the tragic woman willing to throw everything to the wind for love. The decision Garbo's Camille makes is all the more painful as the film dwells upon what she is giving up. Camille is a courtesan in nineteenth-century Paris who must continually secure the affection of a wealthy male patron in order to maintain her lifestyle and manage her considerable debts. At the outset of the film Camille is cynical about her work and both paints herself, and is painted by others, as insincere as a result of this effort to secure wealth. She says to Armand Duval, the man of only a moderate income who she eventually falls in love with, 'I'm not always sincere. One can't be in the world, you know.' She uses her skills to secure the patronage of the wealthy Baron de Varville. A jealous rival for the Baron's affection tells him about Camille, 'She has the reputation of being one of the most extravagant girls in Paris, as well as one of the most insincere… She's the kind who says one thing and thinks another.' Camille's desire to secure wealth is portrayed as a performance that must be engaged in order to secure her goal, but does not allow her to reveal her true self or obtain true love. Part of Camille's willingness to engage in this performance is explained to the audience as the result of her former poverty growing up on a farm and then working in a linen shop. Much had changed since her early days in the city, including her name from Marguerite to Camille, further evidence of the dislocation of her true self caused by her economic aspirations. With Armand, notably, she is called Marguerite.[45]

The central narrative of the film is driven by Marguerite's discovery of her love for Armand and her related abandonment of wealth and its attendant male patronage. Armand stands in stark contrast to the people surrounding

Marguerite. He is fairly quiet and reserved, and when he attends a party that she throws, is generally disgusted by her friends who are intent on eating and dancing. The film contrasts the loud and vulgar consumption of Marguerite's friends, rotund and seated at a table piled high with food, with Armand's quiet reserve. Armand expresses his desire to take Marguerite away from a lifestyle that he considers unhealthy and which seems to be affecting the weak health of Marguerite. She is tempted but learns of his income of 7,000 francs a year and informs him that she spends that amount in a month. He responds, 'Marguerite, you need love more than you need money just now', painting them as mutually exclusive. The next scene of the film illustrates the extent of her work for Baron de Varville, who is portrayed as a cruel possessive man. He pays her debt of 40,000 francs for her but only after slapping her and implying she is a prostitute. He abandons Marguerite and she heads off into the country with Armand. From there, the film dwells upon the wholesome atmosphere of Armand's village and modest home. Marguerite's health starts to recover and it is clear that she no longer has to pretend to love in order to obtain money. Her true love and physical and mental happiness are connected to a lack of wealth.

Yet the ideal life of the country does not last long and Marguerite's past work comes to haunt her. Armand is suspicious of her. Her past performances and her preoccupation with wealth are difficult to forget and he is prone to jealousy. She secretly sells her jewels, which leads to suspicious behaviour as she disguises this and prompts an argument. In the argument, Marguerite utters the phrase quoted at the opening of this chapter and declares her willingness to abandon everything, including wealth, for Armand. He asks that fateful question, 'You mean you'd give up everything for me?', and she responds 'everything in the world. Everything. Never be jealous again. Never doubt that I love you more than the world – more than myself.' Indeed, Marguerite further proves this after Armand's father visits her and begs her to give up Armand so that he can maintain his reputation and his career. Realising that she is damaging Armand's social and economic livelihood, she mounts one last performance when she tells him that she is tired of the little house, the boring life, and the lack of money. She tells him she's going back to the Baron and Armand is bitterly angry, saying, 'your heart is a thing that can be bought and sold … But when it came to a choice the jewels and carriages that he could give you were worth more than my love, my devotion, my life'. The film ends with Armand finally seeing through her performance and the motivation behind it and returning to where she is living out her last days with the debt collectors literally at her door. They reconcile before she dies. In this way, the 1936 film departed from the 1921 version, where Camille is portrayed as rather more heartless and dies penniless and alone.[46] The 1936 version offered up more of a happy ending in the final, although tragic, exchange of love.

Marguerite gives up her means of earning money for love, and her wage earning is constructed in the film as a performance that hides her desire for true love. The attention to the clothes, extravagant homes, parties, and food that *Camille* dwells upon made obvious connections to the newly consumer-driven interwar period, with its multiple goods for sale and its modern ideas about working women and sexual relations. These modern ideas were contained in Marguerite's abandonment of her own particular work and her commitment to Armand's moderate lifestyle in the country. Yet the narrative ultimately demands that Marguerite not simply slip a notch in the scale of comfort but that instead she gives up everything for love even, as she says, herself. In this way the film constructed love again as something removed from class, politics, and society and granted it the similarly timeless kiss of death.

A year after *Camille* was released a picture with a similar lesson regarding love and wealth was the third most popular film in Britain.[47] The American film *A Star Is Born* (1937) featured a farm girl from North Dakota with the inauspicious name of Esther Blodgett who leaves her farm for the bright lights and big city of Hollywood.[48] Esther finds the reality of being a star in Hollywood discouraging and expensive until she meets the film star Norman Maine, who falls in love with her. He gets her an audition with a big film company and her own career ascends just as his own is declining, partly due to his constant drinking. The film follows their trials and tribulations as they marry and Norman's drinking spirals out of control.

The beginning of the film emphasises both Esther's relative poverty and her personal ambitions to become a star. She takes rooms at a boarding house in Hollywood for $6 a week and we later learn that she is $24 in debt to the manager who is too soft-hearted to collect. Eventually an assistant director, Danny McGuire, whom she befriends and who struggles to find work for himself, finds her a job as a waitress at a party given by a director. She waits on different film studio executives in a demure black-and-white maid's uniform and tries out different accents as she serves hors d'oeuvres. (See Figure 3.1.) The ambitions of Esther, which were on display in the first part of the film and in her first moments as a waitress at the party, subside when she meets her love-interest, Norman Maine. Instead of trying out her accents and displaying her desire to become a star Esther simply offers him an hors d'oeuvre, demurely casting her eyes downward. When Maine asks her what she would pick off the

Esther Blodgett as a waitress at a party, hoping to meet a producer, and where   **3.1**
she ultimately meets troubled actor Norman Maine in *A Star Is Born* (1937).

tray, Esther seems embarrassed and says, 'Oh I don't know', her confidence and ambition clearly melted away in the face of the man who would be her husband.

Maine is intrigued by Esther and follows her into the kitchen where she is putting plates away. In this scene, her position as a worker at the party is contrasted with Maine's current girlfriend, who has looked on as Maine first met Esther. Esther wears her severe maid's outfit while Maine's date enters the kitchen wearing symbols of wealth, including a gold lamé dress, jewels, and perfectly coiffed hair. Maine's girlfriend accuses him of infidelity and they break up. Maine then playfully makes Esther leave with him in a rush by breaking all the plates she is putting away. Esther continues to act in a shy manner with Maine in their whirlwind first moments and does not display her ambitions. We realise she must have told him she wants to be a star off-screen when he says to her as he drops her off at her boarding house, 'Do you realise that all I know about you is that you're foolish enough to want to go into pictures?' The film tries to emphasise that Esther is not merely using Maine's connections. Maine, however, immediately takes it upon himself to phone his producer in the middle of the night while drunk and recommend he take on Esther, stating 'She's got that sincerity and honestness [*sic*] that makes great actors'. Maine, like the viewer is intended to, sees Esther as honest and forthright. Her ambitions are not initially problematic in the film and Maine with his own clout and security only wants to help her.

Through Maine's efforts, Esther comes to star opposite him in a film entitled *Enchanted Hour*. However, as the producer listens to the comments of the audience as they leave the theatre, it becomes clear that Esther is the real star of the film and not Maine. The studio hires her and her name is changed to Vicky Lester. Maine is proud of her abilities and shortly after this, and before he realises the true decline of his own star status, they are married. Their honeymoon takes place far from their working world of film in a towed camper in what looks like northern California. In the scenes of the honeymoon, set against a mountainous grandeur emphasising a 'natural' state, they both occupy traditional gendered work patterns. Maine drives the car while Esther makes dinner on the little stove in the caravan. After the honeymoon, Maine attempts to perpetuate this idyllic world when they return to Hollywood and he buys her an expansive home with a garden and pool telling her, 'This is our castle. It used to be in the air. And we'll never use any words like contracts and pictures and careers. When we come in those gates we'll check the studio outside.' Work and ambition are literally displaced by conventional domesticity. Yet this is not to be, as their friend Oliver the producer and a press man quickly show up at the house to publicise their marriage. The first inklings to Maine that his own star has dimmed are when the photographer says in a surly manner, 'What they're asking for is exclusives of Miss Lester … alone'. Oliver and Maine take this moment to discuss Maine's career and Maine asks him, 'Do you think I'm slipping?' Oliver responds, 'Can you take it? The tense is wrong. You're not slipping. You've slipped.' Oliver then informs him that he has a new film for Esther with her in a starring role.

What follows next is a montage of scenes that dramatises Maine's decline in fortune and Vicky's ascendance. A billboard with Maine's name above the film's title *Enchanted Hour* is papered over by Vicky's name instead, visually obliterating his career in favour of hers, and a film magazine reports that Oliver's studio has ended its contract with Maine as well. The film then cuts to a scene of Norman playing indoor golf in his room by himself, rushing to the phone when it rings and saying sarcastically, 'No Miss Lester isn't home yet. No I'm not the butler but I can take a message just as well as he can, honest.' When Esther comes home they are portrayed as very much in love yet suffering a peculiar role reversal in regard to work and gender. Maine comments on how tired she must be from work as he takes her jacket and tells her genially enough that he's made a dinner for them: 'I've been learning to cook in my spare time'. This scene of happy reconciliation is disturbed, however, by a mailman who calls Norman 'Mr Lester'. Norman pauses and looks at him angrily. This role reversal is emphasised as tragic in the film, and as something that prevents the fruition of what would otherwise be a happy and healthy relationship. Normative heterosexual love is constructed through its very absence on the screen.

The rest of the film documents Maine's decline as he begins to drink again and causes a series of public upheavals, not the least of which involves him showing up drunk and disorderly at the Academy Awards while Esther is giving her acceptance speech for best actress. Esther takes all of these scenes in her stride and appears concerned for him, taking his shoes off while he is passed out after the awards and while her Oscar lies on the floor beside them. (See Figure 3.2.) She eventually must bail Maine out of jail, standing beside a dishevelled Maine in her expensive-looking clothing and promising the judge to take care of him. The headline of the paper the next day reads 'Norman Maine released to custody of wife Vicky Lester after drunk conviction'. Vicky's economic ascendance is further extended to include her influence in the halls of justice. The climax comes when Oliver's brash assistant, Matt Libby, explicitly describes the change in economic roles between Maine and Esther to Maine's face: 'You've fixed yourself nice and comfortable. You can live off your wife now.' Maine punches Libby, thus marking this arrangement out as thoroughly unacceptable through his own violent response.

All of this results in Vicky deciding to give up her career as an actress. She tells Oliver while Maine lies in bed in the next room silently listening to their conversation, 'I can't do any more pictures. I'm going away for good with Norman.' Oliver implores her, 'You can't do that Vicky. You're at the very peak of your success and you've worked so hard to achieve it.' Vicky, however, will not be swayed and argues, 'That's what's been wrong. I've thought it all out. Maybe if I hadn't been away from him so much, last night and what went before, it wouldn't have happened. I know it's too late to think about that now but it may not be too late to go away with him and start over somewhere.' Oliver says, 'It's your life you're giving up'. Vicky makes this ultimate sacrifice, saying, 'So I can try to give Norman back his'. As she says this, the camera cuts to Norman who closes his eyes as he hears this. She goes on to ask Oliver, 'Can you honestly tell me I'm wrong to do it?' He says quietly and with feeling, 'No Vicky, I can't honestly tell you that.' As Oliver prepares to leave, he says goodbye to Vicky in way that acknowledges her change in status through her name, 'Goodbye Vicki Lester. You were a grand girl. Good luck Mrs Norman Maine', and kisses her on the forehead.[49]

This scene is remarkable in conveying the mutually exclusive relationship that wealth and love increasingly occupied in interwar popular culture. Esther's own economic success is seen as incompatible with her ability to truly love her husband. She instead gives up her 'life', which is equated with her wage-earning status, in order to maintain Maine's and allow him to presumably take the role as the breadwinner. The moments when he is happiest in the film are

3.2   Esther at the end of her big night, removing Norman's shoes, after he shows up drunk at the Academy Awards ceremony, and causes a scene when she wins in the best actress category.

those where he is in that role on their honeymoon. The film condones this through Oliver's awed and reverent reaction to Esther's decision. Yet Maine himself cannot accept the burden he has become and drowns himself in the ocean in a way that makes Esther and others think it is accidental. Esther is shattered by his death and decides to continue with her decision to give up pictures, but is talked back into it by her grandmother. Nevertheless in the final scene Esther makes it clear that she still values her husband's status over her own, as she says into the microphone at her comeback at the Chinese Theatre and with tears shining in her eyes, 'Hello everybody. This is Mrs Norman Maine.' Esther's return to film and wage-earning status is legitimated only by her public commitment to her husband. The tragedy of her husband occurred nevertheless, we as the audience know, because of this previous upending of the masculine breadwinner ideal within their marriage.

The preponderance of this downward shift in the female character's role was such that even bestselling novels felt its effect when they were adapted into films. Warwick Deeping's *Sorrell and Son* (1925) only briefly features the woman that Sorrell's son Kit marries; yet the 1933 film granted her both a larger role and an occupation that she abandons.[50] After Sorrell diligently devotes his life to funding Kit's education, Kit goes to medical school and meets Molly, the girl who lives above him, when he is driven to distraction by the sound of her typewriter. She is a pretty and feisty modern girl who moves about decisively and wears sensible if somewhat dull clothing. She is making her way in the world writing books and articles. When he offers her any assistance she may need, she retorts, 'I'm quite capable of standing alone thank you very much.' Kit and Molly nevertheless develop a deep friendship. The viewer finds out that Molly writes books about free love and does not believe in marriage. Kit asks her, 'Why do you write such muck? You don't believe it.' In response Molly admits to Kit that she loves him, but that she loves her freedom more. It is revealed that Kit has been telling her he loves her for years and has been enduring her rejection. He makes it clear that he will not be asking her again.

Predictably enough, this all changes when heterosexual love is discovered. Kit performs a surgery in the hospital that is a great success. However, afterwards he realises that there is a small puncture in his surgical glove. The doctors worry that he may contract blood poisoning as a result and he is hospitalised. A telegram is sent to his father in Kit's rooms and Molly happens to be there when he receives it. As they wait to hear of Kit's health, Molly breaks down and confesses to Sorrell how much Kit means to her. Talking at first to Sorrell, she declares that Kit must be all right: 'it means so much to you. And me'. 'To you?' says Sorrell and she replies passionately 'Yes. It means everything. Everything.' At this moment Kit comes back to the rooms with his arm in a sling. Molly excuses herself hastily and the scene cuts to her in her room upstairs crying in the dark with her head in a pillow. Kit following her says, 'Don't cry. I'm not worth it.' She, crying, says, 'I know. For a minute, I thought you were.' He says 'And now?', still crying and with her face away from him, she sobs, 'You'd better ask me to marry you again before I change my mind.' 'Oh darling', says Kit and kisses her. She collapses into his kiss with her head thrown back as he looms over her. The next time we see Molly she is wearing a sparkling and feminine evening gown, rather than the practical clothes of a working girl. She is also filmed in soft focus, the stark edges of the working girl blurred. No more references are made to her writing, which considering the topic has probably gone by the wayside. Instead she appears, in every way, a supportive non-working doctor's wife.

In this moment, then, Molly's role as a wage earner is effectively dismantled in the face of love. Not only is it dismantled; this wage earning and its politics are actively constructed as a performance that had to be abandoned in order for Molly to reveal and express her true love. Molly's character and the process of falling in love are also important within the narrative as a means of redeeming the injustices inflicted by other female characters. Molly, in contrast to Sorrell's scheming ex-wife and the overbearing woman who owns the hotel that he had to work at, is not interested in gaining a man for his money. Rather, she gives up any claims to independent social mobility for love. In this way, the threat of the working girl, not to mention her modern ideas about marriage, were contained and dismantled presumably in order to make her appealing to the audience. This vulnerability, or this truth, which simultaneously makes her a desiring subject and an object of desire, is directly related to Molly's abandonment of claims to economic gain and social power.

The Thirty-Nine Steps (1935), directed by Alfred Hitchcock and based on the popular novel by John Buchan, provided a similar narrative. Pamela is introduced to the viewer from a distance, wearing glasses, reading, and smartly attired in her own compartment on the train. She is haughty and repeatedly gives up the hero Richard Hannay to the police, both in the train and at a political rally where she sees him again. Her involvement with the police and politics indicates her role as an active member of the nation and the public sphere. However, through a series of circumstances, she is later handcuffed to him as he escapes. Hannay drags her after him in his escape, threatening not too convincingly to rough her up as she goes. Pamela's appearance is increasingly dishevelled and tender moments occur when Hannay remedies this by absentmindedly fixing her falling hair and hanging her soiled pantyhose on the fireplace. Eventually Pamela realises that he is telling the truth about being at the centre of a vast conspiracy and the viewer is assured of her own 'true' tender feelings for him, feelings she had been resisting in her pursuit of upright citizenship. She abandons her faith in the law and places it, rather, upon Hannay who, like Kit, becomes the primary conduit of action within the story.

The above depiction of Pamela as well as other heroines I have examined reflected the anxieties of the interwar period about the newfound status of women within the economy and, by extension, the nation. Popular culture obfuscated the burgeoning roles of women by emphasising to both men and women the pleasures of abandoning this modern role. Pamela's performance of citizenship is thus undone in *The Thirty-Nine Steps*, as she abandons that role for one that rewards her with the love of a man who in turn can save the country. Likewise Esther, Marguerite, and others are also presented as choosing love rather than money. That money often rewarded this choice does not diminish that fateful decision. Time and time again, the film and fiction most popular in Britain in the 1920s and 1930s stressed the pleasures of love over work and citizenship. Indeed, as we turn to wealthy women, this pleasure became all the more heady as the scale of what was abandoned grew.

Poor rich women

While working women gave up their independent ways for love, wealthy women provided an even more dramatic shift in the narratives as they staked their inheritances and the only way of life they had known on their commitment to love. This concept of inherited wealth may have had particular resonance with British audiences, but it is impossible to gauge this except by inference from the popularity of certain films and novels. Certainly it is evident that the image of wealthy women choosing love and the sometimes-penniless husband rather than money appealed to audiences of film and fiction alike.

The Middle of the Road (1923) makes the downward shift of circumstances for its protagonist's wife, Joyce, a key aspect of the novel's happy ending. Bertram and Joyce are completely at odds with each other in regard to both wealth and politics. Bertram's socialist leanings stand in stark contrast to those of the wealthy young Joyce Pollard, formerly Ottery. Joyce's family is wealthy, aristocratic, and conservative, with multiple residences including the grand estate Holme Ottery. Her father is active in both politics and business, part of what Gibbs commonly refers to as the 'men of the Old Order … keeping a grip on the machinery of Government, arranging new balances of power'.[51] Wealthy and spoiled, Joyce's character seems to be the epitome of the modern and shocking flapper. Yet, far from being politically uninterested, as most flappers were portrayed in the popular press, Joyce is profoundly outspoken about her own political and economic views. We are first introduced to Joyce in her convalescence from a miscarriage, when she declares her desire to see her good friend Kenneth:

> Joyce, with absurd little bows on her night-dress, excited, thrusting off the bedclothes, stretching out for a cigarette, saying 'Damn' when she dropped the match, laughing when her mother fastened up a little button which revealed too much, announcing her intention of having a tea-party for her 'best boy', careless of shocking this old-fashioned mother.[52]

Joyce's inability to show much feeling towards the event of her miscarriage is an indication of her general lack of sympathy throughout the novel. She is either ambivalent or cutting in her views of the ex-soldier's plight even though Bertram counts as one of these men. Joyce responds to his assessment of the war and the economic order that results, saying, 'you're always harking back to the old war! Let's forget about it. We're talking about the present situation. The working people are thoroughly lazy, utterly demoralised, and infected with Bolshevism. They ought to be kept in their places with a strong hand.'[53] For Joyce and the people that surround her, the interwar unemployment threatens the old order, which had been central to her economic and social foundation. Thus the narrative sets up the struggle between Joyce and Bertram as the struggle between those who fought in the war and received little economic recognition and those who did not fight in the war and harboured the money. Joyce's character heightens Bertram's exile from both the economy and the political and social order. This polarity is further brought home when Joyce's father is forced to sell Holme Ottery because of financial difficulties. In Joyce's estimation, one of those difficulties is her father's annual payment to her and Bertram: Bertram's inability to find a job makes her father's payment necessary and she demands that he finds work.

However, it is the happy ending and a seemingly impossible and somewhat hollow resolution between the two that highlights some of the strange dynamics of the magic moment. In response to Joyce's demands and increasing hostility, they separate and Bertram goes to Russia and meets the impoverished Princess Nadia. Although the narrative bestowed upon Bertram the 'best woman he had ever known', Nadia does not survive the story. She dies of typhus eleven pages later and Bertram is beset by a fever. Throughout the fever, Bertram calls out Joyce's name and eventually she is called to his bedside. In her re-entrance into the narrative it is clear that something in Joyce's life has changed. When Bertram's socialist friends see Joyce, 'She was very pale, and looked ill, but wonderfully young and elegant and exquisite', and when she is told about him calling out her name, 'A little mist came into [her] eyes. "I don't deserve his remembrance. I've been rotten to him", she said humbly.' She tells him that she has returned and 'put her arms around him and wept, so that her tears fell on his face'. Bertram asks how England is and she responds:

> 'England's still there. Holme Ottery's sold. I've a little house close by. We'll go back and live there. It's ready for our home-coming.'
>   'Home-coming!' said Bertram. 'How good that sounds! I've been wandering alone since you left me, Joyce. Always damned lonely.'
>   'I'm with you now', said Joyce. 'Body and soul, Bertram. The past is dead, and I'm changed.'

Joyce has indeed changed. From caustic, haughty, and aristocratic to humbled, crying, and in slightly diminished circumstances, Joyce's character has undergone a fundamental transformation. The sale of her family's estate home do not necessarily indicate a newfound love of socialism or descent into the poverty of Princess Nadia, but somehow this experience of loss allows for a declaration of love and the happy ending to be realised. Bertram, with the work he had been writing on in Russia and Germany, had also already been assured of work. Thus Bertram was resituated in the narrative as a wage earner and a man confident in his beliefs, while Joyce has been humbled, her body and soul, her innermost truth stripped of economic pretension, and now belonging to Bertram.

The title character of *Queen Christina*, played by Greta Garbo, was the subject of Britain's seventh most popular film in 1934.[54] The film also produced a female character whose heterosexual appeal was dependent upon a dramatic shift in her economic and social status. This fictional account of the real-life seventeenth-century Norwegian Queen depicts Christina at the outset of the film as extremely masculine. She wears man's clothing, strides about her home followed by two huge Great Dane dogs, and loves riding horses and hunting. She is well read, has an old crotchety man as her attendant rather than a ladies maid, and does not wish to marry. (See Figure 3.3.) Yet her marriage is of great concern to her court, which wishes to use the marriage as a means of securing a beneficial foreign alliance and ensuring Sweden's continued military success.

Queen Christina in masculine dress at the outset of the film
                          Queen Christina (1933, [UK 1934]).

Christina herself is portrayed as embodying Sweden and its military and financial successes. Yet she is chafing under the constraints of her ongoing duties, saying angrily to her adviser, 'My days and nights are given up to the service of the state. I'm so cramped with duty that I have to read a book in the middle of the night.' She is especially resentful of the clamour of the politicians and military men to continue with European wars and to pressure her into marriage. In a stirring speech, Garbo embodies this frustration, exclaiming: 'Spoils, glory, flags and trumpets. What is behind these high-sounding words? Death and destruction. Triumphals of crippled men. Sweden victorious and a ravaged Europe. An island in a dead sea. I tell you I want no more of it. I want for my people security and happiness.' Such a sentiment may have raised images of World War I with European audiences. Yet Queen Christina's real resentment lies with the pressure of the politicians and the people themselves for her to marry. Her chancellor admonishes her to marry, saying, 'You cannot die an old maid'. Christina's response highlights the particularly masculine role she plays: 'I have no intention, chancellor. I shall die a bachelor.'

In response to these pressures, Christina escapes the court for a hunting trip with her trusty old attendant Aage. On this diversion she encounters the

Queen Christina in decidedly more feminine dress,   **3.4**
preparing for the arrival of her lover Antonio at her palace.

Spanish envoy on its way to Stockholm to represent the marriage proposal
of their king to her. The Spanish carriage becomes stuck in the snow and she
directs them out of the situation. Christina's command of the situation as well
as her masculine attire causes the Spanish ambassador, Antonio, to mistake her
for a boy. He tips her a coin for her trouble, which she takes in surprise as the
camera focuses on her likeness on one side of the coin. Here, her monopoly
of both nation and economy are perfectly captured.

Christina and Antonio meet again that night at an inn where both are
sheltering from a winter storm. Christina has secured the best room in the
inn, telling her servant to give the owner $10 for a $3 room. Antonio and
his entourage arrive and he is introduced to Christina, still masquerading as
a man. They talk of many things and Antonio is impressed by her considerable knowledge of the arts in Spain. They also, under the guise of her masculinity, discuss the differences between Spain and Sweden in highly eroticised
ways. Antonio remarks, 'You understand I admire your country. It's rugged
and strong and impressive. It has all the virile qualities.' Yet he ultimately
declares that Spain has better lovers, saying, 'You cannot serenade a woman in
a snowstorm. All the graces in the art of love, elaborate approaches that will

make the game amusing, can only be practised in those countries that quiver in the heat of the sun.' After this loaded discussion the owner suggests that the two 'gentlemen' share a room. Christina tries to refuse but finally relents as Antonio takes offence. The night predictably results in his discovering her gender but not her identity as Queen. They share a few passionate nights as the inn is snowed in. Before they leave she promises him that they will meet again at the palace but does not reveal her true role.

Back at the palace it is clear that love has transformed the Queen. This is expressed primarily through costuming, as for the first time in the film she is wearing a dress. She stands in front of a mirror in a bejewelled gown, trying on necklaces and generally fussing with her appearance. (See Figure 3.4.) Two lady maids wait on her while the aged Aage leans against a wall sulking and snorting. Heterosexual love has clearly transformed Christina from a masculine figure into a womanly one. When Queen Christina receives the envoy in her throne room, Antonio is clearly shocked to discover her role as ruler. Later in her private chambers she rushes to him excitedly, saying 'Antonio'. He, however, is clearly not happy with her role, bowing to her in a formal manner and stating his official business. Christina notes that he is angry and he replies, 'I appreciate a jest. A royal jest. However, with the diversion being over, may I conclude my mission to your unusual country?' He clearly feels that her superior status allowed her to make a joke of him and he laments, 'Why did you go out of your way to make me seem ridiculous?' She explains herself to him in a way that negates her own social and economic status yet elevates the heterosexual love he offered her: 'it had been so enchanting to be a woman, not a queen. Just a woman in a man's arms.' He asks her what she wants from him and she responds, 'I want back that room in the inn, that snow that fell, the warm fire and the sweet hours, beloved one.' Her desire to return to a time and place where her economic and social status was negligible allows him to takes her in his arms, and she throws her head back as they kiss.

Ultimately Christina chooses to commit herself entirely to a place where her status and wealth mean little. Under pressure from the peasants and her advisers to reject the Spaniards and marry someone of northern blood, she chooses to abdicate her throne, saying to the grief-stricken response of her court, 'I am grateful, but there is a voice in our souls that tells us what to do and we obey. I have no choice.' As such her soul and her heterosexual love are conflated and are removed from concerns about nation and wealth. She rides off to meet Antonio on a boat that will sail for his home in Spain, thus renouncing the strong and virile Sweden in favour of a hot-blooded and passionate country. However, when she arrives at the boat she discovers that Antonio has been fatally wounded in a duel with her former lover and treasurer. She gathers the dying Antonio in her arms and says, 'Are you in pain?'. He weakly responds, smiling, 'no, not now. Have you said goodbye to your country?' She says, 'Yes, to everything but you'. This moment mirrors many of the others I have discussed here in that the former queen renounces everything for the love embodied by the male figure. Even after Antonio dies, Christina chooses to sail for his home in Spain.

The message of *Queen Christina*, that women must abandon social and economic power for love, was echoed in other historical dramas from the period that focused on the lives of female royalty. Films like the American *The Private Lives of Elizabeth and Essex* (1939), as well as the British *Catherine the Great* (1934), both focused on the incompatibility of love with political and economic power; yet instead of featuring a royal figure who abandons her role at the centre of nation and economy these films document the struggle of these women to choose their duty to both over love.[55] Both protagonists are dramatically torn by this choice and the eventual decision to abandon love for duty is dramatised as a selfless one, yet one that will not necessarily bring personal happiness. Both Catherine and Elizabeth I are transformed into ornate symbols for the nation, a process that rejects their individual identity and subsumes this identity under the trappings of royalty and wealth. Thus love, as well as claims to individuality and the 'true' self, is renounced for the collective good. Even films such as *Victoria the Great* (1937) and its sequel (or remake) as *Sixty Glorious Years* in 1938, which revolved around the happy marriage of the Queen and Prince Albert, acknowledged and in some ways subverted their very obvious role reversal within their marriage.[56] In both films, it is the frustration of Albert with his curtailed role as the dominant figure in the marriage that is emphasised throughout and becomes the focus of the narrative. The film compensates for what both Victoria and Albert identify as a lack of appreciation for his talents by the masses and parliamentarians, by putting Albert's unacknowledged actions front and centre. Albert advises Victoria in matters both large and small on screen and his own contributions to the Great Exhibition of 1851 are amplified. Albert checks Victoria's impulsive decisions and brings moderation to her outlook.

These films and their message about gender, love, and nation are especially interesting in light of the abdication of King Edward VIII for the American divorcée Mrs Simpson in 1936. Edward's renouncement of the throne was cast in a very different light, prompting the creation of bodies such as Mass

Observation to measure what was anticipated to be a traumatic event for the masses. The release of *Victoria the Great* in 1937 and *Sixty Glorious Years* in 1938 promoted a vision of a monarchy and a marriage that coexisted and flourished. Yet this success was largely attributed in the films to a traditional gendered arrangement of power that functioned behind the outward exercise of limited feminine sovereign power. The story of Queen Victoria on film, in many ways, took up the messages housed in other popular portrayals of women in power. The humanising of this enduring monarch occurred within a film about her marriage and not the politics of her reign. The roles of a powerful female figure was consequently cast within this film and the others discussed as problematic at the very least, requiring considerable compromise and at times, outright diminishment, of their own roles in favour of their male love-interests.

A similar struggle between great wealth, power, and love appears in *The Sheik*, both in the book by E. M. Hull in 1919 and the silent movie in 1921, released in Britain in 1923.[57] At the outset of both narratives we are introduced to Diane Mayo, who is haughty and aristocratic, wears riding breeches, orders servants about, and rejects men. In the book she is described through the following exchange between an American and an Englishman: "'Not a very human girl', laughed the American. "She was sure meant for a boy and changed at the last moment. She looks like a boy in petticoats, a damned pretty boy – and a damned haughty one", he added, chuckling. "I overheard her this morning, in the garden, making mincemeat of a French officer".'[58] Aside from this evidence of her man-like behaviour, Diana also decides to mount an expedition into the desert, something disapproved of by both by her older brother and those representing 'proper' society. She is able to undertake the expedition regardless because of the incredible wealth bestowed by her parents and her coming of age. Her brother's guardianship had expired months earlier.

Diana's unfeminine behaviour, in terms of actions and wealth, is curtailed when the Sheik Ahmed kidnaps her. In Ahmed's possession Diana has to be broken – a breaking that involves leaving her with none of the wealth or power she possessed among her own people, yet simultaneously revealing her desire as her true aim in life. She is given only what Ahmed chooses to give her and she is also subject to his desire, a desire that seems explicitly about control. In the novel repeated scenes of his forcibly 'taking her' occur; in the film this is done less often but with a very effective closing of a bedroom curtain as she stands in front of the camera terrified.[59] Diana's economic, social, and sexual independence is stripped from her in a way that implies that these were simply a performance and that the real Diana and her love and longing were the truth within.

Diana grows to inexplicably love the Sheik and expresses this early in a revelation at the Sheik's potential deathbed that leaves her physically trembling, in a moment similar to those in *Sorrell and Son* and *The Middle of the Road*. The placement of the man on the deathbed, supine and vulnerable, seemed to have particular resonance in narratives of the interwar period. Undoubtedly, images and experiences of the war had highlighted the romantic tragedy of such a situation, and in many ways this moment seems to indicate the extent of the crisis of masculinity embodied in popular narratives. Here are instances of men that quite tangibly need to be restored through a declaration of love. While such images had been common in how women were conceived, such as in *Camille* and *The Constant Nymph*, the interwar period offers up men in similar positions but with less fatal outcomes. The deathbed moment paired the dynamic, downshifting of the woman's status with the upward-shifting status of the hero. As the woman declares the love that will end her position as a threat, the hero is restored from death. However, as mentioned before, this moment also pairs the dramatic 'reality' of death with the simultaneous 'reality' of love. In Diana's case she realises her love for Ahmed, marries him, and remains in the desert. We are clued into her future in the film's sequel *Son of the Sheik* (1926) where the actress Agnes Ayres reprised her role as Diana. In the sequel, Diana's character functions very much like a Victorian wife, trying to tame the patriarchal temper of her forbidding husband.[60] This particular plot was rehashed in the 1930s in films such as the American *Tarzan the Ape Man* (1932) which brought in 24,377 people to Portsmouth's Regent cinema and also featured a well-to-do British woman physically displaced from her social and economic background who grows to love her captor.[61] In *Tarzan the Ape Man* Jane abandons her role as part of an expedition hoping to secure ivory in the African jungles, in order to stay with Tarzan in the jungle and ultimately resides there in further sequels.[62]

This plot, then, was a staple of films popular in interwar Britain. Hitchcock, who often illustrated ambivalence towards the socially mobile girl, was demonstrating an adherence to this formula early in his career. Films like the silent *Champagne* (1928) featuring tremendously popular British actor Betty Balfour, introduced Betty as a wealthy and spoiled heiress living an indulgent life.[63] She uses and crashes her father's airplane in order to attend a party on a ship that her poorer love-interest, named as 'The Boy' in the casting credits, is on. Although her father fears that the Boy is interested in her only for her money, her wealth becomes problematic for the lovers. When Betty declares that she has arranged for them to marry, the Boy objects, 'You think your money entitles you to do all the arranging.' Betty responds angrily, 'My money enabled me to fly half across the Atlantic to join you.' This exchange ends their engagement, which is renewed later after Betty's father falsely tells her that he has lost his money and she embarks on a seedy life of work as a girl selling flowers. The Boy rescues her when she is most vulnerable, economically and sexually. His love for her is affirmed in spite of her absence of money. She, in turn, assures him that she loves him even with his absence of money. Love is achieved on both sides. Furthermore, the fortune is restored and parental approval bestowed. Hitchcock himself was not happy with the ending and considered the film to be 'dreadful'. He originally pictured a story where the girl is ruined in a whorehouse, but as he remembered, 'they thought it was much too, they didn't use the word "highbrow", but, oh, that wasn't entertainment'.[64] The connection between heterosexuality and love as a trade-off for a girl's abandonment of wealth and status could not exist in Hitchcock's alternate ending, and happy endings were firmly lodged in the domain of the middle or lowbrow.

Wealthy women thus were subjected to a similar abandonment of wealth and status that working women also experienced. Yet while the working girl gave up her wage-earning potential, the wealthy woman offered a much more dramatic image to readers and audiences as she really was often giving up the only way of life she had known. Her economic and social dislocation was often visibly dramatised through a change of geographic location as well as occasionally through the violent dismantling of her own wealth and status. For the wealthy women discussed here who lost their homes as well as their wealth and status, they really did have only love to gain in compensation. They had much more to give up for love, but through this process love was granted a very powerful status. This conference of love was constructed as adequate compensation for their loss, and in case audiences and readers questioned the validity of that exchange, villainous women presented the unsavoury alternative to choosing wealth and status over love. The role of the villainess clearly indicated that even the abandonment of great wealth for love was preferable to a life with wealth, but no love.

Villainous women

Nowhere within popular film and fiction during the interwar period was the mutually exclusive relationship between love and money made more apparent than through the roles of villainous women who strove for wealth at the expense of all else. Their roles provide a caution to readers and viewers as to the negative consequences of pursuing wealth and power over love. The fixation of female villains upon economic prosperity was communicated in popular film and fiction through their concern with class status and social mobility, as well as material beauty. Preoccupation with these was repeatedly presented as negative and was contrasted with their abandonment by the heroine in the magic moment. Consequently, the villainess allowed producers and consumers of popular narratives in the 1920s and 1930s to see love as the ultimate reward through her own example, clearly constructing love as something unrelated to material concerns.

The female villain in her various guises must have been an attractive and sensational figure to audiences. There is some evidence in the amplification of their roles from novels to film that producers and directors were just beginning to realise the visual appeal of the female villain in the interwar period. The villainess covered a range of highly visible roles, from sultry vamp to mannish lesbian, yet the female villain of the 1920s and 1930s must be distinguished from the femme fatale of 1940s film noir. The seemingly innocent woman revealed to be a female villain had not yet made the impact in the 1920s and 1930s that she would in the 1940s.[65] Novels such as *The Maltese Falcon* (1930) by Dashiell Hammett with the duplicitous Brigid O'Shaughnessy at its centre, and James Cain's *The Postman Always Rings Twice* (1934), with its tempestuous Cora tempting men to their doom, had indeed already been penned on the other side of the Atlantic, but did not reach the screen in Britain or the United States until the next decade. Instead, female villainy in the interwar period was largely envisioned as dangerous, yet recognisable through certain key characteristics.[66] The interwar villainess was subsequently seldom granted the intimacy with the hero that the lovely femme fatale later was, as her villainy was marked out early on.

The relatively early identification of the female villain in interwar film and fiction can be accounted for by the discussion in the previous chapter of the knowability of villainy in the interwar period. I argued there that villains could often hold positions of considerable power in institutions equated with Englishness, such as the military, business, or government. The proximity to these powerful institutions made his desire for wealth and power less obvious and effectively disguised it, while speaking to some of the concerns audiences in the post-World War I period had with the roles of real-life politicians and businessmen. Interwar narratives also spoke to audience concerns about women, although audiences at this point were not as concerned with the possibility of women possessing great political or social power as they would be during World War II. Likely this was because it was still highly unrealistic for women to gain access to these seats of power in the 1920s and 1930s. This possibility was only beginning to be acknowledged, more often in the realm of science fiction than anywhere else. By World War II, the more visible role of the mobilised woman on a variety of fronts would be paired with a proportionally greater fear of her ability to possess truly threatening secrets that could imperil the nation.

Sonya Rose's *Which People's War?* aptly demonstrates the potential threat that women posed to the nation during World War II. She argues that both female sexuality and foreigners could disrupt the stability of the British 'family which was actively conceived of in this period'.[67] Women were seen as potential and real threats through a combination of their sexual relations with non-British soldiers and their innate untrustworthiness, all of which made pillow talk a dangerous affair. This was a logical extension of women's increasingly public roles within the economy and the nation itself. Suspicions of women developed into a full-blown paranoia about just how much women knew of state secrets. Antonia Lant notes that the government mounted the 'Careless Talk' poster campaign early in the war because of fears about femininity and collaboration. Posters declaring, 'Keep Mum, She's not so dumb' gave way to ones that admonished soldiers to protect themselves from sexually transmitted diseases, spread by women.[68] Thus a much more treacherous version of femininity was rallied in the popular culture at the outset of the World War II than in the 1920s and 1930s. Even such films as *Mata Hari* (1931), about a female spy during World War I and starring Greta Garbo, highlighted her double life early on and then went on to provide a sympathetic portrayal of her conversion to the 'truth' of true love at the end of her life.[69] Her female villainy was the acknowledged topic of the film rather than the twist at the end, as later envisioned in film noir.

The narratives of the interwar period were not interested in camouflaging women's interest in money; instead they highlighted this early on as both unrealistic and dangerous. The real danger of the interwar villainess was that she would amass money at the expense of the heroic breadwinner. The obviousness that marked out most female villains in the interwar period was directly linked to their overt interest in wealth, making them more often a knowable villain than an unknowable one. Recall that the knowable male villain was most often a figure that performed an upper-class status in fairly unsuccessful and noticeable ways. This male villain was often portly or physically identified through weight, physical deformity, or elaborate dress. Female villains were similarly identified, but in their case overt female sexuality and expensive clothing such as diamonds and furs replaced the symbolic meaning of physical girth for men. The villainess's prominently displayed sexuality and extravagance was often noted by other characters in the film or novel as part of their strategy for wealth and power.

The character of Irma in the *Bulldog Drummond* series saw her role shifted significantly from book to film to emphasise the modern characteristics of the interwar villainess. Her role in the 1929 film was amplified and her appearance was one that emphasised her sexuality as well as her penchant for wealth. In the novels Irma is described as girlish with dark hair, and in the first novel she initially masquerades as Peterson's daughter. She is often in disguise, as her lover Peterson is a master of disguises himself. Irma is thus always vilified by her association with Peterson and takes part in his grand schemes of stealing diamonds and destroying Britain's economy. Yet, for all of Irma's own interest in wealth, in the novels she is very much in love with Peterson. However, in *The Female of the Species* (1928), the fifth Bulldog Drummond novel that followed up on the demise of Peterson, Irma takes on many of the traits of Peterson. After describing her initially as dark and pretty, Drummond goes on to outline her most dangerous traits:

> Far more probably would she be a wizened-up crone covered with spectacles, or a portly dame with creaking corsets. So much for her appearance. Her character is a thing to stand aghast at. She has the criminal instinct to its highest degree: she is absolutely without mercy: she is singularly able. How much of course, was her and how much Carl Peterson in the old days is a thing I don't know. But even if it was him principally to start with, she must have profited considerably by seeing him work. And a final point which is just as important if not more so than those I've already given, she must be a very wealthy woman.[70]

Irma debuted as a significant and wealthy villain in this novel, even though she had played a minor role in the earlier four novels. Perhaps because of this book's release the year before or because of an increased recognition of the cache of the female villain, the 1929 film adaptation of the first Bulldog book considerably enlarged Irma's role. Irma appears in the film in heavy make-up, as a bleached blonde in furs and diamonds and it is she, instead of Carl Peterson, who is the mastermind behind the villainous schemes.[71] Indeed, Peterson simply becomes her boy toy whom she manipulates with the promise of sexual favours in order to get her way. At one point, frustrated with her demands, Peterson embraces her, saying passionately, 'I'd go through anything for you', while she smiles deviously over his shoulder. Irma is clearly performing her desire for Peterson in order to achieve her goal of securing wealth.

Another important aspect of the villainess was her preoccupation with gaining and maintaining the social status that accompanies wealth. Mabel, the awful wife of the unfortunate Mark Sabre in *If Winter Comes*, is very much preoccupied with rank and putting forth to the world an appearance that indicates class status. While Sabre is saddled with Mr Fortune as the expansive villain at his workplace, Mabel is a much more insidious and constant presence in Sabre's home. The first instance of the novel that indicates that Mabel and Mark are poorly matched occurs when some of the local inhabitants, a farming family by the name of Wirks, are invited to their home for tea. The narrative notes, 'Mabel had once considered the Wirks extremely picturesque and, quite early in their married life, had invited them to her house that she might photograph them for her album.' This impersonal description of the Wirks as objects rather than people sets the tone for Mabel's character and an argument arises when Sabre objects to the Wirks taking tea in the kitchen rather than with him and Mabel in the formal setting of the garden.[72] This incident signals their opposing views on class, which deepen throughout the novel. Further into the book, the author treats the reader to an explanatory account of Mabel's views on life and class:

> Her life was living among people of her own class. Her measure of a man or of a woman was, Were they of her class? If they were, she gladly accepted them and appeared to find considerable pleasure in their society … The only quality that mattered was the quality of being well-bred. She called the classes beneath her own standard of breeding 'the lower classes', and so long as they left her alone she was perfectly content to leave them alone. In certain aspects she liked them. She liked 'a civil tradesman' immensely; she liked a civil charwoman immensely; and she liked a civil workman immensely. It gave her much pleasure, real pleasure that she felt in all her emotions, to receive civility from the classes that ministered to her class – servants, trades-people, gardeners, carpenters, plumbers, postmen, policemen – as to meet any of her own class.[73]

For Mabel, maintaining one's class status, and if possible elevating it, was dependent upon a strict subscription to certain class behaviours. An interesting sub-plot of the novel involves her treatment of their two servants, Sarah and Rebecca Jinks, whom Sabre calls Low and Hi-Jinks. They remain loyal to Sabre, even as Mabel is intent on constantly reminding them of their inferior status as servants. Mabel eventually leaves Sabre after he endures a series of scandals due to his repeated lack of concern for propriety and a devotion to doing good deeds for others. Her horror of what the neighbours will say when he brings in a poor, unwed, and pregnant girl into the home is the final straw. Mabel eventually marries Major Millet, an older man whom Sabre nicknames

Hopscotch because he's always 'bounding about to show how agile he is. He's always calling out "Ri – te O!" and jumping to do a thing when there's no need to jump'.

The film and novel of *Sorrell and Son* paints a negative portrait of femininity and greed through the character of Sorrell's ex-wife. Her role in the novel was visually glamorised in the film through the addition of expensive clothing. In the book she is quickly dealt with in the striking opening: 'Two years ago his wife had left him, and her leaving had labelled him a shabby failure. She had had no need to utter the words. And all that scramble after the war, the disillusionment of it, the drying up of the fine and foolish enthusiasms, the women going to the rich fellows who had stayed at home, the bewilderment, the sense of a bitter wrong, of blood poured out to be sucked up by the lips of money-mad materialism.'[74] Although Dora Sorrell is lumped in with the general sense of greed and profiteering that the book identified, the film makes this connection even more explicit. One of the opening shots of the film is of Dora's face looking miserable and saying, 'I can't stand it. Pinching and scraping on nothing.' Sorrell dutifully goes out to look for work, but to no avail and a scene follows of Dora leaving him. Sorrell asks if there is another man and she responds affirmatively. He asks 'Wealthy?' and she says 'Yes' with her head thrown back in a defiant manner. She then gives up all claim to her son and disappears until later in the film.

In the meantime, Sorrell toils away as a porter at an inn owned by a woman unhappily married to a weak, drunken husband, and who is predictably an awful person. When he is granted the job the woman informs him, 'And you'll call me Madam', after outlining the terms. She then asks his name on the way out of the room. He says 'Sorrell, Stephen Sorrell' to which she responds 'Well, Stephen. Remember this, the man who scrubs my floors and cleans my boots mustn't be afraid of getting his hands dirty'; insulting him by calling him by his first name and then forcefully reminding him on which end of their power relationship he lies. This relationship between the ex-soldier employee and female employer is produced as a source of outrage in the film as shots show Sorrell scrubbing the floor as the female employer stands over him supervising. After Sorrell moves on to a better hotel he has the pleasure of carrying the bags for a sumptuously dressed Dora who happens to be staying there with her obese and well-dressed husband. Dora takes on a further role when she shows up later in the film after divorcing her last husband and being left a wealthy widow by the next. Again she is dressed in considerable finery. She discusses seeing Kit with Sorrell, who indicates that Kit can choose to do what he wishes after he sees her. Then, in an interesting acknowledgement of the irreconcilability of the material with motherly love, she wipes off her lipstick and covers her bare shoulders as she waits for Kit. The relationship between Kit and his mother does not amount to much. She offers him financial help and he eventually refuses both it and a relationship with her. Her quest for wealth has left her ultimately alone.

The role of the villainess offered a number of important messages about wealth and love to readers and audiences of popular film and fiction in the 1920s and 1930s. Even in a period of considerable economic hardship consumers of popular culture were reminded that money did not mean happiness, and happiness in the ideology promoted by film and fiction was almost always related to heterosexual love. Thus choosing the right man, the heroic breadwinner, was worth more than furs, diamonds, and fancy dresses. Audiences and readers had both the love-interest and the villainess to remind them of that.

Conclusion

The films and novels discussed in this chapter demonstrate an overriding concern with the social and economic mobility of the modern woman, while also illustrating how that concern was navigated through an emphasis upon a particular type of love that mitigated her status within the economy and the nation. By subscribing to heterosexual love the threat of female mobility was effectively arrested and moderated, while female villains offered up lessons as to what would befall the modern woman if she chose not to give it all up for love. The recurrence of this relationship between love, wealth, and status across popular film and fiction in interwar Britain spoke to an important process by which the economic and political claims of women were cast off in favour of heterosexual desire within the cultural landscape, if not real life. This process, I have argued, reflected the real and imagined anxieties in the interwar period surrounding gender, the economy, and the nation.

The loss that became increasingly necessary for female characters in the fiction and film of the 1920s and 1930s was one that seems to address a perceived loss in economic and socio-political status on the behalf of men and a concurrent rise in status among women. The experience of women within the happy ending, ironically, put them on seemingly equal or less than equal economic and social footing with the protagonist. While men may have given it all up for love of country during the war, in these stories women gave it all up for love of men. Hence, this moment was about asserting the economic and social dominance of a male who no longer had the fortune and title to bestow in the union. Desire and love between the hero and his girl became contingent on a reordering of economic and political privilege, one that situated the hero back at the centre of Britain's interwar economy and its sense of itself as a nation within popular narratives. Also central to this argument in popular film and fiction was the continued construction and dismantling of female performance. While these narratives repeatedly asserted that all one needs is love, they also, more importantly, actively asserted that all a woman, in particular, needs is love; and what she does not need is more economic and social power. These narratives argued with an astonishing persistence that a woman's true happiness and her desirability to men were dependent upon her ability to cast off the false performance of desire for wealth and status and acknowledge that the need for the love of a man was paramount. This was constructed as the truth of her being, something that she was not encouraged to situate within the world of material things.

Certainly the disturbing messages housed in popular fiction and film did little to prevent women from working or gaining political voices. Women worked because they had to and wanted to, and the reality that these narratives reflected was growing political and economic activity on the part of women. Yet, the same theme, as Edward Shortt noted, repeated over and over again is worth noting in the period. Popular culture became an important site for the expression of gender tensions in a so-called escapist mass culture. Popular film and fiction became an increasingly vital and known place for the writing of desire, but which produced a particular type of economic and political subject within its pages and on its screen. The message of heterosexual love and the medium that best expressed it would go on to develop in significant ways beyond World War II, even while the central trope surrounding wealth and desire remained surprisingly static – similarly static as the persistence of the capitalist economy and the expanding roles of women within economies and nations. Ultimately, the argument put forth in the narratives examined here – that all you need is love – was loaded with less than lovely implications.

Notes

1 Sedgwick, *Popular Filmgoing in 1930s Britain*.
2 'Death of the short story', *Daily Express* (9 March 1920).
3 Ruby M. Ayres, 'Well, let them despise me!', *Daily Express* (11 April 1930).
4 'Chaplin Tells the Tale', *Picturegoer* (28 September 1935).
5 Bingham, *Gender, Modernity and the Popular Press in Interwar Britain*.
6 Gates and Gillis (eds), *The Devil Himself*.
7 Butler, *Gender Trouble*; Foucault, *History of Sexuality: Vol. I*; Foucault, *The Use of Pleasure: The History of Sexuality*; Sedgwick, *Epistemology of the Closet*.
8 *Struggle for the Breeches*.
9 S. Alexander, 'Men's Fears and Women's Work: Responses to Unemployment in London between the Wars', *Gender & History* 12:2 (2000), 401–25.
10 Thompson, *Making of the English Working Class*.
11 See Clark, *Struggle for the Breeches*; D. Levine, *Family Formation in the Age of Nascent Capitalism* (New York: Academic Press, 1977); Thompson, *Customs in Common*.
12 Glucksmann, *Women Assemble*; D. Thom, *Nice Girls and Rude Girls: Women Workers in World War I* (London: I. B. Tauris, 2000); S. Todd, 'Poverty and Aspiration: Young Women's Entry to Employment in Inter-war England', *Twentieth Century British History* 15:2 (2004), 119–42.
13 Thom, *Nice Girls and Rude Girls*.
14 M. Savage, 'Trade Unionism, Sex Segregation and the State: Women's Employment in "New Industries" in Inter-War Britain', *Social History* 13:2 (1988), 209–28; Alexander, 'Men's Fears and Women's Work'.
15 Census figures from Savage, 'Trade Unionism, Sex Segregation and the State', 230.
16 Todd, 'Poverty and Aspiration'.
17 T. Davy, '"A Cissy Job for Men: A Nice Job for Girls": Women Shorthand Typists in London 1900–1939', in Leanore Davidoff and Belinda Westover (eds), *Our Work, Our Lives, Our Words: Women's History and Women's Work* (New Jersey: Barnes & Noble, 1986), pp. 124–44; Morag Shiach, 'Modernity, Labour and the Typewriter', in H. Stevens and C. Howlett (eds), *Modernist Sexualities* (Manchester: Manchester University Press, 2000).
18 P. Levine, '"Walking the Streets in a Way No Decent Woman Should": Women Police in World War I', *Journal of Modern History* 66:1 (1994), 34–78.
19 'The Blood of Our Sons'.
20 Hynes, *A War Imagined*.
21 *Gender, Modernity and the Popular Press in Interwar Britain*.
22 E. Wilkinson, 'What is right with Britain', *Daily Express* (June 1930).
23 *Daily Express* (1 and 3 May 1930).
24 *Daily Express* (5 and 2 May 1930).
25 See 'Civil Service typists. Girls "underpaid and under-nourished"' *The Times* (5 March 1932).
26 'Are women workers unfair?', *Daily Express* (18 March 1920).
27 'At the telephone. Women who waste time', *Daily Mail* (19 January 1926).

28 'Women in public', *Daily Express* (17 January 1920).

29 Davy, '"Cissy Job for Men: A Nice Job for Girls"'.

30 It must be noted that cross-class pairings were not typical in the nineteenth century and were, in fact, only condoned within a narrow set of circumstances. Writers for the middle and upper classes such as Jane Austen, Anthony Trollope, and Wilkie Collins all defined their happy endings as the appropriate pairing of men and women from similar class backgrounds or one that elevated a deserving and honourable family that had fallen slightly to the wrong side of shabby genteel. Likewise, in working-class melodramas, upper-class men who romanced working-class girls were usually hiding villainous intentions. If a cross-class romance transpired, it was one that only revealed what was in actuality a natural intra-class pairing of the classes. See L. Metayer, 'What the Heroine Taught, 1830–1870', in Michael Hays and Anastasia Nikolopoulou (eds), *Melodrama: The Cultural Emergence of a Genre* (New York: St Martin's Press, 1996).

31 Oppenheim, *Murder at Monte Carlo*, p. 18.

32 Sedgwick, *Popular Filmgoing in 1930s Britain*.

33 J. Hilton, *Lost Horizon* (London: Macmillan, 1933). *Lost Horizon*. DVD, dir. Frank Capra (1937; Culver City, CA: Columbia TriStar Home Video, 1999).

34 As noted before, according to Sedgwick and Harper, *Mutiny on the Bounty* was the second most popular film in Britain in 1936 and brought in 26,136 people to the Portsmouth cinema.

35 Gibbs, *Middle of the Road*, p. 311.

36 *Ibid.*, p. 335.

37 *The Constant Nymph*, 35 mm, dir. B. Dean (London: Gaumont-British, 1933).

38 *Ibid.*

39 '*The Constant Nymph*: Exhibitors' Catalogue' (1933).

40 Mayer, *Sociology of Film*, p. 217.

41 The preference for adolescent heroines among movie goers is documented in A. Kuhn, 'Cinema Culture and Femininity in the 1930s', in C. Gledhill and G. Swanson (eds), *Nationalising Femininity: Culture, Sexuality and British Cinema in the Second World War* (Manchester: Manchester University Press, 1996).

42 Metayer, 'What the Heroine Taught, 1830–1870', p. 238.

43 Hutchinson, *If Winter Comes*, p. 85.

44 S. Brooke, *Sexual Politics: Sexuality, Family Planning, and the British Left from the 1880s to the Present Day* (Oxford: Oxford University Press, 2011); Pederson, *Family, Dependence and the Welfare State*.

45 *Camille*, DVD, dir. G. Cukor (1936; Burbank, CA: Warner Home Video, 2005).

46 *Camille*, 1936; *Camille*, DVD, dir. R. C. Smallwood (1921; Burbank, CA: Warner Home Video, 2005).

47 Sedgwick, *Popular Filmgoing in 1930s Britain*, p. 313.

48 *A Star Is Born*, VHS, dir. W. A. Wellman (1937; SI: Morningstar Entertainment, 1996).

49 *A Star Is Born*.

50 *Sorrell and Son*, 35 mm, dir. J. Raymond (London: British and Dominion Films Corp., 1933)

51 Gibbs, *Middle of the Road*, p. 54.

52 *Ibid.*, p. 27.

53 *Ibid.*, p. 40.

54 *Queen Christina*, DVD, dir. R. Mamoulian (1933; Burbank, CA: Warner Home Video, 2005).

55 For a discussion of historical drama as a genre, see M. Landy, *British Genres: Cinema and Society, 1930–1960* (Princeton: Princeton University Press, 1991).

56 *Victoria the Great*, DVD, dir. H. Wilcox, 1937; London; *Sixty Glorious Years*, DVD, dir. Herbert Wilcox, 1938.

57 *The Sheik*, DVD, dir. G. Melford (1921; Chatsworth, CA: Image Entertainment, 2002); E. M. Hull, *The Sheik* (Boston: Maynard, 1921 [1919]).

58 Hull, *The Sheik*, p. 2.

59 *The Sheik*, DVD, 1921.

60 *The Son of the Sheik*, DVD, dir. G. Fitzmaurice (1926; Chatsworth, CA: Image Entertainment, 2002).

61 Harper, 'Lower Middle-Class Taste-Community in the 1930s', 580.

62 *Tarzan the Ape Man*, DVD, dir. W.S. Van Dyke (1932).

63 *Champagne*, DVD, dir. A. Hitchcock.

64 P. Bogdanovich, '1963 Interview', *The Cinema of Alfred Hitchcock* (New York: Museum of Modern Art, 1963).

65 E. A. Kaplan (ed.), *Women in Film Noir* (London: BFI, 1999); S. Chibnall and R. Murphy (eds), *British Crime Cinema* (London: Routledge, 1999).

66 C. Willis, 'The Female Moriarty: The Arch-Villainess in Victorian Popular Fiction', in Gates and Gillis (eds), *The Devil Himself*, pp. 57–68.

67 *Which People's War?: National Identity and Citizenship in Wartime Britain 1939–1945* (Oxford: Oxford University Press, 2003).

68 A. Lant, *Blackout: Reinventing Women in Wartime British Cinema* (Princeton: Princeton University Press, 1991).

69 *Mata Hari*, DVD, dir. G. Fitzmaurice (1931; Burbank, CA: Warner Home Video, 2005).

70 H. C. McNeile, *The Female of the Species* (London: Hodder & Stoughton, 1928; reprint, 1935), p. 35.

71 E. Tremper, *I'm No Angel: The Blonde in Fiction and Film* (Charlottesville: University of Virginia Press, 2006).

72 Hutchinson, *If Winter Comes*, p. 13.

73 *Ibid.*, pp. 36–7.

74 Deeping, *Sorrell and Son*, p. 5

4

Building character:
censorship, the Home Office,
and the BBFC

I cannot believe that any single film can have any lasting effect on the public, but the result of the same themes repeated over and over again might be most undesirable.
Edward Shortt, speech to Conference of Cinema Exhibitors' Association,
27 June 1935

When Edward Shortt, president of the British Board of Film Censors (BBFC), spoke to the Cinema Exhibitors' Association in the summer of 1935, he attempted to address what he saw as the growing presence of unacceptable themes in films reaching the BBFC. At that particular moment the BBFC was concerned with the influx of gangster films from the United States. The subject of this chapter is not the censorship of gangster films, a subject which has been amply covered by a number of historians, but rather with the inverse of Shortt's concern, those films and novels with 'themes repeated over and over again' that were desirable to both the BBFC and its literary counterpart in censorship, the Home Office.[1] Censorship typically has two roles: containing and excising particular representations and condoning and promoting others. In the case of literature and film in Britain during the interwar period, censorship was linked to the characters and themes discussed throughout this work.

Censorship of films by the BBFC and of literature by the Home Office in interwar Britain contributed to the construction of a popular narrative formula deemed both healthy and entertaining for the masses. The censoring bodies of the interwar period were very aware of the relationship between popular culture and the social and political climate of the day. Indeed, they thought incessantly about the connection between narrative and audience experience and the cumulative impact of narratives stressing the same themes. One of the main jobs of the censor as he or she saw it in 1920s and 1930s Britain was to break possible connections between the negative realities of the world and film and fiction narratives. The troubles of the real world were not to have a significant place in film or fiction. Censorship in this period consequently aimed to produce an idealised vision of man's and woman's place within the economy and nation, an ideological fantasy that was often separated from the reality of interwar unemployment and disillusionment with Parliament after World War I. I argue that the goals of censors as well as popular novelists and filmmakers were very similar: they collectively sought to reimagine contemporary problems in ways that maintained traditional views of gender, work, and nation.

This story is largely one of success, for the censors succeeded through a type of censorship that was both prohibitive and productive in endorsing and promoting a particular relationship between gender, the economy, and nation within popular film and fiction. Films that adhered to this ideology, including the overwhelming majority of the films and novels discussed up to this point, were not censored and were seldom commented upon in the records examined here. The seal of approval that these films and novels elicited illuminate the ways in which censorship could silently produce texts as well as prohibit them. Many histories of censorship in Britain have viewed censorship as a purely prohibitive activity, but as Annette Kuhn has argued, 'regulation … may be understood not so much as an imposition of rules upon some preconstituted entity, but as an ongoing and always provisional process of constituting objects from and for its own practices'.[2] She argues that censorship should be viewed not merely as an activity that regulates a 'pre-existing reality' but as one that can actually produce its own 'truths' in the process, truths that represent the dominant ideology of the day. Thus, in the Foucauldian sense of the deployment of discourse, the effort to control an image can also invest that image with a certain 'truth' and authenticity.

Censors in this period were grappling with this dual effect of censorship in a tangible way as they showed increasing concern with the sensational aspects of their censorship activity and found new ways of investing their work with a quiet authority. In many ways, silence became the mode of operation for the censorship bodies of the BBFC and the Home Office as they quietly worked to censor images through the early vetting of films or the seizure of literature in the mail. The BBFC and the Home Office also engaged in the equally silent approval of 'the same themes repeated over and over again' in fiction and film. This silent production of ideology was central to modern ideas and debates about censorship and was bound up in the tacit approval of characters such as heroes, villains, and love-interests – characters whom we have seen as being intimately tied to concerns about the economy and nation. Thus censorship's endorsement of these figures contributed to the maintenance and production of a world-view that buttressed the role of the soldier and breadwinner, condemned the wealthy profiteer, and censured women working for money and not love.

This chapter demonstrates that the Home Office and BBFC's encounters with the hero, villain, and love-interest were instrumental in shaping these characters in interwar popular culture. Images of the male hero were of particular importance to both organisations. The BBFC took pains to have him portrayed in ways that allowed ideas of normative masculinity to be invested in the role of the breadwinner and the soldier, while moderating concerns about the real-life experiences of men following World War I. This 'truth' of British masculinity was actively produced by the BBFC through the sanctioning of popular films. The Home Office also addressed the role of the hero, but through his relation to the female love-interest and images of sexuality. In my discussion of the censorship of sexuality in the latter part of this chapter, I demonstrate that the novels the Home Office censored in the interwar period were ones that highlighted the sexual as well as the economic and social futility of the hero. We will see that what was often presumed as the censorship of female sexuality was also a simultaneous recuperation of the figure of the male hero. This seemed to form the basis of the Home Office's and BBFC's approach to censorship in this period and their contribution to Michael Paris's concept of the 'warrior nation'. Male villains, in contrast, continued to embody wealth in incredible ways that were largely uncensored by both agencies, as long as the villain was caught by the hero. Anxieties about gangsters and images of evil on the screen never amounted to much as the BBFC and Home Office chose to concentrate less on the traits of the villainous character than on his fate at the hands of the male hero. In this way the hero was again endorsed through villainous characters, as well as the female love-interest, as the lynchpin of the popular formula and the idealised social and economic centre of the world that the BBFC and the Home Office attempted to promote.

This chapter examines the records of the Home Office regarding obscene literature and the scenario reports of the BBFC in order to illuminate the ways which censors encountered and shaped the character types outlined in previous chapters. Through a close examination of the objections of Home Office and BBFC officials to certain themes and characters, as well as internal discussions within each organisation, and finally a survey of novels banned by the Home Office, we can see a tacit endorsement of the character types that dominated popular film and fiction. I argue that the censorship bodies of the Home Office and the BBFC, to varying degrees and through varying means, promoted and produced specific types of heroes, villains, and love-interests in order to maintain a particularly gendered capitalist ideology that situated men at the centre of the nation and economy.

Government and censorship

Censorship, much like the hero, villain, and love-interest, appears to be timeless. Restrictions on the expression of certain groups and opinions, of course, have a long and chequered history. From monarchs controlling negative views of their own past-times and policies to censorship of the free press as it developed, censorship has played an important role in Britain's past.[3] However, as is the case with the characters discussed in this book, this history is by no means as timeless or static as it is sometimes portrayed. This chapter deals with a distinctively modern censorship that was as particular to the twentieth century as the novels and films under its purview.

The purpose of censorship arguably shifted in the eighteenth and nineteenth century as it became concerned less with regulating politics than with regulating depictions of sexuality that were increasingly divorced from politics. This was a period when overt connections between sexuality and political and social messages were obfuscated. Pornographic political cartoons lampooning the king or members of the aristocracy gave way to pornographic images for the primary purpose of arousal.[4] Perhaps the most striking example of the effort to separate political commentary from sexuality were former Chartists forced to take up their drawing pens in pursuit of a new career in pornography rather than political critique in the early nineteenth century.[5] Although the ongoing connection between politics and pornography has been amply demonstrated, producers and regulators of pornography in the eighteenth and nineteenth centuries constructed pornography as a new and vital industry that, on the surface, was removed from the political and social sphere. This seemingly apolitical pornography was also more available due to the same changes in the printing press that ushered in the cheap bestselling novel. Lisa Z. Sigel claims that postcards in particular made visual representations of sexuality affordable and available for the wider public.[6]

Sigel notes that at the same time that these pornographic images were becoming increasingly available and seemingly apolitical, it became the responsibility of government to think more and more about the interests of the public. Foucault argues that during the nineteenth century government began to conceive of citizens as a population to be managed rather than individuals to be disciplined and punished.[7] Managing the population was related to the utilitarian notion of ensuring the happiness and productivity of its citizens. In this context censorship became an important way through which government and the population interacted with each other, and a way for governments to manage the morality of the population. Above all censorship allowed governing bodies to appear concerned about the population and the images it was exposed to, but also to take a hand in maintaining normative truths such as the 'truth' of sexuality and gender that governed a stable society. Through a number of trials in Britain against shopowners peddling pornography, Parliament seemed intent on prohibiting images of sexuality, while it established its own role in fostering modern normative definitions of sexuality. The government maintained this role into the interwar period through the offices of the Home Office and the BBFC, although it took an increasingly varied approach through its endorsement of certain characters that embodied normative discourses about work, gender, and the nation.

Before embarking on a discussion of these characters within the records of the Home Office and the BBFC, it is necessary to briefly outline the history of both organisations and examine their approaches to censorship. The history of the BBFC has been examined in several works while the Home Office has endured less comprehensive scrutiny.[8] Discussions of the Home Office's work tend to concentrate on major cases of censorship such as the trial of D. H. Lawrence's *The Rainbow* in 1915, the subsequent banning of Lawrence's other works such as *Lady Chatterley's Lover* (1928) in the year of its publication and its later trial in 1960, as well as the trial of Radclyffe Hall's novel *The Well of Loneliness* on its publication in 1928.[9] Both organisations were relatively small departments by today's standards, with one figurehead who had signing authority and made final decisions, and one permanent under-secretary who arguably had a much more involved role in direct censorship.[10] Twelve Secretaries of State led the Home Office in the interwar period. Notable among these were Liberal Party member Edward Shortt (1919–22), who later went on to be the third president of the BBFC, and Sir William Joynson-Hicks (1924–29) of the conservatives, known by supporters and critics alike as 'Jix', who mounted the most infamous cases of censorship against the writers D. H. Lawrence and Radclyffe Hall. The president of the BBFC acted in a similar manner to the Secretary of the Home Office in terms of providing final say, although his position was not as subject to election results. Consequently, the interwar period saw only three presidents of the BBFC: T. P. O'Connor (1916–29), Edward Shortt (1929–35), and William Tyrell (1935–48).

The main difference between the Home Office and the BBFC in terms of state-sanctioned authority was that the BBFC was initially developed by the film trade industry and did not have direct statutory power granted by Parliament. While publications in Britain were subject to scrutiny by the Home Office in accordance with the 1857 Obscene Publications Act, which the Home Office presented as 'anything which has the tendency to corrupt the minds and morals of those into whose hands it might come', the BBFC had no governing statutory law.[11] The film trade chose to erect the BBFC in 1913 rather than face direct government interference. Representatives of the trade elected the president of the BBFC, although the Home Secretary could nominate a candidate. Financing for the BBFC and its president's salary was provided through the fees charged by the board for viewing films and the granting of licences.[12] Although no statutory law came into effect for the content of film, in practice and through various rulings of the courts as well as the actions of the Home Office, the BBFC's powers were gradually increased throughout the 1920s and consequently followed as law. The Home Office increasingly deferred concerns and queries about the content of film to the BBFC in this period. Indeed without the direction of the Obscene Publications Act that governed the Home Office, the BBFC created its own list of censorable subjects in a given year and worked from that on a case-by-case basis.[13] Consequently, few cinemas were locally licensed to display films that did not possess a certificate from the BBFC. This certificate, still visible today in British theatres, indicated in the interwar period that the BBFC had approved the film and had granted it a rating of either U for universal or A for adult. Thus the BBFC's censorship of film still was a form of state-sponsored censorship, much like the Home Office's. The split between the two organisations reflected less an ideological split, but rather the sheer growth of popular culture in the interwar period and the necessity of an enlarged bureaucracy in order to deal with the issues this raised among concerned citizens.

Both the BBFC and the Home Office had to contend with enthusiastic and organised groups, as well as individual complaints. Individual complaints often took the form of letters such as the following sent directly to J. R. Clynes by C. G. Smith:

> I was recently advised by a bookseller who knows I like well-written stuff to buy a book called 'Wolf Solent' by J.C. Powys. This book is exceedingly well

written but it is the foulest concoction of vileness I have ever read … I feel that it would only be necessary to call your attention to this book to have the matter investigated. I do not wish my name to appear in the matter or to involve myself in any proceedings at all.

The writer further detailed the offences of the book by commenting that 'seductions are nothing in present-day literature but I think we might be spared mental sexual perversion … humorous jokes of one boy being seduced by another, of incest between father and daughter, of the shape of canine excrement, of the smell of urinals and the other vapourings of the unsanitary mind of this talented author'.[14] The response of the Home Office to the majority of these letters was a review of the offending book, a brief comment in the file (such as 'not suitable for prosecution' in this case), and a follow-up letter stating as much to the complainant. Both the Home Office and the BBFC provided lengthier responses to organised groups such as the London Public Morality Council (LPMC) and the Birmingham Cinema Enquiry Committee (BCEC), and occasionally were pressed into attending meetings or inquiries into the state of the cinema or literature by such groups.

When responding to the complaints of these organised groups, the Home Office and the BBFC had to take a more nuanced approach than they did with individuals. Both the BBFC and the Home Office dealt directly with the LPMC, which formed in the early twentieth century and was a powerful lobby group headed by the Bishop of London.[15] The LPMC regularly corresponded with the Home Office and may have done so with the BBFC – the destruction of the bulk of the BBFC's correspondence during the Blitz makes certainty impossible, although some surviving records indicate a familiarity with the group. The goal of the LPMC was clearly stated by its name and it involved itself in film, fiction, and theatre. It consisted of a tireless secretary, Howard M. Tyrer, who was the main point of contact. Tyrer wrote to the Home Office on behalf of concerned citizens and over the years the LPMC even organised its own panel of experts that mimicked the work of the BBFC. The BBFC, while dealing with the LPMC, also contended with the BCEC, which took particular issue with the content of films in the 1930s. Annette Kuhn notes that partly in response to pressures from this group, the BBFC introduced a new rating, H for horror, in 1937.[16] Although the rating never took hold and was effectively ignored by theatre operators, these groups were persistent in their efforts to change the content of films; correspondence with these groups clarifies much about the approach by the Home Office, in particular, to censorship.

In terms of the ways in which both censoring organisations viewed the characters discussed in the previous chapters, the Home Office and the BBFC encountered them within either published novels already in circulation, in the Home Office's case, or through scripts about to head into production or the screening of finished films not yet distributed, in the BBFC's case. The Home Office censored works through the seizure of material through the mail or from publishers and booksellers. The BBFC, in contrast, was able to censor at the point of production rather than distribution. This attention to scripts at an early stage by the BBFC was especially encouraged in the 1930s when the censors argued that valuable time could be saved for film producers and directors if the censors were involved at the outset.[17] The BBFC had four examiners in the 1920s, which was then reduced to one main examiner through the early part of the 1930s until a woman joined him in April 1934. The examiner's job was to view the film, briefly summarise it, and write up a scenario report that recommended deletions and commented on the suitability of the film for licensing. These reports, of which ones from the period 1930–39 survive, provide valuable information as to which themes were condemned or passed by the censors. They also highlight the peculiar likes and dislikes of the senior script examiner, Colonel J. C. Hanna, and script reader, Miss N. Shortt, daughter of president Edward Shortt. Jeffrey Richards's excellent article on the composition and content control of the BBFC in the 1930s notes that the two censors could best be described as 'a rather tetchy retired army officer and a sheltered upper-class spinster'.[18] The Home Office, in comparison, did not report on every obscene book the clerks read, but only kept records of those that they received complaints about from either lobby groups or individuals, and books that were prosecuted in some form. A sense of the clerks who read the offending books and their particular objections is not nearly as coherent as what can be gleaned from the BBFC. Nevertheless through the available sources it is still possible to gather an idea of these two bodies' approaches to heroes, villains, and love-interests within film and fiction.

The presence of the hero, villain, and love-interest are palpable within these records, but comprehensive analysis of censorship requires attention to silences. Both the prohibitive and productive aspects of censorship make attention to silences vital. As mentioned previously most of the top films and bestselling novels that I have discussed up to this point do not make much of an appearance in the records of the censors and are consequently not in this chapter. The BBFC's scenario reports on every film they viewed did allow some of that decade's most popular films to enter their gaze, but these generally inspired little to no comment as they were passed, in comparison to those that offended the censor. If hit films mentioned here did arouse comment, this would make for a suspiciously seamless and neat, although immensely satisfying, study of popular culture in interwar Britain. Likewise, few if any records of the Home Office's view of bestselling novels by Philip Gibbs or H. C. McNeile's exist. These, after all, were examples of acceptable formulas for entertainment, and in this case silence was productive rather than restrictive. In this chapter I turn my gaze, for the most part, to those works that defied the acceptable formula and prompted comment and censure. This, then, is an exploration of content and characters that deviated from the culture industry formula endorsed through the characters examined in the previous chapter.

The hero

The most important character that the Home Office and the BBFC encountered in their work was the hero. The hero was the character most central to the meaning of the narrative and in whom the censors of the Home Office and the BBFC were most invested. The hero, like them, was charged with protecting the integrity of the nation. As the hero was associated with the military, concerns about the reputation of soldiers weighed heavily on both the Home Office and the BBFC. The efforts of both organisations were often directed towards representing the hero and other institutions of Englishness as capable, honourable, and moral. This effort, following the boom in the interwar period of books and films emphasising the folly of war, promoted the active rehabilitation of the soldier figure and its associated institutions.[19] A sense of what type of morality should be embodied in these narratives can be read in the comments of the Home Office and the BBFC about what they viewed as misrepresentations of the soldier in fiction and film. This discussion will be revisited further on in the chapter as I examine the censorship of images of sexuality, for that censorship also encompassed the reputations of soldiering men.

The Home Office's views on the hero can be discerned by its response to letters about the boom in 'war books' that was discussed in Chapter 1, and the Home Office's subsequent opening of a file on that topic. This was the extent of its action in favour of the role of the soldier hero, yet it stands out as significant among the usually brief responses to complaints about books. These responses generally said little beyond their assessment that the book did not fall under the Obscene Publications Act and was not suitable for censoring. However, a letter from the British Legion's Scottish Headquarters sent to Prime Minister Ramsay MacDonald and then forwarded by his office to the Home Office, prompted a rare statement by the Home Office through the Prime Minister's office. The letter from General Secretary D. Mathers was the product of a conference of the British Legion in Scotland consisting of 'a large ex-service community', where a small number of resolutions were passed. The first and foremost of the resolutions declared:

> 1. That the British Legion (Scotland) deplores the tendency of writers of War Books to depict the British soldier as a drunken and immoral person, thereby casting a slur on those who fought and those who gave their lives for King and country.
>   Without enlarging upon the great grief and sorrow which has been brought into the hearts of those who gave their nearest and dearest, for their King and country, by the filth in some War Books, I am instructed to urge that the Government take some action so as to exercise a censorship before further publication of such books is permitted.[20]

The British Legion focused explicitly on the characterisation of the soldier himself rather than the general depiction of the war. The Home Office responded by suggesting that a letter sent from the Prime Minister should state:

> The Prime Minister regrets as much as they do the whole tone and outlook of some of the War Books which have been published but he is afraid the remedy cannot be found in any official action … He believes that in the end it will be found that no book about the war will have been successful in detracting from the imperishable memories of endurance, courage and nobility left by the British troops by their general behaviour in the Great War.[21]

Perhaps because this was not the Home Office officially commenting on the tone of the war books but rather the Prime Minister, the Home Office was able to put forth its thoughts on the tone of the war books. It did not recommend action, although a file entitled 'Censorship of War Books' was opened at the Home Office which included complaints and press clippings about the number of war books published, indicating a familiarity with the controversy surrounding them.[22] Instead of formally censoring the war books, the Home Office, we shall see, used its concern with female sexuality as a way to support positive images of the male soldier hero. In this way, the Home Office was able to act in favour of traditional views of the soldier as well as binary views of masculinity and femininity.

The BBFC explicitly made what it deemed acceptable characteristics of the hero and heroic bodies central to its approach to censorship. The subjects of censorship put forth in 1917 were preoccupied with buttressing the role of the hero and military organisations most often associated with the character (see the Appendix to this book). Rule 17 dictated that films were not to include 'scenes tending to disparage public characters and institutions'. Rules 21, 'Scenes holding up the King's uniform to contempt or ridicule;' and 22: 'Subjects dealing with India, in which British Officers are seen in an odious light, and otherwise attempting to suggest the disloyalty of British Officers, Native States or bringing into disrepute British prestige in the Empire', clearly indicate that the soldier was to have a privileged place within films exhibited in Britain.[23] In the interwar period, the censors updated rule 22 with a modern interpretation that censored any negative representation of soldiers in the field, not only in India, while rule 17 was also interpreted to include certain professions linked to public institutions.[24] The widening of heroic ideals beyond the hero itself is apparent. In this way the BBFC actively produced coherent connections between heroes, soldiers, officers, and the Empire and invested the role of hero with the label of British 'characters and institutions'.

One can surmise that it was Colonel Hanna who was particularly passionate about appropriate representations of those representing British institutions, such as the soldier or policeman, and was adamant that those representations were in keeping with the wider characteristics of the hero as courageous, honest, and capable. Although the scenario reports do not name the censors – they are identified merely as first and second reader – the Colonel was the only reporter until April 1934 and had been an examiner with the board since 1923. The occasionally vehement remarks about the depictions of British officers can be confidently attributed to him. Indeed, a number of his complaints about the depiction of officers, the police, and even doctors and judges, were not echoed by the other reader. The second reader may well have been introduced to provide some balance to his rather dogmatic interpretation of the rules. This is unclear, yet it is clear that his role as a soldier was privileged both within the censorship rules as well as within the primary organisation of the board. His appointment in 1923 was discussed in a report released to the press by T. P. O'Connor and circulated to the Home Office defending the relatively new position of the BBFC. In the report O'Connor described Hanna's appointment to fill a vacancy that had arisen due to a death:

> For that vacancy we received applications from many candidates of eminence, men who had served in important judicial, military and official positions in the Empire. Our choice fell on a gentleman with a distinguished military career, who in addition is a man of high education and sound judgment.[25]

Here the Colonel's military career was presented as making him particularly suitable to pass judgement upon the films the board received. His promotion to senior script reader and the longevity of his position indicate the vital importance of the soldier's gaze within the censorship process.

The Colonel took his role very seriously and his interpretation and construction of the British hero emphasised the capability of the military man. The gravity that the Colonel brought to his view of the hero was consistent, although he did exhibit the occasional flash of humour. Edgar Wallace's novel *When the Gangs Came to London* (1932) was submitted in 1932 as a potential film and was met with this initial response by the Colonel, the sole reader at this point: 'The verdict might be given in the words of Mr. Edgar Wallace on Page 234 – "What a grand film this would make! But the Censor would never pass it".' This affectionate salvo quickly dried up as he detailed his grounds for not passing the film:

> In this country we do not allow our police to be shown on screen as incompetent, or accepting bribes from criminals. We do not recognize 'Third Degree' methods, nor do we permit the suggestion that our Police force would arrange for the murder of a criminal if they thought the evidence was too weak to secure a conviction. Wholesale Machine gun murders in the streets of Chicago possibly are deemed to come under the head of 'Topicals', but, in London, would be quite prohibitive. The idea of a junior American police officer being placed in actual, if not nominal, control of the whole of the Metropolitan police is a situation which Police authorities in this country would not allow to be shown on the screen.[26]

While rather dramatic in his assumption of police outrage at the showing of the film, the Colonel explicitly made his point about the responsibilities and behaviour of the police force in interwar Britain. He emphasised their complete control of situations, their inability to be bought, their commitment to the protection of life, as well as their national status as equal to, if not better than, Americans. These policemen were constructed by the Colonel as the linchpin of the British nation and economy, devoted to Britain and distracted by nothing else. Weakness in that position simply could not be allowed on the screen.

Hanna's objection to Hitchcock's *The Man Who Knew Too Much* was based on the film's depiction of ineffectual police. The script was first submitted to the BBFC as a Bulldog Drummond story under the title 'The Hidden Hand'.[27] At that point it was passed without objections by the Colonel, who was still working alone, but when the film version was vetted by both the Colonel and the new reader Miss Shortt later that spring, one censor noted that the general story was mostly unchanged except, 'This version however ends with a sort of Sidney Street battle, an attack on the gang's headquarters in Wapping by armed police and two lorry loads of troops. Machine guns used on both sides. Many casualties shown. The whole attack from Sc. [scene] 493 onwards is quite prohibitive.'[28] The ruling on the final scene of the movie, which encompassed most of the climatic action, prompted a phone call from a Mr Beverly Baxter representing the film. The scenario report related the outcome of the conversation:

> He agreed not to arm the Police, but wanted to retain the soldiers. Mr. Wilkinson told him our objections in detail, and he finally agreed that he would endeavour to alter the ending so as to bring it into accord with ordinary Police methods in London. Mr. Baxter suggested that one young policeman could remark to his sergeant that they ought to send for soldiers, and the sergeant could retort fiercely that the police were quite competent to deal with the situation themselves.[29]

In this instance the implication that the police were unable to do their job adequately and were in need of aid from the national troops was objectionable. Nevertheless, the film as released showed no such alteration and included the lorryloads of troops. Although no record exists in the scenario report, the objections of the reader were overridden, likely because the film itself did no disservice to the police, as the villains were brought to justice in the end by the hero, an upper-class ex-soldier who worked for the government.

The Colonel and Miss Shortt continued to patrol the boundaries of correct behaviour for members of the King's army and the police. In 1939, we can presume that it was the Colonel who summed up the synopsis of a film 'Storm over India' as 'another of those conventional and spectacular stories of frontier fighting in India, written by an American with no knowledge of geography and a complete ignorance of the British army'. The report went on to state, 'I think this is an even worse parody of the English officer than any we have had up to now, and I think we are entitled to say definitely we will not allow such caricatures to go out under our certificate.'[30] The second reader found it less objectionable, but the film was never made. To the film *Father O'Flynn* (1935) the Colonel made a similar objection, which was eventually overruled, to a scene where a soldier froze up when his company went over the top of their trench in World War I. The Colonel noted briskly, 'Incidents and dialogue harmless throughout, except Scenes 8–12 which must be modified. We do not allow English officers in uniform to be shown as cowards in the field. Reluctance, and eventually yielding to persuasion, but not to force, would be permissible.'[31] The film was passed as U nevertheless.

The concern about representations of local authorities also encompassed those that represented other seats of power in Britain, or institutions of Englishness, such as doctors and judges. A play by Bernard Shaw entitled *Doctor's Dilemma* was submitted to the board as a possible film. The play concerned a woman who approaches a doctor about saving the life of her husband. The doctor realises that the husband is a scoundrel, also married to his servant, and chooses to pass his case onto an inferior doctor. He then admits his love for the wife. One reader's response was decisive: 'this play is a cynical and vindictive attack on the Medical profession at large. Most of the characters are distinguished physicians or surgeons. Their ignorance, callousness and general humbug are ridiculed on every page.' The reader continued, 'this story is quite impossible for the films. It is entirely detrimental to the honour of doctors and the medical profession generally. The whole preface is by way of "showing up" doctors. If the unsuitable remarks were removed from the play, there would be little left to create even a story.'[32] The script failed to pass the censors. Another scenario and the partial dialogue of a novel 'The Mind of Mr. Reeder', penned again by the ubiquitous Edgar Wallace for the studio of Gaumont-British Pictures, was subject to minor criticism based on its depiction of a judge. The film was passed as 'Ordinary detective fiction. No objection', but elicited this comment: 'This story is suitable for production as a film with one note: p. 63 As this is not a farce I think the type of magistrate should be modified, and he should not be depicted as ancient, deaf and a semi-imbecile.'[33] The portrayal of the judge within a serious film where the depiction was not obviously a joke did not sit well with the board. The film was finally made in 1939, but does not survive.

It is worth noting some of the minor comments or lack of comments accompanying films that would go on to be popular in the interwar period. Of *Lives of a Bengal Lancer* (1935), the Colonel, still working alone at this point, commented, 'It is Hollywood melodrama pure and simple. The story is quite harmless. It has no political significance, and no discredit is brought on the service.' A film that promoted the bravery and self-sacrificing courage of its lead, a soldier in the British army, would not be censored. Yet he could not refrain from offering the following criticism even as he passed it as an A with no deletions:

> The dialogue and behaviour of the officers is American and very un-English throughout. Especially the attitude of Col. Stone to his son, and the back-chat of Fortescue [*sic*] to McGregor. Swords are never drawn in the orderly room. 'Last Post' is not called 'Taps'. The author's Hindustani does not extend to the difference between a 'punkah' and a 'punkah-wallah'. etc. etc.[34]

The Colonel's concern, often repeated, was with an Americanisation of films and British subject matter that jeopardised the proper representation of British forces, although, as he grudgingly admitted, it did no real discredit. *Lives of a Bengal Lancer* was passed with no objections, and 'The Hidden Hand', when first presented to the board as a Bulldog Drummond story, was passed with only minor changes:

> Incident and dialogue throughout are free from objection.
> Except: Sc. 183,185,186,189,191, showing a liaison between a peer and a demi-mondaine which should be entirely deleted.
> Sc. 187, 480 Delete word 'bloody'.

It was only when 'The Hidden Hand' was rewritten and filmed as the non-Bulldog film *The Man Who Knew Too Much* that the objectionable scene involving the lorry full of troops was included and merited the Colonel's critical response. For the most part, popular films needed little modification at the censor level and passed quite quickly. Seldom did a film that was deemed controversial by the censors go on to great box-office success in the theatres.

The role of the hero and the institutions he was associated with was thus a concern for both the BBFC and the Home Office. Both organisations wished to shore up the hero's place within the economy and the nation as well as emphasise the capability of others in the narrative that represented these institutions. The BBFC, primarily through the personage of Colonel Hanna, was able to protect vigorously the reputation and esteem of the British forces. Instances where the Colonel was overruled nevertheless indicated the extent to which cynicism about the war, the role of the soldier, and institutions that represented the nation had penetrated bodies like BBFC, which sought to refute that narrative. The Home Office, in contrast, exhibited concern over the depiction of the soldier and the presence of war novels, yet seemed to do little to prevent their publication. Its primary concern continued to be depictions of sexuality, a concern that encompassed the character of the hero. It was in the censorship of female sexuality that the Home Office most actively endorsed the integrity of the male hero. However, in the meantime we can surmise from both the limited actions of the Home Office and the more overt actions of the BBFC that a particular version of the hero and his role in the nation's institutions was maintained and encouraged within fiction and film.

The villain

The responses of the Home Office and the BBFC to villains in film and fiction were different, and ultimately it was the BBFC that took the most active role. The Home Office did not seem to trouble itself with representations of villains or the criminal class in novels. Instead it saw uncontrolled heterosexuality and homosexuality, which will be discussed in the following section, as the primary problems for its office. The BBFC, in contrast, was preoccupied with the role of the villain and was particularly concerned with representations of crime on the screen. The explicit concerns by the BBFC with villainy compared to the lacklustre approach of the Home Office was partly due to the activity of pressure groups such as the Birmingham Cinema Enquiry Committee (BCEC), which were alarmed with what children were learning from criminals in films. They and the BBFC saw a connection between images of villainy on the screen and criminal activity in real life. Yet, regardless of the lip service the BBFC paid to the burgeoning visibility of crime in films and mounting pressure from lobby groups, the BBFC was unable to take decisive measures against what types of villainy could be shown on film. In part, few rules that the BBFC could instate could apply to the multiple forms that villains were taking. Instead, the BBFC ultimately sought to strengthen the role of the hero as a counter-measure to the images of crime and villainy.

The rationale driving interwar fears about images of villainous criminals was that these depictions in fiction and film would result in real criminality on the streets. In 1923, the BBFC outlined its logic in regard to the containment of unwholesome images to the Home Office by using its own commitment to not showing drugs on the screen as an example. The BBFC was

> certain that the exhibition of these practices, with their at least temporary allurements, might spread knowledge, and as a consequence of knowledge, a temptation to fall into these pernicious habits; and that from being the vice of but a small section of the populations of a great city like London, the malady might spread to every village and to every boy and girl in the country.[35]

Such logic is not unfamiliar to modern-day readers, yet this was one of the first articulations of the link between popular culture, youth, and crime.[36] Youth was seen as particularly vulnerable to the influence of the cinema, as we shall see in the records of the BBFC and the BCEC. These groups did not believe that audiences resisted or subverted the messages housed in mass culture; rather, they believed that audiences took in these messages and adhered to the formula promoted by them. Their approach in many ways mirrored the arguments of Adorno, with different aims. The BCEC wanted to produce healthy, happy children instilled with the interwar values of the hero, rather than the villain.

The relationship between villainy and film was of great concern to the BBFC and groups like the BCEC in the interwar period because of the sheer popularity of crime films. The survey of cinemagoers in Bolton by Mass Observation in 1937 noted that 'Crime' and 'History' tied for the third most popular genre after 'Musical Romance' and 'Drama'. Crime was above other categories such as 'Society Comedies', 'War', and 'Slapstick'. Men ranked crime as their third favourite type of film, while women marked it as their sixth preference.[37] Although Mass Observation did not break down the results according to age, the BCEC attempted to do so in its own questionnaire to 1,439 children in elementary schools and Girl Guide groups in Birmingham during 1930–31. The questionnaire asked the children to comment on what they learned from the pictures. These were written responses, although it appears that teachers and others wrote down responses of those not able to fill out the questionnaire. The results were quite amazing, allowing the committee to endorse the 'clear-sighted reply of one lad', who wrote, "I have learnt many things, if I see anything I have not seen before, I am bound to learn, whether it is good or bad."[38]

The report dwelt on what children were learning about violence and sex in particular. It noted that out of two groups of Girl Guides, the group from ages 7 to 10 identified 'Murder' as their favourite genre of films, with 'Comics' as second, while those aged 10 to 16 placed 'Cowboy Films' first, 'Murder' second, and then 'Love'. The report inserted one comment after these numbers: 'One child said she would show me how to strangle people'.[39] The report did go on to note, fairly enough, that when the 1,439 responses were considered together, comedy was the most popular type of film, with adventure and detective films following closely behind. The responses were then grouped according to topics such as 'Impressions Regarding Sex' as well as 'Film Philosophy', which were full of telling observations about what children have learned about life ('That when you marry, sometimes you pick the wrong man').[40] Yet the external commentary inserted after the direct quotations of the children becomes rather pitched when it entered the section entitled 'Crime and Violence'. Below two responses from children declaring, 'I have learnt nothing but murder' and 'I have learnt about murders', the compiler commented, 'The references to murder are incessant' without, unfortunately, providing numeric qualification. The report also noted, 'Many references to "gangsters"', with the following comments from children, 'They throw knives', 'I have learnt a lot about American gangster and raketteers [*sic*]'.[41] A section followed this general knowledge of gangsters on 'serious references to Imitation'. These comments were included:

> I have learnt how to shoot through my pocket,
> my sister … when she's angry because she can't have her own way she goes to kill herself with a knife,
> I have seen boys doing the different robberies.
> Not long ago the – Picture House showed an item every week about confident tricksers, which learned me dodges used by people who make their living by frauding innocence people [*sic*].[42]

Through the inclusion of such comments in its own section on imitation, the Committee emphasised the dangers of children viewing these films.

The report was later followed up by a meeting in May 1931 between a deputation of the committee and members of the Home Office, including the Home Secretary J. R. Clynes and an under-secretary, S. W. Harris, who dealt quite often with obscene publications. No members of the BBFC seem to have been present. The goal of the BCEC at this meeting was stated at the outset:

> While we are great believers in the cultural, educational and recreational possibilities of the film, we feel that it will be ever so much more developed if there could be more regulations, more selection and more care in the presentation of films and particularly films which have been seen by children up to the age of 16, so that we are not coming to you as prohibitionists.[43]

The BCEC was careful to note both in the text of the survey and its opening remarks that it believed educational films to be of benefit. However, requests for 'more regulations, more selection and more care' were not exactly specific aims for the censorship bodies, and indeed in the case of the age at which children attended films, some of the issues raised were entirely out of the hands of anyone but the cinema manager. Through the course of the meeting, it became clear that the real issue was that the BCEC did not think the BBFC was doing its job adequately. The somewhat moderate tone of the survey was discarded in favour of explicit complaints about the type of films being shown and what was wrong with them. A Mrs Gledhill on the deputation used a reference to a *Bulldog Drummond* film to make her point about the unhealthy things children were learning:

> I have a niece who went to see one of the Drummond pictures and after it she could not sleep, and she is losing great educational value of the films by not going now. And then it is giving a wrong impression of the different stations in life. They represent the crook as well-dressed man and how easy it is to get money, and they have all the latest inventions in the house by simply being a crook. And

then another thing, murder is represented as a great thing, if you want revenge you want to murder somebody, and the children are so impressed.[44]

Here Mrs Gledhill objected to the link between wealth and villainy on the screen, and indeed the villainous and voluminous Carl Peterson in *Bulldog Drummond* (1929) was shown in an expensive overcoat with cane and white ascot. Although his complex schemes and those of his sidekick Irma were arguably not easy ways to get money, for Mrs Gledhill the link between villainy and wealth generated a false impression of society. She wished to break the association between wealth and those usually associated with upper stations of life such as businessmen and government officials, and subscribed to nineteenth-century views that explicitly equated poverty with immoral character. For her the greatest threat of these representations of crooks on film was that they undermined children's ability to make a link between correct morals and class hierarchy of their world. They would not be able to see through this false performance of wealth and identify the real class status of criminals.

The BBFC refuted much of the claims of the BCEC about the films mentioned as unsuitable in a confidential letter to the Home Office following the deputation, writing, 'I think I should let you know we have found from experience that some members, at least, of this Committee are very prejudiced against the Cinema. They appear incapable of keeping to the facts even in their description of films, for we have noticed in some cases, that their criticisms have completely distorted the sequence of the incidents to which they have referred.'[45] The letter went on to refer explicitly to the popularity of the 1929 *Bulldog Drummond* film by pointing out that a person hired by a film trade organisation visited 417 cinemas in the Midlands and Lancashire and noted that '*Bulldog Drummond* was seen in Liverpool in two cinemas, in Manchester and Northampton: in each town, it was received with applause'.[46] The general public's response outweighed the concerns of the minority of the Birmingham group. The letter went on to detail the reasons why certain films were passed which the BCEC had complained about and to document the response to these films by audiences across Britain. Little came of the deputation and the BCEC's report beyond this, as the Home Office expressed confidence in the BBFC and continued to defer all issues relating to the content of film to it.

Although the BBFC worked to limit the influence of the BCEC's report and deputation, Mrs Gledhill's concern about the association between wealth and villainy was shared by the BBFC, just to a lesser degree. The BBFC's 1929 annual report observed that in regard to gangster films, 'in many cases, there is in addition an admixture of the criminal or bootlegging element, with the introduction of an atmosphere of riotous luxury'.[47] Gangster films were of particular concern to the BBFC, for these depicted not simply a sole criminal but an organised band profiting from illegal trade. Rules outside of the law governed the organisation of criminals in films like the American *Scarface* (1932). This film about the rise of Tony Camonte through the ranks of the Mafia was a not-so-subtle reference to Al Capone and raised considerable concern in Britain and the United States, where it only passed the censors when the title was changed to *Scarface, The Shame of a Nation.* John Springhall notes that the BBFC passed a censored version of the film in 1932 even though local licensing boards in Kent, Beckenham, and Birmingham banned the film.[48] Thus while the BBFC expressed concern over gangster films, as evidenced by the reaction of Colonel Hanna to 'When the Gangs Came to London', little actually came of these concerns.

No strict guidelines were formed to formally regulate the link between villainy and wealth or manage images of villainy in general. O'Connor's rules about images of crime were encompassed in rule 6, which indicated that 'the modus operandi of criminals' was not to be shown. Other images of villainy which were not to be shown were rules 24: 'Gruesome murders and strangulation scenes' and 7: 'Cruelty to young infants and excessive cruelty and torture to adults, especially women'. The guidelines themselves seem to indicate that it may have been difficult to strictly regulate the depiction of the villain as few rules could encompass the multiple situations imagined for villains within mass culture. Gangster films may have attracted so much attention because this was a noticeable genre that followed easily defined patterns, while other types of villains could have existed anywhere and at any time. Certainly the villain was key to the films emerging from Hollywood and in Britain, yet evidence of discussions about villains between the BBFC and members of the film industry is scarce.

Instead of concentrating on drafting guidelines that would contain sprawling depictions of villainy, the BBFC chose to counteract this depravity with an emphasis upon the roles of heroic figures in bringing the villain to justice. Consequently the censors continued to object to films where the villain was not apprehended. Colonel Hanna, reviewing yet another scenario based upon a novel by Edgar Wallace in 1931, expressed in his plot summary a great deal of admiration for the story in general:

> This book is the … last four years of the life of Charles Peace the notorious criminal who was executed for murder in 1879. Mr. Wallace draws the character of this extraordinary man with a very clever pen. Physically very small, but of

great muscular strength due to his early training as an acrobat. Almost illiterate, but constantly swaggering about his superior vacation, a bully, a canting hypocrite, a lover of the ladies, a ruthless, revengeful, and utterly callous. His career of crime included petty thefts and grand larceny, burglary, blackmail and murder. His uncanny cleverness in distinguishing himself and the bold risks that he ran are admirably described. In fact there is almost a romance woven about this eccentric creature.

One suspects that the Colonel was a reader of Edgar Wallace and perhaps not an infrequent attendant of adventure films outside of his work hours. However, despite the admiration Hanna displayed, his ruling was firm:

> But from our point of view of a film based on this story one can say unhesitantly [*sic*] that it would come into our category of 'Crime' film and as such would not be an acceptable subject. Moreover the character is not an imaginary one, but one of the most notorious criminals in the memory of living man. Crime, and not the detection of crime, would be the keynote of a film based on this story.[49]

The distinction between a story about crime and not the detection of crime seems to be how the board found a middle path between the popularity of the crime film and the morally objectionable element of the villain at the centre of such narratives. The capture of the villain was also undoubtedly satisfying to censors and audience member alike, who cannot be distinguished from each other easily. A film entitled 'The Rose and Crown' prompted one of the censors to identify it as a 'crime tale' and to further comment on it as 'a pretty little tale, but I don't think we could take exception to it as a film. The villain certainly gets his deserts in the end at the hands of the law.'[50] This ending soothed any possible objections by reasserting the proper moral order of the world within the narrative. This caveat allowed numerous representations of villainy to make it to the screen.

The villain continued to exist as a lightning rod of controversy and as a popular and indeed necessarily immoral character within film narratives. While the Home Office did not attempt to overtly comment on or police the character within novels, the BBFC was forced through the sheer popularity of the villain on the screen to address the impact of images of evil-doing. Ultimately, however, the BBFC found that it was easier to describe the hero than it was to enforce limitations on the villain's characteristics. Like the narratives they viewed, the BBFC promoted the figure of the hero as embodying an act of justice that brought about the containment of the villain, while the criminal himself enjoyed a more varied and many splendoured characterisation.

The love-interest

The love-interest in popular fiction and film in the 1920s, as discussed in the previous chapter, was ideally a heterosexual female character devoted to the narrative's male hero. The female character within popular narratives tended to see in the hero the embodiment of all that was good about Britain, including its masculine breadwinning and soldier ideals, even while others in the narrative did not always recognise this. Usually by the end of the novel or film she had cast off her own claims to a central place within the nation and the economy by subscribing instead only to the hero's love, and he in turn had been placed back at the centre of both the economy and the nation. This characterisation of the love-interest was supported by the censorship of images of female sexuality in the interwar period. I argue in the following that the Home Office and BBFC's persecution of certain novels and films was an effort to contain narratives that worked against this idealised image of the heterosexual female love-interest. These narratives had to be contained not only because they offered up a vision of dangerous female desire, but also because they jeopardised the final and dominant depiction of the male hero as the economic and social centre of his world. When examining the Home Office's record of censorship in particular, we shall see that books banned and taken to trial by the Home Office threatened the predominance of the breadwinner soldier ideal.

As noted in my discussion of the history of censorship at the outset of this chapter, throughout the nineteenth century government had devoted more and more time to the policing of sex and sexuality within novels and plays. The Home Office in the interwar period continued to perceive its censorship role as one associated primarily with policing images of sexuality. This was especially true during the tenure of Sir William Joynson-Hicks from 1924 to 1929. It was under his reign that Radclyffe Hall's *Well of Loneliness* (1928) was brought to trial and other novels such as D. H. Lawrence's *Lady Chatterley's Lover* (1928) and Norah C. Jones's *Sleeveless Errand* (1929) were seized and banned. After Joynson-Hicks left office, other novels continued to be banned, such as James Hanley's *Boy* (1931), although throughout the 1930s the Home Office consciously avoided the sensational aspects of a trial. Nevertheless the censorship activity in this period through trials and seizure of material offers the historian the rare opportunity to look at a body of censored work. This opportunity is virtually impossible in the realm of film, where censored films either did not make it to theatres or were destroyed. These novels, in contrast, allow us to examine a range of offensive content therein.

The Home Office's motivations for banning these books seemed to centre upon the books' depiction of sex acts, even as the degrees to which each of these represented these images varied. *Lady Chatterley* presented the most descriptive and frank discussions of sexual intercourse, describing sexual anatomy in detail and using words such as 'fuck' in order to do so. *Boy* described both homosexual and heterosexual encounters in vaguer terms and tended to imply these encounters occurred through descriptions of dizziness, etc. *Sleeveless Errand* and *The Well* did not feature scenes of explicit sexual intercourse, although in the former the two main characters share a bed and chat with each other but do not have sex. *Sleeveless Errand* was also cited by the prosecution as containing numerous swear words. As *The Times* commented, 'Filthy language and indecent situations appeared to be the keynote of the book'.[51] *The Well* avoided cursing and was a much more conventional and chaste love story – with the important exception that it featured a woman in the traditional male role – where sexual intercourse was summed up by the author as, 'and that night they were not divided'.[52] Thus it was the implication of sex acts, sex acts themselves, as well as errant female sexuality that seemed to be objects of censorship.

The type of sex acts and sexuality that were censored is a topic of some debate. Excellent work has been done on the Home Office's censorship of representations of homosexuality. The trial of Radclyffe Hall's *The Well of Loneliness* has been interpreted by a number of historians as an effort to police deviant female homosexuality. No doubt it was. Yet Laura Doan's examination of the trial and its press coverage notes that the early and generally benign reaction to the novel was later distorted by the vitriolic response of one reviewer for the *Evening Standard* who notoriously stated that he would sooner offer up someone a vial of prussic acid than let he or she read this novel.[53] From there, reaction to the novel eventually resulted in the highly publicised trial. Doan argues that regardless of the extreme reaction of one journalist and the subsequent trial, widespread homophobia was not as extensive in Britain as it would be in later years.[54] Doan's argument is further strengthened if we take a comprehensive look at the subjects of censorship in this period. Out of *Well of Loneliness*, *Lady Chatterley's Lover*, *Boy*, and *Sleeveless Errand*, only *Well of Loneliness* dealt with homosexuality as its primary theme as it outlines in a conventional way the life and frustrated love of its female heroine, Stephen Gordon. Hanley's novel *Boy* does count homosexual encounters as a secondary theme, for among the many awful trials and tribulations of a young boy who attempts to join the tradition of seafaring by stowing away on a merchant ship is his sexual harassment by coarse and cruel sailors before he succumbs to the heterosexual advances of a prostitute and contracts syphilis. The story ends with the boy being smothered by the ship's captain in an act of mercy. Both *Sleeveless Errand* and *Lady Chatterley's Lover*, however, address heterosexual relationships. It must also be noted that in the same year that *Well of Loneliness* was tried, the Home Office chose not to take action against Compton Mackenzie's *Extraordinary Women* (1928), a scathing satire of a group of socialite lesbians and their romantic intrigues on the island of Sirene.[55] While homosexuality did prompt censorship by the Home Office, it cannot be identified as the only subject of interwar censorship by the Home Office.

Images of deviant heterosexuality seemed to be of at least equal concern to the Home Office when looking at the plots of *Lady Chatterley's Lover* and *Sleeveless Errand*. Lawrence's *Lady Chatterley* deals with the extra-marital affair of the upper-class Lady Chatterley with the male gamekeeper on her husband's estate. Her husband, Clifford, had been paralysed in World War I, thus leading in part to her affair. Her sexual and romantic relationship with Mellors eventually results in her pregnancy and she leaves Clifford for him. The novel, while banned in Britain upon its release, was later published in France and enjoyed healthy sales there until it was put on trial in Britain in 1960 and was absolved under the revised 1959 definition of obscenity. *Sleeveless Errand* by Norah C. Jones could not make the same claims to being as highbrow as *Lady Chatterley*. In style and tone it was quite similar to the middlebrow novels discussed in previous chapters, a fact which did not escape Jones's contemporaries. Author Rebecca West was part of the literary elite who felt compelled to speak out against its censorship even as they found themselves defending somewhat lowbrow novels. West made a comment on both Jones's censorship troubles and her writing style when she wrote, 'She must frequently have regretted that she did not write a nice healthy book such as Miss Dell writes about girls in boys' clothing being horse-whipped by he-men.'[56] The comparison between Jones and Ethel M. Dell, the popular author of *The Sheik* and its sequels, is not entirely unfair, although perhaps slightly overstated. The story of *Sleeveless Errand* begins with Paula Cranford's lover, Philip, ending their relationship. The novel follows Paula over two days as she decides to commit suicide and then befriends a similarly disillusioned young man, Bill Cheland, who has discovered his wife's infidelity. They meet various immoral people as Paula sorts out her affairs in preparation for her death. She then talks Bill out of committing suicide and into returning to his wife. The novel ends with Paula driving over a cliff.

All of the above novels, *Boy*, *Lady Chatterley's Lover*, *Sleeveless Errand*, and *The Well of Loneliness*, contain images of female sexuality not sufficiently contained by a loving and somewhat chaste heterosexual relationship. In *Lady Chatterley*, Lady Chatterley herself, Connie, is operating outside of the bounds of her marriage when she engages in an adulterous, albeit heterosexual, affair; in *Sleeveless Errand* Paula Cranford has been dumped by her male lover but shares a bed with Bill even though they do not have sex; in *Boy* the only women in the story are prostitutes who are paid for their contributions to a heterosexual relationship; and in *The Well*, Stephen Gordon rejects both a heterosexual relationship and a feminine role. In this way, none of the novels conform to ideas of a happy ending bound by heterosexual love, ideas that seemed to form the normative base of the Home Office's ideology. In addition the women within these novels demonstrate a marked cynicism about the heterosexual happy ending. Lady Chatterley is unsatisfied with her initial happy ending – her marriage with Clifford – when it is marred by disability, Paula speaks often and negatively about love, while the prostitutes in *Boy* cynically count sex as an economic transaction. Stephen Gordon stands alone among these female characters as one who does believe in and yearn for the happy ending of mutual love in *The Well*. Yet this happy ending is not achieved in the form of either heterosexual or homosexual love.

Along with featuring women who operate outside of the normative bounds of heterosexual love, the primacy of the soldier figure as both the centre of the nation and centre of the economy was questioned in these novels. The connection between these novels and the war itself has been mentioned by Celia Marshik in her examination of *The Well* and *Sleeveless Errand*.[57] She notes that the war was vital to both books. While she argues that their censorship was an effort to contain images of the war that stressed the sexual freedom that women gained in wartime and which haunted them afterwards, I want to shift the focus from the sexual freedom gained by the women to the negative role attributed to the male soldier within the novels cited above. The theme of the exiled male, which was so vital to the popular film and fiction formula, seems just as vital to the censors, because while the popular formula I have outlined resolved the exile of the male by resituating him at the centre of the nation and the economy and through heterosexual love, none of the above novels achieve that resolution. The soldier is left conspicuously exiled at the novels' ends in terms of his war service, his position as the superior breadwinner, and his contribution to a heterosexual union. In many ways, the censoring of these novels reflected the Home Office's concerns about the depiction of the hero; concerns that we have seen were shared and acted upon by the BBFC.

Lady Chatterley by D. H. Lawrence presented the censors with a nuanced and damning portrait of the soldier undone socially, physically, and mentally by the war. Lord Clifford Chatterley is the wealthy son of a conservative landowner and businessman. After his marriage to the new Lady Chatterley he 'was shipped home smashed' in 1918, paralysed from the waist down; he then takes up writing.[58] This physical paralysis was the outward reflection of a mind almost as damaged. The effect of the war is referred to as a bruise that spreads through Clifford and taints him. Lawrence attributes his state directly to the war:

> The colliers at Tevershall were talking again of a strike, and it seemed to Connie there again it was not a manifestation of energy, it was the bruise of the war that had been in abeyance, slowly rising to the surface and creating the great ache of unrest, and stupor of discontent. The bruise was deep, deep, deep … the bruise of the false inhuman war.[59]

A connection between paralysis of the economy, the nation, and the figure of Clifford as the soldier was made explicit. All the former ideals of heroism, nobility, and a healthy economy were as smashed as the soldier himself. Indeed the actual war, as it also was in popular fiction, was not described at all. It was merely an absence in the novel, marking the hollowness and meaninglessness of all that had been associated with the soldier role before the war. Instead the reader is left only with the consequence of the war in Clifford's paralysed body, his weak mind, and his inability to maintain any connection with his wife.

Clifford's wartime role as soldier is undermined throughout the novel. Little about him offers up a vision of heroic strength or honour. He becomes an increasingly pathetic figure as his physical and emotional separation from Connie progresses. Connie had initially taken responsibility for his personal care after his wounding, but this becomes too much for her and she throws off this role in a way that make it clear that she sees him as a grasping, weak, and contaminating figure: 'a bulb stuck parasitic on her tree of life, and producing to her eyes, a rather shabby flower'.[60] Clifford is instead entrusted to the energetic Mrs Bolton, a woman from the working class who considers herself somewhat above that class because of her profession as nurse. Mrs Bolton's nursing role becomes valuable to Clifford and she quickly diagnoses his state of mind upon learning of Connie's affair as 'male hysteria', a term that Elaine Showalter has noted was not easily accepted when dealing with the shell-shock of soldiers.[61] Mrs Bolton takes charge of Clifford physically and mentally with an approach that conceives of all men as 'babies, just big babies'.[62] He is shaved and catered to by Mrs Bolton and gradually emerges as a more juvenile figure.

Clifford's wartime credentials are further insulted by Mellors's position in the novel as the one who undermines his manhood being a soldier himself who produces a child with Lady Chatterley and secures Connie's sexual and romantic satisfaction. In the very first moment that Connie sees Mellors in the narrative he is introduced as a soldier. When he is called by Clifford, a further description is offered: 'The man at once slung his gun over his shoulder, and came forward with the same curious swift, yet soft movements, as if keeping invisible. He was moderately tall and lean, and was silent.' This in many ways seems to define pre-war ideas of soldiers, yet we soon discover that even Mellors's service does not fit with British or at least English ideas of soldiering and heroism. He had served in India, rather than France, and had been out there for years, learning in Clifford's eyes nothing but to think beyond his proper station in life. Moreover when Mellors contemplates his own time in the service it is in a negative way, as something that necessitates his desire for solitude from the world. His soldiering in the east, his working-class status, and his social mobility through a sexual affair with Lady Chatterley all make him an exiled figure, yet one who is not returned to the economic and social centre of the novel as the ideal hero.

While Clifford's identity as a soldier is revealed as hollow, he does maintain a significant role at the centre of Britain's economy through his increasing involvement with his coal mine. Yet this is undermined by the personal insights the reader is given into his life and the general treatment of the mines as always on the edge of striking and as a 'mechanical' part of 'this terrifying new and gruesome England'.[63] It is clear that Clifford's return to power and authority is fostered by the older, working-class nursemaid Mrs Bolton.[64] Mrs Bolton talks to him of the mine's productivity and the possibility of its being closed down and Clifford sees the opportunity of capturing what Lawrence feminises as 'the bitch-goddess of success' through industry rather than literary fame:

> Under Mrs. Bolton's influence, Clifford was tempted to enter this other fight, to capture the bitch-goddess by brute means of industrial production. Somehow, he got his pecker up. In one way, Mrs. Bolton made a man of him, as Connie never did. Connie kept him apart, and made him sensitive and conscious of himself and his own states. Mrs. Bolton made him aware only of outside things. Inwardly he began to go soft as pulp. But outwardly he began to be effective.[65]

Mrs Bolton abets Clifford's economic success but the manhood he claims from the pit is diluted by her involvement and Clifford's own inner lack of strength. Not only were Clifford and Mrs Bolton acting outside of normative age-appropriate gender roles but they were also subverting class hierarchy. This demonstrates that the connection between the economy and masculinity, and its subversion by female involvement, is very much central to the novel.

Mrs Bolton is clearly in charge of Clifford and by the end of the novel his need of her is so great that he looks to her for business advice, personal care, and physical contact. The last images of Clifford are him at his most childlike under her care:

> He would gaze on her with wide, childish eyes, in a relaxation of Madonna-worship. It was sheer relaxation on his part, letting go of all his manhood, and sinking back to a childish position that was really perverse. And then he would put his hand into her bosom and feel her breasts, and kiss them in exultation of perversity, of being a child when he was a man.[66]

In this way Clifford was completely subject to the greater female authority of Mrs Bolton. Her reaction is one of mingled disgust and admiration, as well as a realisation of her power:

> Mrs. Bolton was both thrilled and ashamed, she both loved and hated it. Yet she never rebuffed nor rebuked him. And they drew into a closer physical intimacy, an intimacy of perversity, when he was a child stricken with an apparent candour and an apparent wonderment … While she was the Magna Mater, full of power and potency, having the great blond child-man under her will and her stroke entirely.

Earlier in the novel Connie realises she has a similar degree of power over Clifford and is more thoroughly disgusted by it. Clifford declares to Connie, 'I mean, but for you I am absolutely nothing. I live for your sake and your future. I am nothing to myself.' This indeed is Clifford's 'magic moment', yet Connie is appalled by his declaration'.[67] Connie instead turns to the strong but silent Mellors who does not offer her a link to the nation or the economy but rather to sexual fulfilment. Consequently the role of the upright soldier at the centre of the nation and the economy, and as the focus of the narrative's heterosexual relationship is destabilised on all fronts.

The masculinity of the soldier figure continued to be threatened in the other novels censored by the Home Office, including the *Well of Loneliness*, which offered up the ideal soldier yet in the form of a woman. In many respects, Stephen Gordon is the perfect man but she is a woman. Stephen grows up in the country with considerable wealth and an interest in horses, cars, and education. At 21 she is described as 'a rich, independent woman'.[68] She longs to care financially for her female lover Mary and 'give the girl luxury, make her secure so that she need never fight for her living; she could have every comfort that money could buy'. Stephen showers Mary with gifts, buying expensive jewellery and clothing and taking long vacations.

Stephen is also devoted to Britain and at the outbreak of war she feels compelled to fight for her country, yet is frustrated by the limits of her own sex:

> Every instinct handed down the men of her race, every decent instinct of courage, now rose to mock her so that all that was male in her make-up seemed to grow more aggressive, aggressive perhaps as never before, because of this new frustration … England was calling her men into battle, her women to the bedsides of the wounded and dying, and between these two chivalrous, surging forces she, Stephen, might well be crushed out of existence.[69]

Stephen finds a way of serving, joining the 'London Ambulance Column', and is eventually sent to the western front to drive. This activity in the war is portrayed as her limited acceptance into British institutions: 'England had taken her, asking no questions – she was strong and efficient, she could fill a man's place, she could organise too, given scope for her talent.'[70] The column she serves in is entirely made up of women like her: 'Miss Smith who had been breeding dogs in the country; or Miss Oliphant who had been breeding nothing since birth but a litter of hefty complexes; or Miss Tring who had lived with a very dear friend in the humbler purlieus of Chelsea. One great weakness they all had, it must be admitted, and this was for uniforms.'[71] This group did well in the war and Stephen behaves honourably at the front, earning the Croix de Guerre as well as the companionship of her fellow ambulance driver, Mary.

As Marshik points out, the connection between the war and the love affair between Stephen and Mary was a bone of contention at Hall's trial. Hall herself seemed to anticipate this when she penned the author's note at the outset of the novel:

> A motor ambulance unit of British women drivers did very fine service upon the Allied front in France during the war, but although the unit mentioned in this book, of which Stephen Gordon becomes a member, operates in much the same area, it has never had any existence save in the author's imagination.[72]

The prosecution focused on this depiction of women at the front, causing Hall to interrupt the judge in protest. In a letter to Bernard Shaw she wrote that she saw the prosecutors' interpretation of her description of the front as a site of sexual indulgence as slander against the units themselves.[73] Such a heated debate about the proper depiction of those engaged in wartime activities was not unfamiliar to censorship authorities in this period, as I have demonstrated. A culture of censorship around the soldier figure had survived the war, even if it appeared increasingly archaic. Hall's book challenged the sexed and hetero-sexual assumption surrounding soldiering, even if it conformed to some of the aspects of the ideal soldier as the centre of Britain's economy and its sense of self as a nation.

James Hanley's *Boy* offered up a vision of a sailor that would have shocked and appalled the BBFC's Colonel Hanna, even if these sailors were not tied to the Royal Navy.[74] The sailors that the boy, Arthur Fearon, encounters are crude, coarse, and often interested in having sex with him. One of these sailors lures him into a heterosexual situation with a prostitute who ends up infecting him with syphilis, while the other sailor looks on. The only somewhat honourable figure in the novel is Captain Wood, whose smothering of the boy at the end is presented as an alternative to a painful death by syphilis. The novel seemed intent on puncturing romantic conceptions of service to the sea: 'I gamble you are quite a romantic young person so far as the sea is concerned. But, my boy, there is something associated with the sea that you have not yet learned. The day you learn it you will know the meaning of slavery. That's all the sea ever was.'[75] Lawyers for the prosecution of the novel concentrated upon the crude language used by the sailors, the images of homosexuality, and the wrapper on the book, which depicted a scantily clad prostitute dancing for two sailors.[76] The Council for Civil Liberties, headed up by E. M. Forster and including J. B. Priestley and H. G. Wells as vice-presidents, protested the prosecution and banning of the book to no avail, basing their objections upon the reputation of the author and publisher rather than the book itself: 'We offer no opinion on the book itself, though we point out that Mr. Hanley is a writer of standing and that Messrs. Boriswood, the publisher, against whom the prosecution was brought, are a firm of repute.'[77] Such a tepid defence of the book carefully avoided its content as well as the controversial portrayal of sailors at the heart of it.

Norah C. James's *Sleeveless Errand*, banned in the same year as *The Well of Loneliness*, presented a critique of the soldier figure and the war in general. The protagonist Norah complains to Bill:

> We seem to have lost our moral sense. My own brothers are a good example of what I'm saying. I had four. Decent ordinary boys when the war came. They were all in it, and now the two who are still alive are just wasters – not really bad, but slipshod and weak. They live for to-day alone – to-morrow they may be dead – if not, they muddle through that day too, because the next may never come. Isn't that the direct outcome of the war psychology?[78]

Norah's brothers are painted as weak and unstable, not at all the type of soldier maintained in popular film and fiction. The theme of the unstable war generation is repeated throughout the novel in rather awkward and repetitive moments where Norah holds forth on the topic: 'Look at our generation, Bill, and the next; by the next I mean the people who were born just before or during the War. Haven't they struck you as all hopelessly at sea? As a whole we don't seem to have any moral values left at all.'[79] Indeed, the novel demonstrates this lack of morality following the war as Norah and Bill visit multiple seedy bars and encounter people devoted to drinking and drugs.

Sleeveless Errand also takes aim at the institutions and ideologies at the heart of wartime Britain. Norah complains that the war itself revealed the hollowness of such beliefs:

> The War banged every preconceived theory to bits. What chance had we of keeping our heads when all around us we saw the extremes that are a part of it? Excess and intense privation, ruthless discipline and loose living; the highest awards made to men for the destruction of the enemy, and hanging the murderer for the same action of taking human life. Imprisoning men whose conscience would not let them fight, and shouting that war was altogether wrong and must never again be allowed. The Church too! What a failure![80]

According to Norah, the government failed to distinguish between murder and heroism, and she hints at the great divide between images of the profiteer and those who suffered economically in the war. Religion is also judged lacking in light of the war. Norah goes on to declare that the post-World War I period held its most bitter pills for those still wanting to believe in the efforts of the state:

> Those of us who had cared a bit about reconstruction and all that came down with even a greater bang, for we found that there wasn't going to be any reconstruction at all. That all the politicians could do was to try and get votes by slogans. Things like 'Hang the Kaiser and make the world safe for Democracy'. Democracy. Christ! What a farce.[81]

For Norah, democracy has become a farce in the period after the war and she has realised that politicians work for power and not the good of the people. This, again, was the enduring legacy of the interwar period, when the government took on an increasingly villainous character within film and fiction. Such cynicism about everything from democracy and the church, to politicians and men in general, illuminates her multiple reasons for suicide beyond the ending of her relationship with her lover. Collectively these books describe a society of women unhappy in heterosexual relationships and men unable to fulfil their roles as soldiers, breadwinners, and lovers.

While the Home Office provides the historian an opportunity to survey a body of banned novels, the BBFC's censorship of films makes it difficult to access a similar body. Annette Kuhn, however, has assembled a survey of the early period of British film until 1925 which indicates that the BBFC followed a similar path to the Home Office.[82] Looking at the scenario reports throughout the 1930s, one can see that the BBFC stayed true to the Home Office's pattern by objecting to depictions of nudity and situations which suggested intimacy between non-married couples. To Hitchcock's *Thirty-Nine Steps*, the first reader's only suggested revisions are regarding the heterosexual relationship of the hero and his love-interest:

> Story is harmless melodrama, with various improbable adventures.
> Sc. 105. Delete reference to sex appeal.
> Sc. 219–223. Crofter and wife must not be shown in bed together.
> Sc. 421. Hannay and Pamela handcuffed together on bed. This must be modified.[83]

The second reader disagreed with the objections, stating:

> Sc. 219 Showing crofter and wife in bed. I see no harm in the way it is shown.
> Sc. 417 and 418 Pamela and Hannay lying on the bed. I consider perfectly harmless.

The film was passed with no deletions, perhaps because it culminated in a happy heterosexual ending.

A film version of *Lady Chatterley's Lover*, however, met a quick end at the hands of the BBFC when it was submitted as a scenario in 1935. The first reader, presumably Colonel Hanna, noted at the outset of his scenario report that it is 'based on a notorious book which I understand was banned in Britain' and declared, 'I fear I cannot find any excuse for Constance. Her liaison with Mellors is just plain animal passion. There is nothing else in the story. I do not advise the production of a film based on the story as submitted.' Lawrence's novel and the undermined masculinity of Sir Clifford Chatterley doubtless had little appeal to the Colonel in light of his thoughts on the depictions of soldiers. The second reader was a little more circumspect about the film, comparing it to other films that had been exhibited and also providing some suggestions for how it could see the light of day:

> I do not like this story being produced as a film, but it is difficult to call it prohibitive in view of the fact that a French film 'Remous' was shown in London recently and dealt with a similar situation. I do not know if 'Remous' was given a certificate. In any case the outcome of the stories differ. In 'Remous' the husband commits suicide to leave the woman free to marry her lover. In this story (Lady Chatterley) the sympathy is entirely with the woman and the writer condones her infidelity, which I consider has a lowering moral effect.

If this story is to be produced I think the complete scenario should be submitted and the following impossible scenes be omitted:–

p. 6 Mellors naked body at tub

p. 21 Connie and Mellors taking off their clothes in the rain and submitting to their passions.[84]

No information is given about whether another scenario was submitted but the film was not produced.

For the most part, the script readers at the BBFC concentrated on unnecessary depictions of skin and nudity within films. In response to the film based on bestselling author Michael Arlen's novel *Lily Christine*, the single script reader in 1932 objected to the dress of women in the film:

Sc. 33. … There seems no necessity to show these details of the lady in various stages of undress. She could be perfectly decently clothed in a dressing grown without affecting the story.

Sc. 107. Delete Ivor in bed with Lily. He can sit on the outside of the bed and chat. Delete the following dialogue in this scene. 'Bloody good' and 'I'll commit any wickedness to get you'.

Sc. 123. Another undressed lady scene which is quite unnecessary to the story and dragged in gratuitously. It would be much better to delete it altogether.[85]

The script readers thus concentrated on what they saw as unnecessary displays of the female body. Little mention exists in the records about display of male bodies but it was already the norm of this period for films to display the female more often than the male. For the most part, however, the unease expressed in the scenario reports with depictions of sexuality and the body was proportionate to its other concerns with criminality and proper depictions of the hero.

Images of love and sexuality were also of concern to groups like the Birmingham Cinema Enquiry Committee, yet their reports exhibited greater concern with issues such as crime on the screen. The Birmingham group recorded the responses of children about 'Impressions in regards to Sex' that they learned from films in its 1931 report:

I have learnt:

'How to love and to murder people at the same time'

'A lot about murdering and love'

'How to kiss' (Boy of 13)

'I have learnt about love'

'I have learnt a lot about love'

'Women without any clothes are love stories'

'Love pictures is teaching children very young' (Girl of 12)

'Nothing at all except the art of love' (Boy of 12)[86]

Those comments followed by the ages clearly indicated the BCEC's thoughts on such an education in love. But in general, what the children learned about love seemed less objectionable to the group than the age at which they learned it. As well, in comparison to the concern about misleading depictions of crime, no similarly heightened rhetoric about the false messages of love existed in the report. Little was said about the false impressions of love and the happy endings that were being generated on-screen, or that images of love should be banned at all. Rather the concern seemed to be about the age and means by which children achieved this education. Such a concern over the age rather than the 'truth' of film love is an indication of the degree of success that censors as well as film producers achieved in bringing palatable images of heterosexuality to the screen.

What the censorship efforts of the Home Office and the BBFC in regard to sexuality and the character of the love-interest indicate is that both organisations were heavily engaged in promoting a normative masculine ideal through the endorsement of a particular type of female heterosexuality. Female heterosexuality became an important underpinning to the presentation of a vital masculinity that could sustain the love of a good woman and play an integral role at the centre of Britain's nation and economy. Narratives and images that did not fit with this ideal tended to be censored as a result. Consequently the censorship of sexuality by the Home Office was not simply about the frank depiction of sex acts and naughty bits, but rather about the political implications of this sexuality. I have demonstrated that the sexuality within the censored novels discussed was tied to negative portrayals of the soldier and the ideals that he represented after World War I. Containing these images of errant female sexuality allowed censors to maintain an image of an idealised Britain that could still subscribe to heroic ideals. Censors in this period, like the producers of bestselling novels and popular films, worked to reform a capitalist democracy based upon the primacy of the heroic soldier and the male breadwinner.

Conclusion

The interwar censorship of film and fiction can be understood only when viewed through the lens of World War I. Through this lens we can see that censorship was, for all intentions, a continuation of wartime censorship, which did not allow for negative portrayals of the soldier. Organisations such as the BBFC and the Home Office continued to foster the culture of censorship that had surrounded images of soldiers during wartime. Soldiers were persistently portrayed as brave and honourable men who got the girl, who believed in the nation and the government in charge of it, and who, after they vanquished the villain, ultimately subscribed to a capitalist economy. Film and fiction that worked against these images was simply unacceptable.

Thus we can see that censoring bodies saw the maintenance of this soldiering ideal as key to the continuation of Britain's economy and nationalism. The rupture between the soldier, the nation, and economy that I outlined in Chapter 1 was not one that was easily acknowledged by government bodies. Instead they worked tirelessly to maintain this relationship through the alternating endorsement and censoring of specific characters and relations in popular narratives. Censorship was not simply a prohibitive and productive act; it was a defensive effort to manage the ideological impact of the war upon Britain, an impact that threatened to be expressed through the powerful media of popular culture. This was the theme 'repeated over and over again' that was deemed most undesirable by the Home Office and the BBFC.[87]

Notes

1 M. Glancy, 'Temporary American Citizens? British Audiences, Hollywood Films and the Threat of Americanization in the 1920s', *Historical Journal of Film, Radio and Television* 26:4 (2006), 461–84; P. Marshall, 'The Lord Chamberlain and the Containment of Americanization in the British Theatre of the 1920s', *New Theatre Quarterly* 19 (2003), 381–94; J. C. Robertson, 'The Censors and British Gangland, 1913–1990', in S. Chibnall and R. Murphy (eds), *British Crime Cinema* (New York: Routledge, 1999); J. Springhall, 'Censoring Hollywood: Youth, Moral Panic and Crime/Gangster Movies of the 1930s', *Journal of Popular Culture* 32:3 (1998), 135.

2 A. Kuhn, *Cinema, Censorship and Sexuality, 1909–1925* (New York: Routledge, 1988), p. 7.

3 M. Kinservik, *Disciplining Satire: The Censorship of Satiric Comedy on the Eighteenth-Century London Stage* (London: Associated University Presses, 2002).

4 R. Weil, 'Sometimes a Sceptre is Only a Sceptre: Pornography and Politics in Restoration England', in L. Hunt (ed.), *The Invention of Pornography: Obscenity and the Origins of Modernity, 1500–1800* (New York: Zone Books, 1993), pp. 125–53.

5 Foucault, *History of Sexuality: Vol. I*; Lynn Hunt (ed.), *The Invention of Pornography: Obscenity and the Origins of Modernity, 1500–1800* (New York: Zone Books, 1993); McCalman, *Radical Underworld*.

6 *Governing Pleasures: Pornography and Social Change in England, 1815–1914* (New Brunswick: Rutgers University Press, 2002).

7 *Discipline and Punish*.

8 A. Kuhn, 'Children, "Horrific" Films, and Censorship in 1930s Britain', *Historical Journal of Film, Radio and Television* 22:2 (2002), 197–202; Richards, 'British

Board of Film Censors and Content Control in the 1930s', 95–116; J. C. Robertson, *The British Board of Film Censors: Film Censorship in Britain, 1896–1950* (London: Croom Helm, 1985); J. C. Robertson, *The Hidden Cinema: British Film Censorship in Action, 1913–72* (London: Routledge, 1993); M. Dickenson and S. Street, *Cinema and the State: The Film Industry and the British Government 1927–84* (London: BFI, 1985); J. Trevelyan, *What the Censor Saw* (London: Michael Joseph, 1977); J. Pellew, *The Home Office 1848–1914: From Clerks to Bureaucrats* (London: Heinemann Educational, 1982).

  9 A. Parkes, 'Lesbianism, History, and Censorship: *The Well of Loneliness* and the Suppressed Randiness of Virginia Woolf's *Orlando*', *Twentieth Century Literature* 40:4 (1994), 434–60; C. Pollnitz, 'The Censorship and Transmission of D. H. Lawrence's Pansies: The Home Office and the "Foul-Mouthed Fellow"', *Journal of Modern Literature* 28:3 (2005), 44–71; A. Wee, 'Trials & Eros: the British Home Office v. indecent publications 1857–1932' (University of Minnesota, Ph.D. thesis, 2003); L. Doan, *Fashioning Sapphism: The Origins of a Modern English Lesbian Culture* (New York: Columbia University Press, 2000).

10 At the BBFC, Joseph Brooke Wilkinson occupied the position as Secretary of the Board from 1913 to 1948. At the Home Office there were three under-secretaries: Sir Edward Troup (1908–22), Sir John Anderson (1922–32), and Sir Russell Scott (1932–38), followed by Sir Alexander Maxwell as Britain entered the war. The under-secretary was an especially vital role at the Home Office, where the major figurehead of the Secretary of State changed with each election.

11 HO 144/14042, File 544688/16, letter of 24 March 1930.

12 N. Pronay, 'The "Moving Picture" and Historical Research', *Journal of Contemporary History* 18:3 (1983), 365–95.

13 See the Appendix to this book, which lists material deemed objectionable in 1917.

14 HO 45/15139, File 511182/95.

15 Lucy Bland dates the formation of the LPMC to 1901 ('"Purifying" the Public World: Feminist Vigilantes in Late Victorian England', *Women's History Review* 1:3 (1993), 397–412).

16 Kuhn, 'Children, "Horrific" Films, and Censorship in 1930s Britain', 3.

17 Richards, 'The British Board of Film Censors and Content Control in the 1930s'.

18 *Ibid.*, 101.

19 Watson, *Fighting Different Wars*.

20 HO 144/14042, File 544688/33, letter of 19 June 1930.

21 HO 144/14042, File 544688/33, letter of 5 August 1930.

22 HO 144/14042, File 544688/33 is entitled 'Censorship of War Books'.

23 Reproduced in N. March Hunnings, *Film Censors and the Law* (London: Allen & Unwin, 1967), 408–9. See also the Appendix to this book.

24 'Father O'Flynn' 29 August 1935, BBFC Scenario Reports 1935; 'The Mind of Mr. Reeder' 13 September 1935, BBFC Scenario Reports, 1935.

25 HO 45/11191, File 373422/64, press release, 29 January 1923.

26 'When the Gangs Came to London' 3 November 1932, BBFC Scenario Reports, 1930–32.

27 'The Hidden Hand' 27 February 1934, BBFC Scenario Reports, 1934.

28 'The Man Who Knew Too Much' 10 May 1934, BBFC Scenario Reports, 1934.
29 *Ibid.*
30 'Storm over India' 22 June 1939, BBFC Scenario Reports, 1939.
31 'Father O'Flynn' 29 August 1935.
32 'Doctor's Dilemma' 18 February 1935, BBFC Scenario Reports, 1935.
33 'The Mind of Mr. Reeder' 13 September 1935.
34 'Lives of a Bengal Lancer' 24 January 1934, BBFC Scenario Reports, 1934.
35 HO 45/11191, File 373422/64, letter from the BBFC, 29 January 1923.
36 Springhall, 'Censoring Hollywood'.
37 *Mass-Observation at the Movies*, 34–5.
38 HO 45/14276, File 551004/92, Birmingham Cinema Enquiry Committee: Reports of Visits to Cinemas Autumn 1930, spring 1931, received at HO, 15 May 1931.
39 *Ibid.*, 6.
40 *Ibid.*, 17.
41 *Ibid.*
42 *Ibid.*, 18–19.
43 HO 45/14276, File 551004/92, Deputation from the Birmingham Cinema Enquiry Committee to the Home Secretary, 8 May 1931.
44 *Ibid.*, 13–14.
45 HO 45/14276, File 551004/92, letter marked 'Private and Confidential', 19 May 1931.
46 *Ibid.*
47 BBFC Annual Report, 1929.
48 'Censoring Hollywood', 102–3.
49 'The Devil Man' 6 August 1931, BBFC Scenario Report, 1930–32.
50 'The Rose and Crown' 10 Oct 1934, BBFC Scenario Report, 1934.
51 'Seized novel condemned', *The Times* (3 March 1929).
52 R. Hall, *The Well of Loneliness* (Paris: Pegasus Press, 1928), p. 365.
53 Quoted in Doan, *Fashioning Sapphism*.
54 *Ibid.*
55 The reasons for *Extraordinary Women* escaping censorship are difficult to ascertain. The Home Office reported in its file that the chief magistrate's opinion of the book consisted of the following: 'that the end of the book certainly did not indicate that these persons had done otherwise than ruin their own lives and happiness, the book ending on rather a tragic note'. If dismal endings allowed novels about lesbians to remain uncensored, then surely *The Well of Loneliness* should have escaped uncensored. This indicates something beyond same-sex sex or love was objectionable (9 August 1928, HO 45/15727, File 5282/84).
56 Rebecca West, 'A Jixless errand', *Time and Tide* (15 March 1929), p. 285.
57 'History's "Abrupt Revenges": Censoring War's Perversions in *The Well of Loneliness* and *Sleeveless Errand*', *Journal of Modern Literature* 26:2 (2003), 145–59.
58 D. H. Lawrence, *Lady Chatterley's Lover* (Middlesex: Penguin, 1961 [1928]), p. 13.
59 *Ibid.*, p. 53.
60 *Ibid.*, p. 86.
61 *Ibid.*, 301; E. Showalter, 'Rivers and Sassoon: The Inscription of Male Gender

Anxieties', in Margaret Randolph Higonnet *et al.* (eds), *Behind the Lines: Gender and the Two World Wars* (New Haven: Yale University Press, 1987), pp. 61–9.

62 Lawrence, *Lady Chatterley's Lover*, p. 103.

63 *Ibid.*, p. 163.

64 *Ibid.*, p. 109.

65 *Ibid.*, pp. 111–12.

66 *Ibid.*, p. 303.

67 *Ibid.*, p. 117.

68 Hall, *Well of Loneliness*, p. 152.

69 *Ibid.*, 315.

70 *Ibid.*, 319.

71 *Ibid.*, 320.

72 *Ibid.*, 9.

73 Quoted in Marshik, 'History's "Abrupt Revenges"', 152.

74 HO 144/22430, File 648756/32.

75 J. Hanley, *Boy* (London: Boriswood, 1931), p. 176.

76 J. Armstrong, 'The Publication, Prosecution, and Re-publication of James Hanley's *Boy* (1931)', *Library* 6–19:4 (1997), 351–62.

77 'Prosecutions of Publishers', *Spectator* (26 April 1935).

78 N. C. James, *Sleeveless Errand* (Paris: Henry Babou and Jack Kahane, 1929 [1928]), pp. 59–60.

79 *Ibid.*, p. 202.

80 *Ibid.*, pp. 202–3.

81 *Ibid.*, p. 205.

82 *Cinema, Censorship and Sexuality.*

83 'The Thirty-Nine Steps', 14 January 1935, BBFC Scenario Report, 1935.

84 'Lady Chatterley's Lover', 14 June 1935, BBFC Scenario Report, 1935.

85 'Lilly Christine', 8 February 1932, BBFC Scenario Report, 1930–32.

86 BCEC 'Report of Questionnaire Addressed to School Children' 5 May 1931, HO 45/14276, File 551004/92.

87 E. Shortt, speech to the Conference of the Cinema Exhibitors' Association, 27 June 1935.

Conclusion: thoughts on heroes, villains, and love-interests beyond 1939

This monograph has highlighted the existence of a persistent ideology about gender, the economy, and the nation within the film and fiction most popular with British audiences between World War I and the outset of World War II. Over and over again, popular film and fiction narratives worked to buttress the role of the male breadwinner and soldier as the centre of the nation and economy. These chapters have charted the multiple paths through which this ideology was shaped: in villainous characters, love-interests, heroes as well as government bodies. The creation and maintenance of such an ideology, which drew upon two powerful media, the work of many character and narrative devices, as well as censoring bodies, was not a light undertaking.

The need for such an ideology, as I have demonstrated, was great in the interwar period. The impact of World War I upon conceptions of the soldier, of government, and business, and changing patterns of male and female employment all contributed to the production and consumption on a large scale of a message that promoted pre-war views of work, gender, and the nation. The narratives of popular film and fiction, produced by both British and American authors and filmmakers, consumed by British audiences, and further sanctioned by the British government, offered images of stability to eager audiences that moderated fears about the viability of a capitalist economy and the roles of men and women within it. Heroes working for the good of the nation and in support of an existing system continued to vanquish the villains who were abusing their roles within both. Working women were less threatening as workers when they demonstrated in popular narratives that work would always be secondary to a heterosexual relationship with a heroic man. Messages such as these were repeated throughout the interwar period and continued to persist beyond 1939. Although it is sometimes thought to be out of form for the historian to connect studies of the past to years beyond it, an analysis of a war's impact upon narratives within popular culture unfortunately offers up more instances beyond World War I as comparison. I will mention only briefly the possibilities for studies of popular culture's shifting ideologies beyond this book's time-frame.

By far, the greatest benefit to the historian of extending a study of the dominance of the breadwinner ideology beyond 1939 is the variety of sources available for gauging the impact of popular culture on audiences. The interwar period is unique not only in the dominance of fiction and film as powerful media, but also in the scarce sources available on audience responses to this media. Even World War II offers more opportunity for the historian to gauge this effect. Studies by the social survey group Mass Observation can grant historians some insight into the dialectic between the narratives of film and fiction and the audience. Presumably sources from the latter half of the twentieth century would offer similar insights. The ways in which television, independent film, and the Internet both subvert and build upon the ideology I have outlined here, could also indicate the extent to which this ideology has informed the worldviews of those who have spent their lifetimes consuming it.

We can, for instance, gain a greater understanding of how media impacted ordinary people during World War II due to the widespread concern, both official and unofficial, with home-front morale during the war and the role of media in this. Certainly, the production and consumption of a stable ideology involving the heroic breadwinner underwent some significant shifts with the beginning of World War II. Although the hero continued to work tirelessly for the nation and his family, men had to face further challenges to their exclusive status as soldiers and breadwinners. Soldiers endured an intensification of the mechanised warfare that had been introduced in World War I as bombs, tanks, planes, and submarines were used on a larger scale. The popular film directed by Noël Coward and David Lean, *In Which We Serve* (1942), concentrated upon submarine warfare as the heroic captain, Captain Kinross, led his men and his ship through numerous battles.[1] The film reflected not just the challenge posed to the soldier situating himself behind tanks and within ships, but also the changing role of Britain within the war and within the world. *In Which We Serve* was about a ship that ultimately sank in service of country and cause. The stiff upper lip of its hero, played by Coward himself, and the combined efforts of sailors of all different classes were celebrated in the film more than any definitive victory.

The wartime bombing of Britain would further contribute to storylines that celebrated community and ordinary people as heroes, such as the elderly, the young, and women. British film began to look noticeably different to American film in this period, as the early role Britain played in the war, its experience of direct and sustained bombing, and its effort at nationwide mobilisation emphasised different narratives from the US in films such as *Millions Like Us* (1943), *A Canterbury Tale* (1944), and *Went the Day Well* (1942).[2] Wartime films increasingly promoted survival and perseverance as key heroic characteristics of the modern British citizen. Not surprisingly the efforts of documentary filmmakers such as Humphrey Jennings and others associated with the Crown Film Unit found great success dramatising the everyday role of people in the war. The role of the masculine hero underwent significant changes as a result of this broadening of the heroic ideal.[3] Changes such as these mark out the popular narratives produced in World War II as worthy of their own study.

A study of popular media during World War II must also grapple with government's increasingly sophisticated understanding and deployment of ideology within popular culture to suit nationalist aims. Propaganda was used to a much greater and devastating effect by all sides during World War II than it had been during World War I. Official British propaganda was partly aimed at addressing the need to mobilise women workers, one more feature that distinguishes that world war from the previous. This mobilisation was much larger than during World War I and posed a considerable challenge to the government, which had a better grasp of both the need to enforce the male breadwinner ideology for those on the fighting front as well as a greater sense of the substantial impact of women's work in sustaining the wartime economy. Representations of women thus had to walk a fine line between deploying heroic narratives around their roles and still emphasising women as heterosexual objects in service to the male heroes on the fighting front. Such complexities often resulted in singular images, and the works of Penny Summerfield as well as Sonya Rose both highlight the conflicting messages about gender and work within government-sponsored propaganda from that period.[4] Antonia Lant has highlighted similarly mixed messages within popular films from the time as well.[5]

Beyond World War II, we might assume a destabilisation of popular culture's promotion of the breadwinner ideology on a number of levels. Film and fiction, for one, became harder to define as the dominant producer of a coherent and popular ideology, as new media threatened to usurp their hold upon audiences. Television and other forms of entertainment such as rock 'n' roll, and of course the Internet, have vied with film and fiction as powerful media after World War II. Film and fiction have struggled ever since to regain the domination that they enjoyed in the 1920s and 1930s. Innovations in home viewing as well as production techniques have resulted in dramatic changes within the production and consumption of film. Reading patterns have also been affected in the last half of the twentieth century and into the twenty-first. As a result the ideology promoted by film and fiction in the interwar period was somewhat singular in the coherence of its message and in its captive audience. This is not to imply that ideology is less powerful in the current age, but it poses a greater challenge for the historian to identify the multiple media through which the ordinary person imbibes and engages with ideology.

Contributing to these changes was the development of a growing youth culture from the 1950s onwards that saw teenagers rejecting the films and fiction that their parents watched. Youth culture both responded to imposed trends and manufactured their own, as 'youth' were increasingly constituted as a recognisable demographic.[6] Youth culture in the late 1950s and 1960s tended to coalesce around groups that aggressively marked themselves out as unique from their peers through distinctive clothing, music, film and fiction. This again resulted in an audience that arguably demonstrated greater diversity of taste. The dominance of an ideology within popular culture that revolved around work, gender, and nation in the 1920s and 1930s certainly still held sway within the youth culture of the period, but was also subject to sharp criticism from a generation emerging from war and in the age of affluence.

What is perhaps most clear is that the male breadwinner ideology faced considerable challenges in attaching itself to the military as an institution of Englishness in post-war Britain. This new lack of emphasis upon the role of the soldier was due to a number of factors, including Britain's aggressive decolonisation after 1947, Britain's visible and embarrassing inability after 1956 to wage war without the international and economic sanction of the United States, and yet another shift in military engagement resulting from the introduction of nuclear weapons during World War II. Popular films from the 1950s tended to hark back to World War II as a site of nostalgia in light of these changes and stress images of manly cooperation over military victory. Prisoners-of-war films such as *The Colditz Story* (1955) showed British prisoners among many other nationalities in a German camp.[7] The film stressed cooperation among the nations as the most effective means of gaining escape. Other films such as *The Bridge on the River Kwai* (1957) also featured the imprisonment of British soldiers, this time by the Japanese, and stressed the role of an American soldier in sabotaging the plans of the enemy. This film openly questioned the validity of traditional British military ideals as the rigid Colonel Nicholson commits

British efficiency to a bridge that will ultimately aid the Japanese until he realises his folly, with the American's prompting, at the last minute and blows the bridge up.

Post-war movements like the 'Angry Young Men' in post-war Britain, which consisted of a number of young novelists and filmmakers, further produced caustic diatribes against these very conceptions of soldiers even while mourning the loss of these institutions, and Britain's past imperial glory in particular.[8] The protagonist of the play *Look Back in Anger* (1956), performed in the same year as *Bridge on the River Kwai* and the year of the Suez Crisis, declared bitterly that, 'there aren't any good, brave causes left', and yearned for the certainty of the Edwardian age.[9] Decolonisation and the triumph of the United States on the international scene seemed to make the heroic imperial tales of Edgar Wallace and the Korda brothers look ridiculous. As Wendy Webster notes, it was a much more fraught effort to produce films that defended Empire as Britain decolonised in the 1950s and early 1960s.[10] Britain's imperial might had been vastly undercut by the rise of the United States as the world's policeman. Developments such as these after World War II mark out the media produced during the interwar period as exceptional in important ways.

The interwar period also offered the government access to and control over the message of popular culture in ways that it has not seen since. As I argued in Chapter 4, the behind-the-scenes censorship engaged in by the Home Office and the British Board of Film Censors allowed the government to substantially shape and contribute to the ideology of popular culture. This contribution intensified during World War II, resulting in the relatively open manipulation of the media for the purpose of nationalist rhetoric. The propaganda produced by the government was explicitly productive rather than prohibitive, marking a somewhat new relationship to the government's control over the media. The government was no longer vetting the productions of other narratives but instead was an active producer in itself, influencing the production of film and fiction. Not surprisingly, from the 1930s onwards both the government and the ordinary citizen demonstrated increasing awareness about government's relationship to popular culture. The change in obscenity laws in 1959 to allow literary merit as a defence against censorship reflected government's inability to quietly affect changes in film and fiction.[11]

Yet although the interwar period was exceptional in its dissemination of the breadwinner and soldier ideology through popular culture, and although we can see shifts within this ideology beyond 1939, it is ultimately this formula's persistence that is so striking to the modern consumer of popular fiction and film. After all, this story has been one about the impact of capitalism upon conceptions of work, gender, and the nation, and that story continues well beyond the 1920s and 1930s. The end of this study by no means signals the end of that ideology, nor the end of capitalism as the dominant economic system in Britain, or indeed the west. Just as capitalism continues to define people primarily as working units, popular film and fiction just as persistently refine this category to define 'real' workers as men who can save the world. Heroes in big-budget blockbusters persevere in their work for the nation and as independent breadwinners. Villains continue to work against the ability of the hero to maintain his breadwinner status and his role as worker for the nation. Perhaps, most shocking of all, female love-interests still continue to renounce their economic and social mobility for the love of the male hero.

Examples of the popularity of these tropes immediately after World War II abound. Martin Francis points out in his examination of the Ealing Studio film, *Scott of the Antarctic* (1948), that images of masculinity in the late 1940s continued to be tied up with powerful discourses of empire, class, and 'Englishness'.[12] This film featured the doomed expedition of Captain Scott to the Antarctic in the early twentieth century, but stressed the noble British nature of such ambition and sacrifice and the male camaraderie that motivated it. Scott was a hero whose last words in his journal, used to great effect in the film, 'For God's sake, look after our people', clearly positioned him as a hero and protector of the nation who was passing on that very role to others. Even a film that seemed to be about the failure of heroic ideals ultimately enforced them. This, if anything, seems to be a theme of the late 1940s and 1950s.[13]

Films made after the war emphasised the benefits of community, survival, and endurance as noted, but as Penny Summerfield argues, these films also had a hand in rewriting the public history of World War II to affirm older notions of the male hero-soldier. Women largely disappeared from popular films about the war, made after the war.[14] Gone were films that attempted to mobilise women or even ordinary people as home-front soldiers and workers. Instead the war was rewritten as a largely masculine endeavour that empha-sised interwar notions of the breadwinner and the soldier ideal. *The Colditz Story* glorified the position of male prisoners of war by giving imprisoned British soldiers a unique leading position among other nationalities in order to ensure freedom for the people within the Colditz camp. Even the noir film *They Made Me a Fugitive* (1947) represented a dialogue with the idea that a hero should be both a soldier and a breadwinner by illustrating the tragic result when heroes were denied that role. Much like the tragic Baron in *Grand Hotel*, the hero in *They Made Me a Fugitive*, Clem Morgan, is an ex-soldier forced into black-market crime as a result of poverty. The film ends tragically, not with Morgan's death, but with the villain, Narcy, falsely condemning him in his dying moments, and sentencing him to a life of imprisonment and estrangement from his female love-interest. Both films, over a decade apart, and in the context of rebuilding, stress the tragedy of ex-soldiers cast out of their rightful roles at the centre of economy, nation, and heterosexual love.

While films such as *They Made Me a Fugitive* emphasised what could happen to misdirected heroes, many others continued to glorify heroes that worked for king and country. One need only think of the appeal of the James Bond films of the 1960s and onwards and the Ian Fleming's novels of the 1950s and 1960s as evidence of this.[15] Bond, while working for the nation, represented by the British secret service, and obviously benefiting from its payroll with his upper-class dress and impressive gadgets, saves Britain as well as the United States from villains, often in communist attire, working to destroy Britain and America's capitalist economy, or to steal wealth in underhanded and diabolical ways. Bond continued to work for the British Empire beyond decolonisation. Wendy Webster has also pointed out that despite the difficulties of articulating a coherent British position on decolonisation, films such as *Guns at Batasi* (1964) and *Simba* (1955) did just that by again reasserting the role of the British in serving the Empire by ultimately gracefully exiting it.[16] These narratives mourned the end of empire and the end of the British soldiering ideal while promoting the role of the British as silent heroes. This narrative has come under much deserved scrutiny of late as new evidence of the role of the British government at the end of Empire is emerging. The popular narrative of peaceful abdication promoted in film and fiction and by politicians may not survive such an examination.[17] Yet this narrative was evident within popular film and fiction in the post-war period. British heroes worked for Britain and the world as they took on the new evils of a post-war world.

Certainly the relationship of women to wealth and labour continued to occupy problematic places within popular culture after the war, particularly as women entered the workforce in earnest in the 1970s. In popular narratives, women continue to be female love-interests who either abandon their own positions in order to affirm the male hero's or had their own working roles complicated within the narrative. In the case of the Bond films, they often showed a range of women, some who were working for the villain, some who were not, continually give up their jobs for a usually fleeting roll in the hay. Bond succeeded every time in saving the world as well as getting the girl, even if the character did not last until the next film. Other films, as part of the new permissive movement, such as 1965's *Darling* with Julie Christie continued to highlight the problems of the new modern and liberated woman who slept her way to fortune but not happiness. Popular narratives demonstrated the continuation of stories that privileged male breadwinners working for institutions of Englishness. The explicitly sexual and sometimes misogynist relationships that male heroes had with the modern woman of the 1960s and the 1970s further emphasised women's role as heterosexual object rather than worker within popular narratives. The revitalisation of James Bond in the early twenty-first century with the actor Daniel Craig has yet to disrupt this pattern, even as the franchise has made room for women as government agents and not only objects. Bond nevertheless remains particularly good at subverting a female agent's commitment to her job, often with morbid results.

What I have ultimately demonstrated is the uniqueness of the interwar period as the foundation of an ideology, steeped in economic anxiety and the aftermath of war, which has persisted well into the twentieth century. This was a period when mass media had an immense and largely captive audience, and before a growing cynicism about the relationship between the media and the masses would emerge. Low and middlebrow novels were readily available for a fully literate British public and films were just as accessible. The British embraced the new forms of media available to them, just as historians must embrace the novels and films they consumed as a vital entrance into the period itself. The contours of escapism, outlined in the film and fiction that ordinary people consumed, tells us much more about what ordinary people wanted to escape from than anything. The anxieties of the period are writ large across these sources. War, a jobless future, money for the wrong men, and women working and liking it, were all captured on the page and the screen.

In examining the literature and film that Britons actually read and watched I have demonstrated that the role of the idealised soldier and breadwinner as constructed within mass culture held a powerful place in Britain after the trauma of war and within a period of great economic, political, and social uncertainty. Ordinary people, by choosing the books they did at the local bookseller or library, and by attending local cinemas, consumed idealised images of the soldier-hero getting the job done, vanquishing the money-hungry profiteer, and convincing women to give it all up for love. The breadwinning soldier, crafted so carefully in a previous century, was constructed within low and middlebrow works as central to the rebuilding of a great nation, and able to withstand the forces aligned against him. Endurance and the status quo was the message while radical reform was not. Conceptions of villainy, of love, and of heroics were actively tied to this rebuilding then in a period of anxiety about the economy, the effects of war, profiteering, and the ongoing effects of feminism. The extent to which we, as consumers and occasional producers of popular culture, have imbibed this ideology and perhaps reproduce it in what we teach our children about being 'good' and what it means to be 'bad', and in what we look for in love, is a dubious but powerful testament to the legacies of the age of anxiety.

Notes

1 Lant, *Blackout*; A. Aldgate and J. Richards, *Britain Can Take It: British Cinema in the Second World War* (London: I. B. Tauris, 2007).
2 Cull, *Selling War*; D. Welky, *The Moguls and the Dictators: Hollywood and the Coming of World War II* (Johns Hopkins University Press, 2008).
3 Spicer, *Typical Men*.
4 Rose, *Which People's War?*; P. Summerfield, '"The Girl that Makes the Thing that Drills the Hole that Holds the Spring…": Discourses of Women and Work in the Second World War', in Gledhill and Swanson (eds), *Nationalising Femininity*, pp. 35–53.
5 *Blackout*.
6 B. Osgerby, '"Well. It's Saturday Night an' I Just Got Paid": Youth, Consumerism, and Hegemony in Post- War Britain', *Contemporary Record* 6 (1992), 287–305.
7 Landy, *British Genres*, pp. 172–6.
8 S. Brooke, 'Gender and Working Class Identity in Britain during the 1950s', *Journal of Social History* 34 (2001), 773–95.
9 J. Osborne, *Look Back in Anger: A Play in Three Acts* (London: Faber & Faber, 1965 [1957]).
10 *Englishness and Empire 1939–1965*.
11 A. Aldgate, *Censorship and the Permissive Society: British Cinema and Theatre 1955–1965* (London: Clarendon Press, 1995).
12 'A Flight from Commitment? Domesticity, Adventure and the Masculine Imaginary in Britain after the Second World War', *Gender & History* 19:1 (2007), 163–85.
13 S. Brooke, 'Screening the Postwar World: British Film in the Fifties', *Journal of British Studies* 44:3 (2005), 562–9.
14 'Public Memory or Public Amnesia? British Women of the Second World War in Popular Films of the 1950s and 1960s' *Journal of British Studies* 48:4 (October 2009), 935–57.
15 Chapman, *Licence to Thrill*.
16 Webster, *Englishness and Empire 1939–1965*.
17 D. M. Anderson, 'Mau Mau in the High Court and the "Lost" British Empire Archives: Colonial Conspiracy or Bureaucratic Bungle?', *Journal of Imperial and Commonwealth History* 39:5 (2011): 699–716; C. Elkins, *Imperial Reckonings: The Untold Story of Britain's Gulag in Kenya* (New York: Jonathan Cape, 2005).

Appendix
Censorable items compiled in 1917 from the BBFC's Annual Reports of 1913–15

1. Indecorous, ambiguous and irreverent titles and subtitles
2. Cruelty to animals
3. The irreverent treatment of sacred subjects
4. Drunken scenes carried to excess
5. Vulgar accessories in the staging
6. The modus operandi of criminals
7. Cruelty to young infants and excessive cruelty and torture to adults, especially women
8. Unnecessary exhibition of under-clothing
9. The exhibition of profuse bleeding
10. Nude figures
11. Offensive vulgarity, and impropriety in conduct and dress
12. Indecorous dancing
13. Excessively passionate love scenes
14. Bathing scenes passing the limits of propriety
15. References to controversial politics
16. Relations of capital and labour
17. Scenes tending to disparage public characters and institutions
18. Realistic horrors of warfare
19. Scenes and incidents calculated to afford information to the enemy
20. Incidents having a tendency to disparage our Allies
21. Scenes holding up the King's uniform to contempt or ridicule
22. Subjects dealing with India, in which British Officers are seen in an odious light, and otherwise attempting to suggest the disloyalty of British Officers, Native States or bringing into disrepute British prestige in the Empire
23. The exploitation of tragic incidents of the war
24. Gruesome murders and strangulation scenes
25. Executions
26. The effects of vitriol throwing
27. The drug habit, e.g. opium, morphia, cocaine, etc
28. Subjects dealing with White Slave traffic
29. Subjects dealing with premeditated seduction of girls
30. 'First Night' scenes

31. Scenes suggestive of immorality
32. Indelicate sexual situations
33. Situations accentuating delicate marital relations
34. Men and women in bed together
35. Illicit relationships
36. Prostitution and procuration
37. Incidents indicating the actual perpetration of criminal assaults on women
38. Scenes depicting the effect of venereal disease, inherited or acquired
39. Incidents suggestive of incestuous relations
40. Themes and references relative to 'race suicide'
41. Confinements
42. Scenes laid in disorderly houses
43. Materialisation of the conventional figure of Christ

Bibliography

Novels

Ambler, E. *Cause for Alarm*. London: Penguin Books, 2009 [1938].

Arlen, M. *The Green Hat: A Romance for a Few People*. London: Collins, 1924.

Bennett, A. *Lord Raingo*. New York: G. H. Doran, 1926.

Buchan, J. 'The Thirty-Nine Steps'. In *The Complete Richard Hannay*. London: Penguin, 1992 [1915].

— 'The Three Hostages'. In *The Complete Richard Hannay*. London: Penguin, 1992 [1924].

Charteris, L. *Enter the Saint*. London: Hodder & Stoughton, 1930.

— *Prelude for War*. London: Hodder & Stoughton, 1938.

Deeping, W. *Old Pybus*. New York: Grosset & Dunlap, 1928.

— *Sorrell and Son*. New York: Alfred A. Knopf, 1925.

Gibbs, P. *The Middle of the Road*. New York: G. H. Doran, 1923.

— *Now It Can Be Told*. London: Harper & Brothers, 1920.

— *Young Anarchy*. New York: G. H. Doran, 1926.

Haggard, H. R. *King Solomon's Mines*. New York: Longmans, Green, 1916 [1885].

Hall, R. *The Well of Loneliness*. Paris: Pegasus, 1928.

Hanley, J. *Boy*. London: Boriswood, 1931.

Hilton, J. *Lost Horizon*. London: Macmillan, 1933.

Horler, S. *Tiger Standish*. New York: Crime Club, 1933.

Hull, E. M. *The Sheik*. Boston: Maynard, 1921 [1919].

Hutchinson, A. S. M. *If Winter Comes*. Toronto: McClelland & Stewart, 1921.

Innes, H. *Sabotage Broadcast*. London: Herbert Jenkins, 1938.

James, N. C. *Sleeveless Errand*. Paris: Henry Babou and Jack Kahane, 1929 [1928].

Lawrence, D. H. *Lady Chatterley's Lover*. Middlesex: Penguin, 1961 [1928].

McNeile, H. C. *Bulldog Drummond*. New York: Doubleday, Doran, 1934 [1920].

— *The Female of the Species*. London: Hodder & Stoughton, 1928. Reprint, 1935.

— *The Third Round*. London: Hodder & Stoughton, 1925.

Oppenheim, E. P. *Curious Happenings to the Rooke Legatees: A Series of Stories*. London: Hodder & Stoughton, 1937.

— *Envoy Extraordinary*. Boston: Little, Brown, 1937.

— *Exit a Dictator*. Boston: Little, Brown, 1939.

— *Murder at Monte Carlo*. Boston: Little, Brown, 1933.

— 'An Opportunist in Arms'. *The Curious Happenings to the Rooke Legatees*. London: Collier, 1938.

— *The Profiteers*. Boston: Little, Brown, 1921.

— *The Spymaster*. Boston: Little, Brown, 1938.

Pain, Barry. *If Winter Don't*. New York: Frederick A. Stokes, 1922.

Remarque, E. M. *All Quiet on the Western Front*. Translated by A. W. Wheen. Toronto: McClelland & Stewart, 1929.

Sabatini, R. *Captain Blood: His Odyssey*. New York: Grosset & Dunlap, 1922.

Wallace, E. *The Double*. London: Hodder & Stoughton, 1928.

— *The Green Rust*. London: Hodder & Stoughton, 1919.

— *The Joker*. London: Hodder & Stoughton, 1926.

Films

Arrowsmith. DVD, dir. J. Ford. 1931; Los Angeles, CA: MGM, 2005.

Bulldog Drummond. 35 mm, dir. F. R. Jones. Hollywood, CA; Samuel Goldwyn, 1929.

Bulldog Drummond's Peril. DVD, dir. J. Hogan. 1938; Narberth, PA: Alpha Video, 2003.

Camille. DVD, dir. R. C. Smallwood. 1921; Burbank, CA: Warner Home Video, 2005.

Camille. DVD, dir. G. Cukor. 1936; Burbank, CA: Warner Home Video, 2005.

Captain Blood. DVD, dir. M. Curtiz. 1935; Burbank, CA: Warner Home Video, 2005.

Cavalcade. VHS, dir. F. Lloyd. 1933; Beverly Hills, CA: Fox Video, 1993.

Champagne. DVD, dir. A. Hitchcock. 1928; Los Angeles, CA; Brentwood Home Video, 2005.

The Constant Nymph. 35 mm, dir. B. Dean. London, UK: Gaumont-British Corp., 1933.

The Drum. DVD, dir. Z. Korda. London, UK: Alexander Korda Films, 1938.

The Four Feathers. DVD, dir. Z. Korda. London Film Productions. 1939.

Frankenstein. Dir. James Whale, 1931, Universal Pictures.

Grand Hotel. DVD, dir. E. Goulding. 1932; Burbank, CA; Warner Home Video, 2005.

Gunga Din. DVD, dir. G. Stevens. 1939; Burbank, CA; Warner Home Video, 2004.

It Happened One Night. DVD, dir. F. Capra. Columbia Pictures, 1934.

King Kong. VHS, dir. M. C. Cooper. 1933; New York; Turner Home Entertainment, 1992.

The Lady Vanishes. Dir. A. Hitchcock. 1938. Gainsborough Pictures, Gaumont-British.

Lives of a Bengal Lancer. DVD, dir. H. Hathaway. 1935; Universal City, CA: Universal Studios Home Entertainment, 2005.

Lost Horizon. DVD, dir. F. Capra. 1937; Culver City, CA: Columbia TriStar Home Video, 1999.

The Man Who Knew Too Much. DVD, dir. A. Hitchcock. 1935; Los Angeles, CA: Laserlight DVD, 1999.

Mata Hari. DVD, dir. G. Fitzmaurice. 1931; Burbank, CA: Warner Home Video, 2005.

Mr Deeds Goes to Town. DVD, dir. Frank Capra. 1936; Culver City, CA: Columbia TriStar Entertainment, 2002.

Mutiny on the Bounty. VHS, dir. F. Lloyd. 1935; Burbank, CA: Warner Home Video, 2001.

Queen Christina. DVD, dir. R. Mamoulian. 1933; Burbank, CA: Warner Home Video, 2005.

Roman Scandals. VHS, dir. F. Tuttle. 1933; New York, NY: HBO Video, 1995.

Sanders of the River. DVD, dir. Z. Korda. London Film Productions. 1935.

Shanghai Express. Videodisc, dir. J. Von Sternberg. 1932; Los Angeles, CA: Paramount [year unknown]. *The Sheik*. DVD, dir. G. Melford. 1921; Chatsworth, CA: Image Entertainment, 2002.

Snow White and the Seven Dwarfs. VHS, dir. D. Hand. 1938; Burbank, CA: Walt Disney Home Video, 1994.

The Son of the Sheik. DVD, dir. G. Fitzmaurice. 1926; Chatsworth, CA: Image Entertainment, 2002.

Sorrell and Son. 35 mm, dir. J. Raymond. London, UK: British and Dominion Films Corp., 1933.

A Star Is Born, VHS, dir. W. A. Wellman (1937; SI: Morningstar Entertainment, 1996).

Tarzan the Ape Man. Dir. W. S. Van Dyke, 1938.

The Thirty-Nine Steps. DVD, dir. A. Hitchcock. 1935; Los Angeles, CA; Brentwood Home Video, 2005.

You Can't Take It with You. Dir. F. Capra. Columbia Pictures. 1938.

Other published primary material

Cole, G. D. H. *Out of Work: An Introduction to the Study of Unemployment*. New York: Alfred A. Knopf, 1923.

Clynes, J. R. 'Food Control in War and Peace', *Economic Journal* 30:118 (1920), 147–55.

Davison, R. C. *The Unemployed: Old Policies and New*. London: Longmans, Green, 1929.

Engelbrecht, H.C. and F. C. Hanighen. *Merchants of Death: A Study of the International Armament Industry*. London: Routledge, 1934.

Graves, R. *Good-Bye to All That: An Autobiography*. London: Jonathan Cape, 1929.

Leavis, Q. D. *Fiction and the Reading Public*. London: Chatto & Windus, 1932.

Mayer, J. P. *Sociology of Film: Studies and Documents*. London: Faber & Faber, 1945.

Orwell, G. 'Bookshop Memories', in Sonia Orwell and Ian Angus (eds), *The Collected Essays, Journalism and Letters of George Orwell: Volume I: An Age Like This 1920–1940*, pp. 273–7. London: Penguin, 1968.

The Pilgrim Trust. *Men without Work: A Report Made to the Pilgrim Trust*. Cambridge: Cambridge University Press, 1938.

The Profiteering Act, 1919, Fully Annotated. London: Stevens, 1919.

Newspapers and periodicals

Bioscope
Daily Express
Daily Mail
Film Weekly
Manchester Guardian
New Statesmen
Observer

Picturegoer (Weekly)
Times
Times Literary Supplement

Archival sources

Board of Trade
British Board of Film Censors Scenario Reports 1930–39
British Film Institute Special Collections
Department of Public Prosecutions
Home Office

Secondary sources

Adorno, T. W. 'Culture Industry Reconsidered', *New German Critique* 6 (1975): 12–19.
Adorno, T. W. and M. Horkheimer. *Dialectic of Enlightenment: Philosophical Fragments.* Translated by Edmund Jephcott. Stanford, CA: Stanford University Press, 1947. Reprint, 2002.
Aldgate, A. *Censorship and the Permissive Society: British Cinema and Theatre 1955–1965.* London: Clarendon Press, 1995.
Aldgate, A. and J. Richards, *Britain Can Take It: British Cinema in the Second World War.* London: I. B. Tauris, 2007.
Alexander, S. 'Men's Fears and Women's Work: Responses to Unemployment in London between the Wars', *Gender & History* 12:2 (2000), 401–25.
— 'Women, Class and Sexual Difference in the 1830s and 1840s: Some Reflections on the Writing of a Feminist History', *History Workshop Journal* 17:1 (1984), 125–49.
Anderson, D. 'Mau Mau in the High Court and the "Lost" British Empire Archives: Colonial Conspiracy or Bureaucratic Bungle?', *Journal of Imperial and Commonwealth History* 39:5 (2011), 699–716.
Armstrong, J. 'The Publication, Prosecution, and Re-publication of James Hanley's *Boy* (1931)', *Library* 6–19:4 (1997), 351–62.
Auerbach, S. *Race, Law, and 'The Chinese Puzzle' in Imperial Britain.* New York: Palgrave Macmillan, 2009.
Bailey, P. *Popular Culture and Performance in the Victorian City.* Cambridge: Cambridge University Press, 1998.
— 'White Collars, Gray Lives? The Lower Middle Class Revisited', *Journal of British Studies* 38:3 (1999), 273–90.
Banner, D. 'Why Don't They Just Shoot Him?: The Bond Villains and Cold War Heroism', in Stacy Gillis and Philippa Gates (eds), *The Devil Himself: Villainy in Detective Fiction and Film.* London: Greenwood, 2002.
Beaven, B. *Leisure, Citizenship and Working-Class Men in Britain, 1850–1945.* Manchester: Manchester University Press, 2009.
Beers, L. *Your Britain: Media and the Making of the Labour Party.* Cambridge, MA: Harvard University Press, 2010.
Bergman, A. *We're in the Money: Depression America and Its Films.* New York: Harper & Row, 1972.

Bingham, A. *Gender, Modernity and the Popular Press in Interwar Britain*. Oxford: Oxford University Press, 2004.

Bland, L. '"Purifying" the Public World: Feminist Vigilantes in Late Victorian England', *Women's History Review* 1:3 (1993), 397–412.

Bloom, C. *Bestsellers: Popular Fiction since 1900*. New York: Palgrave Macmillan, 2002.

— ed. *Literature and Culture in Modern Britain: Volume I: 1900–1929*. London: Longman, 1993.

— ed. *Spy Thrillers: From Buchan to le Carré*. New York: St Martin's Press, 1990.

Bogdanovich, P. '1963 Interview', *The Cinema of Alfred Hitchcock*. New York: Museum of Modern Art, 1963.

Bourke, J. *Dismembering the Male: Men's Bodies, Britain, and the Great War*. Chicago: University of Chicago Press, 1996.

Boyd, K. *Manliness and the Boys' Story Paper in Britain: A Cultural History, 1855–1940*. Basingstoke: Palgrave Macmillan, 2003.

Bracco, R. *Merchants of Hope: British Middlebrow Writers and the First World War, 1919–1939*. Oxford: Berg, 1993.

Brooke, S. 'Gender and Working Class Identity in Britain during the 1950s', *Journal of Social History* 34 (2001), 773–95.

— '"A New World for Women?" Abortion Law Reform in Britain during the 1930s', *American Historical Review* 106:2 (2001), 431–59.

— 'Screening the Postwar World: British Film in the Fifties', *Journal of British Studies* 44: 3 (2005), 562–69.

— *Sexual Politics: Sexuality, Family Planning, and the British Left from the 1880s to the Present Day*. Oxford: Oxford University Press, 2011.

Butler, J. *Gender Trouble: Feminism and the Subversion of Identity*. New York: Routledge, 1999 [1990].

Caesar, A. *Taking It Like a Man: Suffering, Sexuality and the War Poets Brooke, Sassoon, Owen, Graves*. Manchester: Manchester University Press, 1993.

Caven, H. 'Horror in Our Time: Images of the Concentration Camps in British Media, 1945', *Historical Journal of Film, Radio, and Television* 21:3 (2001), 205–53.

Chapman, J. *The British at War: Cinema, State, and Propaganda 1939–1945*. I. B. Tauris, 1998.

— *Licence to Thrill: A Cultural History of the James Bond Films*. New York: Columbia University Press, 2000.

Clark, A. *The Struggle for the Breeches: Gender and the Making of the British Working Class*. Berkeley, CA: University of California Press, 1995.

Colls, R. *Identity of England*. Oxford: Oxford University Press, 2002.

Cooke, L. 'British Cinema: From Cottage Industry to Mass Entertainment', in Clive Bloom (ed.), *Literature and Culture in Modern Britain: Volume I, 1900–1929*, pp. 167–88. London: Longman, 1993.

Cregier, D. M. 'Robinson, Sir Joseph Bejamin, first baronet (1840–1929)', *Oxford Dictionary of National Biography*, Oxford University Press-Online Edition, May 2006.

Crozier, A. J. *Appeasement and Germany's Last Bid for Colonies*. London: Macmillan, 1988.

Cull, N. J. *Selling War: The British Propaganda Campaign Against American 'Neutrality' in World War II*. Oxford: Oxford University Press, 1995.

Daunton, M. J. 'How to Pay for the War: State, Society and Taxation in Britain,

1917–24', *English Historical Review* 111:443 (1996), 882–919.

Davies, A. *Leisure, Gender, and Poverty: Working-Class Culture in Salford and Manchester, 1900–1939*. Buckingham: Open University Press, 1992.

— 'The Scottish Chicago? From "Hooligans" to "Gangsters" in Inter-War Glasgow', *Cultural and Social History* 4:4 (2007), 511–27.

Davy, T. '"A Cissy Job for Men: A Nice Job for Girls": Women Shorthand Typists in London 1900–1939', in Leanore Davidoff and Belinda Westover (eds), *Our Work, Our Lives, Our Words: Women's History and Women's Work*, pp. 124–44. New Jersey: Barnes and Noble, 1986.

Dawson, G. 'The Blond Bedouin: Lawrence of Arabia, Imperial Adventure and the Imagining of English-British Masculinity', in Michael Roper and John Tosh (eds), *Manful Assertions: Masculinities in Britain since 1800*, pp. 113–44. London: Routledge, 1991.

— *Soldier Heroes: British Adventure, Empire, and the Imagining of Masculinities*. London: Routledge, 1994.

Doan, L. *Fashioning Sapphism: The Origins of a Modern English Lesbian Culture*. New York: Columbia University Press, 2000.

Dodd, P. 'Englishness and the National Culture', in Robert Colls and Philip Dodd (eds), *Englishness: Politics and Culture 1880–1920*, pp. 1–22. London: Croom Helm, 1986.

Elkins, C. *Imperial Reckonings: The Untold Story of Britain's Gulag in Kenya*. New York: Jonathan Cape, 2005.

Etlin, R. ed. *Art, Culture, and Media under the Third Reich*. Chicago: University of Chicago Press, 2002.

Finn, M. C. *The Character of Credit: Personal Debt in English Culture, 1740–1914*. Cambridge: Cambridge University Press, 2003.

Foucault, M. *Discipline and Punish: The Birth of the Prison*. Translated by Alan Sheridan. New York: Vintage, 1979.

— 'Governmentality', in Paul Rabinow and Nikolas Rose (eds), *The Essential Foucault: Selections from the Essential Works of Foucault 1954–1984*, pp. 229–45. New York: New Press, 2003.

— *The History of Sexuality: Volume I: An Introduction*. Translated by Robert Hurley. New York: Vintage, 1978. Reprint, 1990.

— *The Use of Pleasure: The History of Sexuality: Volume II*. New York: Vintage Books, 1990.

Francis, M. 'A Flight from Commitment? Domesticity, Adventure and the Masculine Imaginary in Britain after the Second World War', *Gender & History* 19:1 (2007), 163–85.

— *The Flyer: British Culture and the Royal Air Force, 1939–1945*. Oxford: Oxford University Press, 2009.

Fussell, P. *The Great War and Modern Memory*. Oxford: Oxford University Press, 1975, 2000.

Gates, P. and S. Gillis, eds. *The Devil Himself: Villainy in Detective Fiction and Film*. London: Greenwood, 2002.

Glancy, M. 'Temporary American Citizens? British Audiences, Hollywood Films and the Threat of Americanization in the 1920s', *Historical Journal of Film, Radio and Television* 26:4 (2006), 461–84.

— *When Hollywood Loved Britain: The Hollywood 'British' Film 1939–45*. Manchester: Manchester University Press, 1999.

Gledhill, C. *Reframing British Cinema 1918–1928: Between Restraint and Passion*. London: BFI, 2003.

— ed. *Stardom: Industry of Desire*. London: Routledge, 1991.

Glucksmann, M. *Women Assemble: Women Workers and the New Industries in Inter-War Britain*. London: Routledge, 1990.

Gray, J. *et al.* eds. *Fandom: Identities and Communities in a Mediated World*. New York: New York University Press, 2007.

Green, M. *The Adventurous Male: Chapters in the History of the White Male Mind*. University Park, PA: Pennsylvania State University Press, 1993.

Grieveson, L. and C. MacCabe, eds. *Empire and Film*. London: BFI, 2011.

Gullace, N. F. *'The Blood of Our Sons': Men, Women, and the Renegotiation of British Citizenship During the Great War*. New York: Palgrave Macmillan, 2002.

Hall, C. *White, Male, and Middle-Class: Explorations in Feminism and History*. New York: Routledge, 1992.

Hall, C. and L. Davidoff. *Family Fortunes: Men and Women of the English Middle Class 1780–1850*. Revised edition. London: Routledge, 1997.

Harper, S. 'Fragmentation and Crisis: 1940s Admissions Figures at the Regent Cinema, Portsmouth, UK', *Historical Journal of Film, Radio and Television* 26:3 (2006), 361–94.

— 'A Lower Middle-Class Taste-Community in the 1930s: Admission Figures at the Regent Cinema, Portsmouth, UK', *Historical Journal of Film, Radio, and Television* 24:4 (2004), 565–87.

— *Picturing the Past: The Rise and Fall of the British Costume Film*. London: BFI, 1994.

Harrison, B. and H. C. G. Matthew. *Oxford Dictionary of National Biography: In Association with the British Academy: From the Earliest Times to the Year 2000*, 62 vols. Oxford: Oxford University Press, 2004.

Higson, A. 'National Cinema(s), International Markets and Cross-cultural Identities', in Ib Bondebjerg (ed.), *Moving Images, Culture and the Mind*, pp. 205–14. Luton: University of Luton Press, 2000.

— 'Re-Presenting the National Past: Nostalgia and Pastiche in the Heritage Film', in L. Friedman (ed.), *Fires Were Started: British Cinema and Thatcherism*, pp. 109–29. Minneapolis: University of Minnesota Press, 1993.

— ed. *Young and Innocent? The Cinema in Britain 1896–1930*. Exeter: University of Exeter Press, 2002.

Hiley, N. 'Nothing More than a "Craze": Cinema Building in Britain from 1909 to 1914', in Andrew Higson (ed.), *Young and Innocent: The Cinema in Britain 1896–1930*, pp. 111–27. Exeter: University of Exeter Press, 2002.

Hinton, J. 'The "Class" Complex: Mass Observation and Cultural Distinction in Pre-War Britain', *Past and Present* 199 (May 2008), 207–36.

Hoggart, R. *The Uses of Literacy*. London: Essential Books, 1957.

Houlbrook, M. '"The Man with the Powder Puff" in Interwar London', *Historical Journal* 50:1 (2007), 145–71.

— 'A Pin to See the Peep Show: Culture, Fiction, and Selfhood in Edith Thompson's Letters, 1921–22', *Past & Present* 207:1 (2010), 215–49.

— *Queer London: Perils and Pleasures in the Sexual Metropolis, 1918–1957*. Chicago: University of Chicago Press, 2005.

Howlett, P. and S. Broadberry. 'The United Kingdom during World War I: Business as Usual?', in Stephen Broadberry (ed.), *The Economics of World War I*, pp. 206–35. Cambridge: Cambridge University Press, 2005.

Humble, N. *The Feminine Middlebrow Novel, 1920s to 1950s: Class, Domesticity, and Bohemianism*. Oxford: Oxford University Press, 2001.

Hunnings, N. M. *Film Censors and the Law*. London: Allen & Unwin, 1967.

Hunt, L. ed. *The Invention of Pornography: Obscenity and the Origins of Modernity, 1500–1800*. New York: Zone Books, 1993.

Hynes, S. *A War Imagined: The First World War and English Culture*. London: Bodley Head, 1990.

Ingman, H. *Women's Fiction between the Wars: Mothers, Daughters, and Writing*. New York: St Martin's Press, 1998.

James, R. *Popular Culture and Working-Class Taste in Britain, 1930–39: A Round of Cheap Diversions?* Manchester: Manchester University Press, 2010.

Joannou, M. ed. *Women Writers of the 1930s: Gender, Politics, and History*. Edinburgh: Edinburgh University Press, 1999.

John, J. *Dickens's Villains: Melodrama, Character, Popular Culture*. Oxford: Oxford University Press, 2001.

Jones, M. 'What Should Historians do with Heroes? Reflections on Nineteenth- and Twentieth-Century Britain', *History Compass* 5:2 (2007), 439–54.

Kaplan, E. Ann, ed. *Women in Film Noir*. London: BFI, 1999.

Kingsley Kent, S. *Making Peace: The Reconstruction of Gender in Interwar Britain*. Princeton: Princeton University Press, 1993.

Kinservik, M. *Disciplining Satire: The Censorship of Satiric Comedy on the Eighteenth-Century London Stage*. London: Associated University Presses, 2002.

Kuhn, A. 'Children, "Horrific" Films, and Censorship in 1930s Britain', *Historical Journal of Film, Radio and Television* 22:2 (2002), 197–202.

— *Cinema, Censorship and Sexuality, 1909–1925*. New York: Routledge, 1988.

— 'Cinema Culture and Femininity in the 1930s', in C. Gledhill and G. Swanson (eds), *Nationalising Femininity: Culture, Sexuality and British Cinema in the Second World War*. Manchester: Manchester University Press, 1996.

— *An Everyday Magic: Cinema and Cultural Memory*. London: I. B. Tauris, 2002.

Landy, M. *British Genres: Cinema and Society, 1930–1960*. Princeton: Princeton University Press, 1991.

Langhamer, C. *Women's Leisure in England, 1920–1960*. Manchester: Manchester University Press, 2001.

Lant, A. *Blackout: Reinventing Women in Wartime British Cinema*. Princeton: Princeton University Press, 1991.

Laqueur, T. W. 'The Queen Caroline Affair: Politics as Art in the Reign of George IV', *Journal of Modern History* 54 (September 1982), 417–66.

Lears, T. J. Jackson. 'Making Fun of Popular Culture', *American Historical Review* 97:5 (1992), 1417–26.

LeMahieu, D. L. *A Culture for Democracy: Mass Communication and the Cultivated Mind in Britain between the Wars*. Oxford: Clarendon Press, 1988.

Levine, D. *Family Formation in the Age of Nascent Capitalism*. New York: Academic Press, 1977.

Levine, L. W. 'The Folklore of Industrial Society: Popular Culture and Its Audiences', *American Historical Review* 97:5 (1992), 1369–99.

Levine, P. '"Walking the Streets in a Way No Decent Woman Should": Women Police in World War I', *Journal of Modern History* 66:1 (1994), 34–78.

Light, A. *Forever England: Femininity, Literature and Conservatism between the Wars.* London: Routledge, 1991.

Low, R. *The History of the British Film: Filmmaking in 1930s Britain*, 7 vols, vol. 7. London: Allen & Unwin, 1948–.

McAleer, J. *Passion's Fortune: The Story of Mills & Boon.* Oxford: Oxford University Press, 1999.

McCalman, I. *Radical Underworld: Prophets, Revolutionaries, and Pornographers in London, 1795–1840.* Cambridge: Cambridge University Press, 1988.

McDermott, J. '"A Needless Sacrifice": British Businessmen and Business as Usual in the First World War', *Albion* 21:2 (1989), 263–82.

MacKenzie, J. M. ed. *Imperialism and Popular Culture.* Manchester: Manchester University Press, 1986.

— ed. *Popular Imperialism and the Military 1850–1950.* Manchester: Manchester University Press, 1992.

McKibbin, R. 'Class and Conventional Wisdom in Interwar Britain', *Ideologies of Class: Social Relations in Britain 1880–1950*, pp. 259–93. Oxford: Oxford University Press, 1990.

— *Classes and Cultures: England 1918–1951.* Oxford: Oxford University Press, 1998.

— *The Ideologies of Class: Social Relations in Britain 1880–1950.* Oxford: Oxford University Press, 1990.

McLaren, A. *Reproduction by Design: Sex, Robots, Trees, and Test-Tube Babies in Interwar Britain.* Chicago: University of Chicago Press, 2012.

MacMillan, M. *Paris 1919: Six Months that changed the World.* New York: Random House, 2003.

McVeagh, J. *Tradefull Merchants: The Portrayal of the Capitalist in Literature.* London: Routledge & Kegan Paul, 1981.

Maltby, R. and A. Higson. *'Film Europe' and 'Film America': Cinema, Commerce and Cultural Exchange 1920–1939.* Exeter: University of Exeter Press, 1999.

Marshall, P. 'The Lord Chamberlain and the Containment of Americanization in the British Theatre of the 1920s', *New Theatre Quarterly* 19 (2003), 381–94.

Marshik, C. 'History's "Abrupt Revenges": Censoring War's Perversions in *The Well of Loneliness* and *Sleeveless Errand*', *Journal of Modern Literature* 26:2 (2003), 145–59.

— *Popular Reading and Publishing in Britain 1914–1950.* Oxford: Clarendon Press, 1992.

Melman, B. *Women and the Popular Imagination in the Twenties: Flappers and Nymphs.* New York: St Martin's Press, 1988.

Melosh, B. *Engendering Culture: Manhood and Womanhood in New Deal Public Art and Theatre.* Washington, DC: Smithsonian Institution Press, 1991.

Metayer, L. 'What the Heroine Taught, 1830–1870', in Michael Hays and Anastasia Nikolopoulou (eds), *Melodrama: The Cultural Emergence of a Genre.* New York: St Martin's Press, 1996.

Michie, R. C. *Guilty Money: The City of London in Victorian and Edwardian Culture, 1815–1914.* London: Pickering & Chatto, 2009.

Miller, M. B. *Shanghai on the Metro: Spies, Intrigue and the French between the Wars.* Berkeley, CA: University of California Press, 1995.

Morgan, K. O. *Consensus and Disunity: The Lloyd George Coalition Government*

1918–1922. Oxford: Clarendon Press, 1979.

Morris, A. J. A. 'Bottomley, Horatio William (1860–1933)', in H. C. G. Mathew and Brian Harrison (eds), *Oxford Dictionary of National Biography*. Oxford: Oxford University Press, 2004.

Mosse, G. L. *Nationalism and Sexuality: Respectability and Abnormal Sexuality in Modern Europe*. New York: Howard Fertig, 1985.

Murphy, R. and S. Chibnall, eds. *British Crime Cinema*. London: Routledge, 1999.

Napper, L. 'A Despicable Tradition? Quota Quickies in the 1930s', in Robert Murphy (ed.), *The British Cinema Book*, pp. 37–47. London: BFI, 1997.

Osgerby, B. '"Well. It's Saturday Night an' I Just Got Paid": Youth, Consumerism, and Hegemony in Post-War Britain', *Contemporary Record* 6 (1992), 287–305.

Overy, R. *The Morbid Age: Britain between the Wars*. London: Allen Lane, Penguin Books, 2009.

Palmer, J. *Thrillers: Genesis and Structure of a Popular Genre*. New York: St Martin's Press, 1979.

Paris, M. *Warrior Nation: Images of War in British Popular Culture, 1850–2000*. London: Reaktion, 2000.

Parkes, A. 'Lesbianism, History, and Censorship: The Well of Loneliness and the Suppressed Randiness of Virginia Woolf's Orlando', *Twentieth Century Literature* 40:4 (1994), 434–60.

Pederson, S. *Family, Dependence and the Welfare State: Great Britain and France, 1914–45*. Cambridge: Cambridge University Press, 1994.

Pellew, J. *The Home Office 1848–1914: From Clerks to Bureaucrats*. London: Heinemann Educational, 1982.

Perkin, H. *The Rise of Professional Society: England since 1880*. London: Routledge, 1989.

Pick, D. *Faces of Degeneration: A European Disorder, c.1848–1918*. Cambridge: Cambridge University Press, 1993.

Pollnitz, C. 'The Censorship and Transmission of D. H. Lawrence's Pansies: The Home Office and the "Foul-Mouthed Fellow"', *Journal of Modern Literature* 28:3 (2005), 44–71.

Poovey, M. *Genres of the Credit Economy: Mediating Value in Eighteenth- and Nineteenth-Century Britain*. Chicago: University of Chicago Press, 2008.

Pronay, N. 'The "Moving Picture" and Historical Research', *Journal of Contemporary History* 18:3 (1983), 365–95.

Radway, J. *Reading the Romance: Women, Patriarchy, and Popular Literature*. Chapel Hill, NC: University of North Carolina Press, 1991.

Richards, J. 'The British Board of Film Censors and Content Control in the 1930s: Images of Britain', *Historical Journal of Film, Radio and Television* 1:2 (1981), 95–116.

— ed. *The Unknown 1930s: An Alternative History of the British Cinema, 1929–39*. London: I. B. Tauris, 1998.

Robert, J. 'The Image of the Profiteer', in J. Winter and J. Robert (eds), *Capital Cities at War: Paris, London, Berlin,1914–1919*, vol. I, pp. 104–32. Cambridge: Cambridge University Press, 1997.

Robertson, J. C. *The British Board of Film Censors: Film Censorship in Britain, 1896–1950*. London: Croom Helm, 1985.

— 'The Censors and British Gangland, 1913–1990', in Steve Chibnall and Robert Murphy (eds), *British Crime Cinema*. New York: Routledge, 1999.

— *The Hidden Cinema: British Film Censorship in Action, 1913–72*. London: Routledge, 1993.

Rogers, N. *Crowds, Culture, and Politics in Georgian Britain*. Oxford: Oxford University Press, 1998.

Rollings, N. 'Whitehall and the Control of Prices and Profits in a Major War, 1919–1939', *Historical Journal* 44:2 (2001), 517–40.

Rose, J. *The Intellectual Life of the British Working Classes*. New Haven: Yale University Press, 2001.

Rose, S. *Limited Livelihoods: Gender and Class in Nineteenth-Century England*. Berkeley, CA: University of California Press, 1992.

— *Which People's War? National Identity and Citizenship in Wartime Britain 1939–1945*. Oxford: Oxford University Press, 2004.

Sandvoss, C. *Fans: The Mirror of Consumption*. Cambridge: Polity, 2005.

Sauerberg, L. *Secret Agents in Fiction: Ian Fleming, John le Carré and Len Deighton*. New York: St Martin's Press, 1984.

Savage, M. 'Trade Unionism, Sex Segregation and the State: Women's Employment in "New Industries" in Inter-War Britain', *Social History* 13:2 (1988), 209–28.

Schwartz, V. *Spectacular Realities: Early Mass Culture in Fin-de-Siècle Paris*. Berkeley, CA: University of California Press, 1998.

Sedgwick, E. Kosofsky. *Epistemology of the Closet*. Berkeley, CA: University of California Press, 1990.

Sedgwick, J. *Popular Filmgoing in 1930s Britain: A Choice of Pleasures*. Exeter: University of Exeter Press, 2000.

Shafer, S. C. *British Popular Films, 1929–1939: The Cinema of Reassurance*. London: Routledge, 1997.

Sheridan, D. and J. Richards, eds. *Mass-Observation at the Movies*. London: Routledge, 1987.

Shiach, M. 'Modernity, Labour and the Typewriter', in Hugh Stevens and Caroline Howlett (eds), *Modernist Sexualities*. Manchester: Manchester University Press, 2000.

Showalter, E. 'Rivers and Sassoon: The Inscription of Male Gender Anxieties', in Margaret Randolph Higonnet *et al.* (eds), *Behind the Lines: Gender and the Two World Wars*. New Haven: Yale University Press, 1987.

Sigel, L. Z. *Governing Pleasures: Pornography and Social Change in England, 1815–1914*. New Brunswick: Rutgers University Press, 2002.

Smith, M. and P. Miles. *Cinema, Literature & Society*. London: Croom Helm, 1987.

Spicer, A. 'Review Article: Film Studies and the Turn to History', *Journal of Contemporary History* 39:1 (2004), 147–55.

— *Typical Men: The Representation of Masculinity in Popular British Cinema*. London: I. B. Tauris, 2001.

Springhall, J. 'Censoring Hollywood: Youth, Moral Panic and Crime/Gangster Movies of the 1930s', *Journal of Popular Culture* 32:3 (1998), 135.

Squillace, R. *Modernism, Modernity, and Arnold Bennett*. Lewisburg, PA: Bucknell University Press, 1997.

Standish, R. *The Prince of Storytellers: The Life of E. Phillips Oppenheim*. London: P. Davies, 1957.

Steedman, C. *Landscape for a Good Woman: A Story of Two Lives*. London: Virago, 1986.

Stern, R. *Home Economics: Domestic Fraud in Victorian England*. Columbus: Ohio State University Press, 2008.

Stevenson, J. *British Society 1914–45*. London: Penguin, 1984.

— 'Myth and Reality: Britain in the 1930s', in Alan Sked and Chris Cook (eds), *Crisis and Controversy: Essays in Honour of A. J. P. Taylor*. London: Macmillan, 1976.

Stevenson, J. and C. Cook. *The Slump: Britain in the Great Depression*. London: Longman, 2009.

Street, S. *British National Cinema*. London: Routledge, 1997.

— *Transatlantic Crossings*. New York: Continuum, 2002.

Street, S. and M. Dickinson. *Cinema and the State: The Film Industry and the British Government 1927–84*. London: BFI, 1985.

Summerfield, P. '"The Girl that Makes the Thing that Drills the Hole that Holds the Spring…": Discourses of Women and Work in the Second World War', in C. Gledhill and G. Swanson (eds), *Nationalising Femininity*, pp. 35–53. Manchester: Manchester University Press, 1996.

— 'Public Memory or Public Amnesia? British Women of the Second World War in Popular Films of the 1950s and 1960s', *Journal of British Studies* 48:4 (October 2009), 935–57.

Swann, P. *The Hollywood Feature Film in Postwar Britain*. London: Croom Helm, 1987.

Swanson, G. '"So Much Money and So Little to Spend It on": Morale, Consumption, and Sexuality', in C. Gledhill and G. Swanson (eds), *Nationalising Femininity*, pp. 70–86. Manchester: Manchester University Press, 1996.

Taylor, J. *Creating Capitalism: Joint Stock Enterprise in British Politics and Culture, 1800–1870*. Woodbridge: Royal Historical Society 2006.

Thom, D. *Nice Girls and Rude Girls: Women Workers in World War I*. London: I. B. Tauris, 2000.

Thompson, E. P. *Customs in Common*. London: Merlin Press, 1991.

— *The Making of the English Working Class*. London: Penguin, 1963.

Thompson, K. 'The Rise and Fall of Film Europe', in Andrew Higson and Richard Maltby (eds), *'Film Europe' and 'Film America': Cinema, Commerce and Cultural Exchange 1920–1939*, pp. 56–81. Exeter: Exeter University Press, 1999.

Todd, S. 'Poverty and Aspiration: Young Women's Entry to Employment in Inter-war England', *Twentieth Century British History* 15:2 (2004), 119–42.

— *Young Women, Work, and Family in England, 1918–1950*. Oxford: Oxford University Press, 2005.

Tosh, J. *A Man's Place: Masculinity and the Middle-Class Home in Victorian England*. New Haven: Yale University Press, 1999.

Tremper, E. *I'm No Angel: The Blonde in Fiction and Film*. Charlottesville: University of Virginia Press, 2006.

Trentmann, F. and P. MacLachlan. 'Civilizing Markets: Traditions of Consumer Politics in Twentieth-Century Britain, Japan and the United States', in Mark Bevir and Frank Trentmann (eds), *Markets in Historical Contexts: Ideas and Politics in the Modern World*. Cambridge: Cambridge University Press, 2004.

Trevelyan, J. *What the Censor Saw*. London: Michael Joseph, 1977.

Usborne, R. *Clubland Heroes: A Nostalgic Study of Some Recurrent Characters in the Romantic Fiction of Dornford Yates, John Buchan and Sapper*. London: Constable, 1953.

Wahrman, D. '"Middle-Class" Domesticity Goes Public: Gender, Class, and Politics from Queen Caroline to Queen Victoria', *Journal of British Studies* 32:4 (1993), 396–32.

Waites, B. A. 'The Effect of the First World War on Class and Status in England, 1910–20', *Journal of Contemporary History* 11:1 (1976), 27–48.

Walkowitz, J. *City of Dreadful Delight: Narratives of Sexual Danger in Late-Victorian London*. Chicago: University of Chicago Press, 1992.

— *Nights Out: Life in Cosmopolitan London*. New Haven: Yale University Press, 2012.

Waters, C. '"Dark Strangers" in Our Midst: Discourses of Race and Nation in Britain, 1947–1963', *Journal of British Studies* 36 (1997), 207–38.

— 'Beyond "Americanization": Rethinking Anglo-American Cultural Exchange between the Wars', *Cultural and Social History* 4:4 (2007), 451–59.

Watson, C. *Snobbery with Violence: Crime Stories and Their Audience*. London: Eyre & Spottiswoode, 1971.

Watson, J. S. K. *Fighting Different Wars: Experience, Memory, and the First World War in Britain*. Cambridge: Cambridge University Press, 2004.

Webster, W. *Englishness and Empire 1939–1965*. Oxford: Oxford University Press, 2005.

Wee, A. 'Trials & Eros: the British Home Office v. indecent publications 1857–1932'. Ph.D. thesis, University of Minnesota, 2003.

Weil, R. 'Sometimes a Sceptre is Only a Sceptre: Pornography and Politics in Restoration England', in Lynn Hunt (ed.), *The Invention of Pornography: Obscenity and the Origins of Modernity, 1500–1800*, pp. 125–53. New York: Zone Books, 1993.

Welky, D. *The Moguls and the Dictators: Hollywood and the Coming of World War II*. Baltimore, MD: Johns Hopkins University Press, 2008.

Wilkinson, G. R. *Depictions and Images of War in Edwardian Newspapers, 1899–1914*. New York: Palgrave Macmillan, 2003.

Winter, J. *Sites of Memory, Sites of Mourning: The Great War in European Cultural History*. Cambridge: Cambridge University Press, 1995.

Woolf, M. 'Ian Fleming's Enigmas and Variations', in Clive Bloom (ed.), *Spy Thrillers: From Buchan to le Carré*. New York: St Martin's Press, 1990.

Woolf, V. *A Moment's Liberty: The Shorter Diary*. Edited by Anne Olivier Bell. San Diego: Harcourt Brace Jovanovich, 1990.

Zweiniger-Bargielowska, I. *Managing the Body: Beauty, Health, and Fitness in Britain, 1880–1939*. Oxford: Oxford University Press, 2010.

Index

Abyssinia 25, 123–5
Adorno, Theodore 6–8, 40, 85, 192
    see also culture industry
All Quiet on the Western Front (film) 18, 67
All Quiet on the Western Front (novel) 96
Ambler, Eric 43, 61, 122
American film 2, 10, 15, 17, 19–20, 25–9, 50
'An Opportunist in Arms' 25, 123–5
anti-semitism 126
    see also Jewish
appeasement 61, 125–7
aristocracy 15–16, 84, 88, 180
Arlen, Michael 16, 22, 26, 39, 209
armaments 61, 96, 122–4
    see also munitions
Arrowsmith 68, 147
audience of popular culture 2–31
Ayres, Ruby M. 133–4, 137

Birmingham Cinema Enquiry
    Committee (BCEC) 20, 183,
    192–5, 209–10
Board of Trade 121
Bolsheviks 41, 44, 48–50, 65–6, 85, 96,
    106, 120, 158
Bond, James 87, 90, 221–2
Boy 198–201, 206
The Bridge on the River Kwai 218–19
British Board of Film Censors (BBFC) 4,
    13, 20, 23, 31, 49, 67, 78, 103,
    144, 177–98, 202, 206–11, 219

British Broadcasting Corporation (BBC)
    124–5
Bulldog Drummond (film) 39, 113–14,
    169, 188, 191, 194–5
Bulldog Drummond (novel) 3, 17, 22, 25,
    44, 50, 57, 65, 77, 91, 103, 115,
    120, 169
Bulldog Drummond's Peril 113

Camille 27, 133, 135, 148–50, 157, 165
A Canterbury Tale 217
capital levy 92–3, 95
Capra, Frank 17, 27, 50, 59, 65, 105,
    123, 126
Captain Blood 57, 67, 70
Catherine the Great 163
Cause for Alarm 61, 122
Cavalcade 16, 39, 52, 67–8
Champagne 116, 165
Chaplin, Charlie 28, 29, 71, 134
Charteris, Leslie 24, 25, 43, 49, 50–1,
    96, 102, 122, 126
China 104, 143
Chinese 104
Christie, Agatha 15, 26, 89–90
Churchill, Winston 49
The Colditz Story 218, 220
The Constant Nymph (film) 23, 145
The Constant Nymph (novel) 22–3,
    145–6, 165
Coward, Noel 16, 52, 216
culture industry 6–8, 31, 40, 85, 185

Darling 222
decolonisation 218–19, 221
Deeping, Warwick 17, 21, 26, 38–9,
    54–5, 85, 90–100, 155
Defence of the Realm Act 45
Dell, Ethel M. 21, 200
detective novels 26, 47, 89, 137, 190,
    193
diamonds 114, 120, 169, 172
Doyle, Arthur Conan 88, 92

empire 3, 46, 59, 72, 103–5, 125, 187,
    219–21
Exit a Dictator 76, 124, 126
Extraordinary Envoy 75, 125

fascism 2, 5, 6, 48–9, 51, 84, 85, 96,
    122, 124–7
The Female of the Species 169
finance 76–7, 88–9, 100, 112, 123–4
foreigners 102, 168
Foucault, Michel 6, 8, 136, 181
The Four Feathers 59, 104

gangsters 10, 179, 193–4
Germans 43, 48, 60, 66, 75–6, 102–3,
    106, 114
Germany 6, 13, 48, 54, 61, 75, 91, 95,
    102, 106, 111, 122
Gibbs, Philip 1–3, 15, 22, 26, 44–6,
    48–50, 52–4, 62–3, 84–5, 87,
    114, 137, 145, 158, 185
Goods and Services Act 127
Grand Hotel 3, 46, 59, 78, 90, 103, 220
The Green Hat 16, 22
Guns at Batasi 221

Hall, Radclyffe 181, 198–9, 205–6
Hanley, James 198–9, 206
Hanna, (Colonel) J. C. 184, 187–91,
    196–7, 206, 208
Hilton, James 26, 143, 148
Hitchcock, Alfred 27–9, 76, 90, 103,
    116, 156, 165–6, 188, 208
Home Office 4, 13, 19–20, 31, 78,
    178–87, 191–2, 194–5, 197–201,
    204, 207–8, 210–11, 219

honours scandal 94, 110
Horler, Sydney 15, 90, 106, 107
Hull, E. M. 105, 164

If Winter Comes 15, 44–6, 52, 56, 63–4,
    83–4, 97–9, 114, 117, 146–7,
    170
If Winter Don't 98
In Which We Serve 216
India 72–5, 187, 189, 203
Indian 74, 104, 119–20
inflation 14, 41, 91–2
Ireland 119
Irish 119–20
Italian 76, 124, 143
Italy 27, 61, 76, 122–4, 126

Jewish 102, 126, 130
    see also anti-semitism
The Joker 115
Jones, Nora. C. 198, 200
Joynson-Hicks, William 181, 198

Korda brothers 59, 104, 219

Lady Chatterley's Lover (film) 208–9
Lady Chatterley's Lover (novel) 181,
    198–203
The Lady Vanishes 76
Lawrence, D. H. 21, 44, 181, 198–203,
    208
Leavis, Q. D. 4, 21, 87
Lives of a Bengal Lancer 15, 28, 39, 67,
    70, 72, 104, 190–1
Lloyd George, David 33, 41, 48–9, 93–4
London Public Morality Council
    (LPMC) 20, 183
Look Back in Anger 219
Lord Raingo 110–13
Lost Horizon 26, 27, 143–4, 148

The Man Who Knew Too Much 90, 103,
    113, 121, 188–9, 191
Mass Observation 10, 15, 25, 28, 67, 70,
    193, 216
Mata Hari 168
McCurdy, Charles A. 93–4

McNeile, H. C. 3, 17, 21, 22, 39, 44, 57, 90, 106, 185
melodrama 87–90, 143, 146, 175
The Middle of the Road 1–2, 26, 44, 46, 48, 49, 53–4, 62–3, 114, 145, 146, 157–9, 165
Millions Like Us 217
Modern Times 71, 134
motherhood 146–7
Mr Deeds Goes to Town 27, 50, 59, 65, 69–70, 105, 120–1
munitions 92, 95, 105, 123–4, 140
    see also armaments
Murder at Monte Carlo 101–2, 120–1, 143
Mutiny on the Bounty 2–3, 28, 39, 70–2, 107–10, 137, 144

national insurance 52
newspaper press 2, 19, 22, 140–2
Now It Can Be Told 45–6, 48, 84–5

O'Connor, T. P. 182, 187–8, 196
obesity 83, 97, 105–6, 112, 169
Obscene Publications Act 182, 185, 200, 219
Old Pybus 99–101
Oppenheim, E. Phillips 24, 25, 39, 43, 75, 76, 87, 101, 102, 106, 114, 121, 123–4, 125, 137, 143

Peace Ballot 123
Pilgrim Trust 51
pornography 180–1
Prelude for War 49–51, 76, 96, 102, 122, 124, 126
printing press 20, 137, 180
prisoner of war 111–12, 218–19, 220
The Private Lives of Elizabeth and Essex 163
Profiteering Act 83–4, 93–5, 121–2, 127
The Profiteers 106, 121

Queen Christina 159–63

The Rat 103
rationing 91–3, 95, 106, 127

Robinson, Joseph 94
Roman Scandals 50, 105, 120
romance novels 25–6, 28, 133–4, 137
Russia 48–9, 54, 75, 124–6, 145, 158, 159
    see also Bolsheviks
Russian Civil War 49

Sabotage Broadcast 122, 124–5
Sayers, Dorothy 26, 89, 102, 130
Scott of the Antarctic 220
Shanghai Express 104
The Sheik (film) 27, 105, 164–5
The Sheik (novel) 21, 105, 164–5, 200
Shortt, Edward 173, 177, 181–2, 184
Shortt, N. 184, 188–9
silent film 20, 87
Simba 221
Sixty Glorious Years 163–4
Sleeveless Errand 198–201, 206–7
Snow White and the Seven Dwarfs 24
socialism 6, 47–51, 66–7, 69
The Son of the Sheik 27, 165
Sorrell and Son (film) 12, 54, 64–5, 155–6, 171–2
Sorrell and Son (novel) 17, 38–9, 46, 54–5, 64, 85, 99, 155, 165, 171
spies 61, 76, 87, 113, 117, 126, 168
The Spymaster 75–6, 124
Squibs Wins the Calcutta Sweeps 16
A Star is Born 59, 150–5

Tarzan the Ape Man 165
They Made Me a Fugitive 220–1
The Third Round 115
The Thirty-Nine Steps 116–17, 156–7, 208
Tiger Standish 106–7
Tyrell, William 182

unemployment 1–2, 5, 6, 14–15, 17, 29–30, 38–41, 43, 46–8, 51–62, 95, 137, 138, 141

Victoria the Great 163–4
villainess 3–4, 136, 141–2, 166–73

Wallace, Edgar 102, 106, 112, 115–16, 121, 188, 190, 196–7, 219
The Well of Loneliness 181, 198–201, 204, 206, 213
Went the Day Well? 217
women's work 41, 137, 138–42, 147–57, 173, 217

Woolf, Virginia 21, 44, 87, 110
World War II 13, 23, 42–3, 61, 75–7, 168, 215–21

You Can't Take It with You 105, 123
youth culture 218